Smart VR/AR/MR Systems for Professionals

Smart VR/AR/MR Systems for Professionals is a comprehensive guide that explores the ground-breaking applications of virtual reality (VR), augmented reality (AR), and mixed reality (MR) in various industries. This book aims to equip practicing professionals with the knowledge and insights they need to harness the full potential of these immersive technologies in their respective fields.

Through this book, the authors aim to explore the experimental breakthroughs and cutting-edge methodologies that have emerged in the realm of VR/AR/MR. The book delves deeper into the profound impact these technologies have had on the design process, computer-aided design, healthcare product development, manufacturing, human-robot collaboration, medical imaging, rehabilitation, and even phobia therapy.

In each chapter of this book, we delve into specific topics, uncovering the principles, methodologies, and best practices that professionals can adopt. Examples of these topics range from empowering design processes with virtual reality to revolutionizing computer-aided design, and from exploring AR/VR/MR technologies in healthcare to transforming manufacturing with digital twins and metrology in VR.

The book aims to provide practitioners with valuable insights, real-world examples, and practical guidance to navigate the ever-evolving landscape of VR/AR/MR systems.

Smart VR/AR/MR Systems for Professionals

Edited by

Karupppasamy Subburaj
Aarhus University, Aarhus, Denmark

Sunpreet Singh
National University of Singapore, Singapore, Singapore

Saša Ćuković
Swiss Federal Institute of Technology – ETH Zurich,
Zurich, Switzerland

Kamalpreet Sandhu
Lovely Professional University, Phagwara, India

Gerrit Meixner
Heilbronn University, Heilbronn, Germany

Radu Emanuil Petruse
Lucian Blaga University of Sibiu, Sibiu, Romania

CRC Press
Taylor & Francis Group
Boca Raton London New York

CRC Press is an imprint of the
Taylor & Francis Group, an **informa** business

Designed cover image: ©ShutterStock Images

First edition published 2024
by CRC Press
2385 NW Executive Center Drive, Suite 320, Boca Raton FL 33431

and by CRC Press
4 Park Square, Milton Park, Abingdon, Oxon, OX14 4RN

CRC Press is an imprint of Taylor & Francis Group, LLC

ISBN: 978-1-032-30651-3 (hbk)
ISBN: 978-1-032-30652-0 (pbk)
ISBN: 978-1-003-30607-8 (ebk)

DOI: 10.1201/9781003306078

Typeset in Sabon
by SPi Technologies India Pvt Ltd (Straive)

Contents

Editor biographies

Karupppasamy Subburaj, PhD, is an associate professor at Aarhus University's Department of Mechanical and Production Engineering in Denmark. He leads the interdisciplinary Medical Engineering and Design (MED) laboratory, focusing on designing medical devices and developing image analysis methods and computing tools for musculoskeletal disorders. With a belief in the power of collaboration, he brings together scientists, researchers, engineers, and physicians to conduct clinically relevant research. Dr. Subburaj holds a PhD from the Indian Institute of Technology Bombay and has conducted postdoctoral research at the University of California San Francisco. He has published extensively, with four patents, three books, and over 150 articles and presentations in international journals and conferences. He also received the SUTD Outstanding Education Award for his contribution to design education and teaching.

Sunpreet Singh, PhD, is a researcher at the National University of Singapore's Department of Mechanical Engineering. His research focuses on additive manufacturing and the application of 3D printing in developing biomaterials for clinical use. Singh has authored over 150 research papers and 27 book chapters, with publications in prestigious journals such as the *Journal of Manufacturing Processes* and *Composite Part: B*. He is also the editor of three books on bio-manufacturing and 3D printing in biomedical engineering. Collaborating with esteemed institutions and experts, Singh contributes significantly to the field. He is a guest editor for various journals and actively participates in advancing the field of metrology in materials and advanced manufacturing.

Saša Ćuković, PhD, is a group leader at the Institute for Biomechanics at ETH Zurich, Switzerland. His research interests include CAD/CAM systems, reverse engineering, non-invasive 3D reconstruction and modeling, computational biomechanics, augmented reality, and computer vision. With experience as a postdoctoral fellow and grant holder at renowned institutions in Austria and Germany, Ćuković has published four books and over 90 papers. Dassault Systems also recognizes him as a CATIA Champion for his dedication to promoting and using the Product Life-cycle Management (PLM) System CATIA. Additionally, he is a scientific member of the Research

Institute for Artificial Intelligence of Serbia, contributing to the advancement of information technology.

Kamalpreet Sandhu, MS is an assistant professor at Lovely Professional University in India, specializing in product and industrial design. His research focuses on designing and developing footwear products and injury prevention in podiatric medicine. Sandhu has conducted various projects and published papers in the field, including a publication on the effect of shod walking on plantar pressure. He is the editor of several books on sustainability, revolutions in product design for healthcare, food printing, and 3D printing in podiatric medicine. Additionally, Sandhu serves as an Editorial Review Board member for international journals and a review editor for *Frontiers in Manufacturing Technology*.

Gerrit Meixner, PhD is a research professor for human-computer interaction at Heilbronn University in Germany. He is also the managing director of the Usability and Interaction Technology Laboratory (UniTYLab). Furthermore, he is Affiliate Professor for Human-Computer Interaction at the School of Electrical Engineering and Computer Science at KTH Royal Institute of Technology Stockholm and Associate Professor in the Medical Faculty of Heidelberg at Heidelberg University. Prof Meixner has a solid academic background, with a diploma and master's degree in computer science and a doctoral degree in Mechanical Engineering. He has published over 140 articles in conferences, journals, and books, focusing on usability engineering and innovative interaction technologies like augmented and virtual reality. In addition, Prof Meixner holds various leadership roles in research clusters and technical committees, emphasizing his commitment to advancing human-computer interaction. He is also a member of editorial boards for reputable healthcare informatics and information technology journals.

Radu Emanuil Petruse, PhD is a lecturer at Lucian Blaga University of Sibiu in Romania. He holds a PhD in Industrial Engineering focusing on industrial augmented reality applications. He has extensive experience in research projects and industrial collaborations, including coordinating projects for Continental Automotive Systems. Petruse is also a certified trainer for Siemens and has multiple certifications from Dassault Systems. As a lecturer at Lucian Blaga University of Sibiu in Romania, he has coordinated international practice seminars and contributed to the Digital Factory project. With research interests in cyber-physical systems, additive manufacturing, augmented reality, and bioengineering, Petruse has published 37 research articles and actively contributes to the engineering field.

List of contributors

Jamil Ahmad
Department of Computer Sciences
and IT, University of Malakand
Malakand, Pakistan

Amjad Aldarwish
Imam Abdulrahman Bin Faisal
University
Dammam, Kingdom of Saudi
Arabia

Fatimah Alhamoud
Imam Abdulrahman Bin Faisal
University
Dammam, Kingdom of Saudi
Arabia

Noor Aljabr
Imam Abdulrahman Bin Faisal
University
Dammam, Kingdom of Saudi
Arabia

Huda Al-Mubarak
Imam Abdulrahman Bin Faisal
University
Dammam, Kingdom of Saudi
Arabia

Maheera Amjad
National University of Sciences &
Technology (NUST)
Islamabad, Pakistan

Umer Asgher
National University of Sciences &
Technology (NUST)
Islamabad, Pakistan

Przemysław Bąbel
Jagiellonian University, Institute of
Psychology
Kraków, Poland

Valerio Belcamino
Politecnico di Torino
Torino, Italy

Enrique Calderon-Sastre
Hiroshima University
Hiroshima, Japan

Jean-Rémy Chardonnet
Arts et Metiers Institute of
Technology, LISPEN, HESAM
Université, UBFC
Chalon-sur-Saône, France

Rida Ayub Chaudary
National University of Sciences &
Technology (NUST)
Islamabad, Pakistan

Saša Ćuković
Institute for Artificial Intelligence of
Serbia
Novi Sad, Serbia

Francesco De Pace
TU Wien
Wien, Austria

Paolo Forteleoni
Politecnico di Torino
Torino, Italy

Kamran Hameed Khawaja
Imam Abdulrahman Bin Faisal
    University
Dammam, Kingdom of Saudi
    Arabia

Yuichi Kurita
Hiroshima University
Hiroshima, Japan

Jacek Lebiedź
Gdańsk University of Technology,
    Faculty of Electronics,
    Telecommunications and
    Informatics, Dept. of
    Intelligent Interactive
    Systems
Gdańsk, Poland

Federico Manuri
Politecnico di Torino
Torino, Italy

Gerrit Meixner
Heilbronn University, Usability
    and Interaction Technology
    Laboratory (UniTyLab)
Heilbronn, Germany

Muhammad Mohsin
Department of Engineering, School
    of Interdisciplinary Engineering
    and Sciences (SINES) National
    University of Sciences &
    Technology (NUST)
Islamabad, Pakistan

Zartasha Mustansar
Department of Engineering, School
    of interdisciplinary Engineering
    and Sciences (SINES) National
    University of Sciences &
    Technology (NUST)
Islamabad, Pakistan

Poongavanam Palani
Indian Institute of Technology
    Madras
Chennai, Tamil Nadu, India

Rehan Zafar Paracha
National University of Sciences &
    Technology (NUST)
Islamabad, Pakistan

Radu Emanuil Petruse
Lucian Blaga University of Sibiu
Sibiu, Romania

Agnieszka Popławska
SWPS University of Social Sciences
    and Humanities, Faculty of
    Psychology in Sopot
Sopot, Poland

Priyanka Ramasamy
Hiroshima University
Hiroshima, Japan

Gunarajulu Renganathan
Hiroshima University
Hiroshima, Japan

Andrea Sanna
Politecnico di Torino
Torino, Italy

Sebastian Stadler
Faculty of Media, Ansbach
    University of Applied Sciences
Ansbach, Germany

Slavenko Stojadinovic
Faculty of Mechanical Engineering,
   Department for Production
   Engineering, University of
   Belgrade
Belgrade, Serbia

Saadia Talay
Department of Engineering, School
   of Interdisciplinary Engineering
   and Sciences (SINES) National
   University of Sciences &
   Technology (NUST)
Islamabad, Pakistan

Mahbubunnabi Tamal
Imam Abdulrahman Bin Faisal
   University
Dammam, Kingdom of Saudi Arabia

Preface

Smart VR/AR/MR Systems for Professionals aimed to serve as a comprehensive reference for professionals, offering an in-depth examination of the innovative applications of virtual reality (VR), augmented reality (AR), and mixed reality (MR) within a multitude of industries. The primary objective of this book is to provide professionals with the requisite knowledge and insights, allowing them to leverage the full potential of these immersive technologies within their respective domains.

In recent years, there has been a notable surge in the adoption of VR/AR/MR systems across diverse industries. With the advent of Industry 4.0 and the rapid advancements in artificial intelligence, these technologies have become invaluable assets for engineering and design applications. They have revolutionized the approach to product development, design analysis, visualization, process design, safety protocols, and quality assurance.

Within the pages of this book, we delve into the pioneering breakthroughs and leading-edge methodologies that have emerged in the VR/AR/MR domain. We attempted to focus on the profound influence these technologies have had on various aspects, including the design process, computer-aided design, healthcare product development, manufacturing, human-robot collaboration, medical imaging, rehabilitation, and even phobia therapy.

The immersive experiences, 360° content views, high-fidelity simulations, and actionable analytical insights offered by VR/AR/MR systems have captured the attention of professionals spanning multiple industries. Manufacturing sectors are adopting these technologies to enhance efficiency and productivity and foster innovation. Healthcare practitioners and patients are reaping the benefits of tailored VR experiences, which improve medical education, rehabilitation, and pain management. The potential for these technologies is immense, and the opportunities that they present are limitless.

In each chapter of this book, we scrutinize specific subjects, unveiling the underlying principles, methodologies, and best practices that professionals can integrate into their work. From enhancing design processes with virtual reality to redefining computer-aided design and from exploring the applications of

AR/VR/MR technologies in healthcare to revolutionizing manufacturing through digital twins and metrology in VR, we will leave no stone unturned.

This collection has been curated to provide practitioners with invaluable insights, real-world examples, and pragmatic guidance, enabling them to navigate the ever-evolving landscape of VR/AR/MR systems. By gaining a deep understanding of the core concepts and embracing these technologies, professionals will be better prepared to excel in their respective fields and contribute to the progress of their industries.

We sincerely anticipate that *Smart VR/AR/MR Systems for Professionals* will become your primary resource, inspiring you to unlock the boundless potential of VR/AR/MR on your professional journey. Let us embark on this transformative exploration together and collectively reshape the future with smart, immersive technologies.

The Editors
Karupppasamy Subburaj
Sunpreet Singh
Saša Ćuković
Kamalpreet Sandhu
Gerrit Meixner
Radu Emanuil Petruse

Acknowledgments

We would like to express our sincere gratitude to all the contributors who made this edited book on smart VR/AR/MR technologies for professional applications possible. Their dedication, expertise, and diverse research interests have greatly enriched the content of this book, making it a valuable resource for professionals in various domains.

We extend our heartfelt appreciation to each author who has generously shared their knowledge and insights in this field. The collective efforts of these authors, hailing from different parts of the world, have resulted in a comprehensive exploration of smart VR/AR/MR technologies and their applications across diverse domains, including healthcare, design, and manufacturing.

We would like to thank the authors for their meticulous research, thoughtful analysis, and compelling contributions that have contributed to the depth and breadth of this book. Their commitment to advancing the understanding and application of smart VR/AR/MR technologies is commendable, and we are grateful for their significant contributions.

We would also like to acknowledge the reviewers who provided valuable feedback and suggestions during the peer-review process. Their expertise and critical evaluation have helped enhance the quality and rigor of the book, ensuring its relevance and reliability.

Furthermore, we are grateful to the editorial and production teams for their diligent efforts throughout the book's development. Their professionalism, attention to detail, and commitment to excellence have played a crucial role in bringing this project to fruition.

Lastly, we would like to express our most profound appreciation to our families, friends, and colleagues for their unwavering support and understanding during this endeavor. Their encouragement and patience have been instrumental in successfully completing this book.

To all who have contributed to this edited book, we sincerely thank you for your invaluable contributions and collaborative spirit. Your expertise and dedication have made this book a valuable resource for professionals seeking insights into the world of smart VR/AR/MR technologies.

Thank you all.

Part 1

Revolutionizing design with immersive technologies

Chapter 1

Embracing virtual reality
Empowering professionals in the design process

Sebastian Stadler
Ansbach University of Applied Sciences, Faculty of Media, Ansbach, Germany

Jean-Rémy Chardonnet
Arts et Metiers Institute of Technology, LISPEN, HESAM Université, UBFC, Chalon-sur-Saône, France

1.1 INTRODUCTION

Design processes help professionals to have standardized approaches to changing projects and circumstances and thus, have proved their value over time. As technologies evolve, new utilizations arise that enhance and change the way professionals design products[1] and apply the design process. Computer-aided design (CAD), for instance, revolutionized prototyping activities in product development as it improved and accelerated modeling capabilities, allowed design changes in an efficient manner, and increased accuracy (and thus, decreased tolerances in production) which eventually led to products with better quality. CAD further impacted the design process as it increased the efficiency of designing products in terms of time and money spent as well as increased flexibility and improved data management (Akca, 2017; Cross, 2006; Stadler et al., 2020c). In recent years, virtual reality (VR) has become increasingly prominent for product development and design-related professions as well. Cross (2006) already foresaw more than twenty years ago that VR has the potential to enhance traditional design methods such as sketching and drawing.

In this chapter, virtual reality is defined as a computer-generated simulation that can be interacted with, consisting of images, videos, and/or sound that represents an environment that the viewer can experience by using electronic equipment. Even though the main application domain for VR is still the entertainment industry, the technology is already used in professional fields such as engineering, training, marketing, exposure therapy, and ergonomics (Krauß et al., 2022). Moreover, VR has already been applied in product development and design fields. First insights indicate that VR has the potential to further disrupt and enhance the design process for professionals. Nevertheless, since VR is still considered a niche product, its impacts on the design process remain to be investigated.

DOI: 10.1201/9781003306078-2

3

1.1.1 Aim and contribution

In the present investigation, the overall aim is to elaborate and discuss the potential impacts that the technology of virtual reality can have on the design process, mainly from the perspective of engineering and design. To allow a holistic assessment, the impacts of VR will be discussed on the levels of professionals and other stakeholders, users, technology, and design as a profession. As a tangible outcome for fostering further research and active usage of VR during the design process, a set of general major guidelines for using VR in the design process for professionals is proposed and human-centered approaches to facilitate the acceptability and acceptance of VR will be developed.

1.2 DESIGN PROCESSES

In order to define design processes, an attempt is made toward a definition of the term "design" as its application fields, goals, and objectives are not uniformly defined but undergo permanent changes (based on Hauffe, 2008). In this chapter, design is defined as the activities designers carry out to develop products out of underlying problems, needs, or ideas resulting in the fulfillment of user needs as well as the needs of all stakeholders. To achieve this, the designers need to consider influences such as ergonomics, technology, sociology, psychology, ecology, philosophy, ecology, and finance (based on Frenkler, 2020). Consequently, the term "design process" can be defined as the stages, approaches, techniques, and activities that designers undergo to design products (British Design Council, 2020). In this context, Cross (2008) states that manufacturing cannot commence before the design is done. Thus, the goal of the design process is to describe the way of designing and to finally give a clear description of the artifact. Similar to the term "design", there is no unique definition of the design process, but various attempts were made to visualize it, for instance by describing the chronological sequence of activities that were carried out while designing a product (i.e., descriptive models). Alternative process models tried to prescribe patterns of activities (i.e., prescriptive models) (Cross, 2008). Comparative analyses of design processes already were published in the field of industrial design, mechanical engineering, and further transdisciplinary professions, concluding that design processes generally describe or prescribe activities that should be considered while designing. These activities include research and problem identification, ideation, prototyping, evaluation, and presentation (Gericke and Blessing, 2012; Pahl et al., 2007; Wynn and Clarkson, 2005).

To allow an assessment of potential impacts that VR can have on the design process, a representative design process model was chosen. Since the "Double Diamond" introduced by the British Design Council (2020) embodies the majority of activities that professionals undergo while designing products, this design process was selected as a representative model for this chapter. Figure 1.1 shows a visualization of the Double Diamond.

The Double Diamond visualizes a stage-based strategy consisting of the following four iterative stages: *discover, define, develop,* and *deliver.* The name and the shape of this design process is derived by the visualization of convergent and divergent thinking throughout the process that results in two diamond-like shapes that touch each other at the point of the design brief. While the first two stages aim to define the right problem by applying divergent and convergent thinking, the same approach is applied in the third and fourth stage to derive the right solution. Similar to the design thinking process, the Double Diamond is divided into a problem space (the first diamond) and a solution space (second diamond). Each stage of the Double Diamond involves its own objective (British Design Council, 2020):

- **Discover:** start the process by questioning the challenge(s) and understanding the users and other stakeholders, eventually leading to the identification of user needs;
- **Define:** understand findings as well as how the problem(s) and user needs are aligned, resulting in a design brief that clearly defines the challenge(s) based on the gathered insights (i.e., design synthesis);
- **Develop:** develop, test, and refine multiple potential solutions;
- **Deliver:** select a single solution and prepare it for launch.

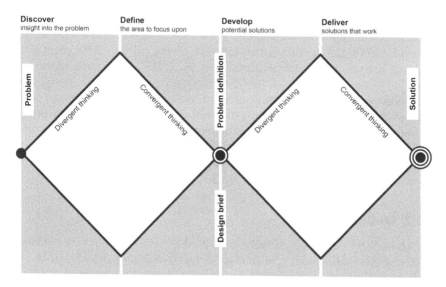

Figure 1.1 Double Diamond design process. (Based on British Design Council, 2020.)

While applying the design process, a range of different design principles are suggested including a human-centered approach for allowing the involved designers to understand the people they are designing for as well as a visual and inclusive communication to help people to understand the problem and ideas. Furthermore, collaborative and co-creative activities should be considered and iterations especially during the development should strongly be focused (British Design Council, 2020).

1.3 USING VR IN THE DESIGN PROCESS

In the following four paragraphs, a non-exhaustive selection of representative usages of VR during the design process is presented in order to demonstrate potential utilizations of VR for design activities.

1.3.1 Discover

In the first stage of the design process, VR has already been applied to allow designers to create empathy, for instance for users and further stakeholders. The technology has great capabilities to allow users to have the illusion of ownership of their virtual representation (i.e., avatar) (Kilteni, 2013). Schutte and Stilinović (2017) investigated whether VR experiences can lead to greater empathy than experiences that are visualized as two-dimensional formats. The results indicate that VR has the potential to lead to greater engagement and interpersonal emotions such as empathy. This implies that VR could allow designers to step into the shoes of those people they are designing for as well as experience environments through their eyes. Beyond the creation of empathy, the usage of VR allows experiences in a wide range of conditions and scenarios, for instance involving cultural differences and physical limitations (based on Coburn et al., 2017). Moreover, scenarios could be visualized that might not be practical or even feasible in real-life conditions. In summary, the usage of VR during this stage of the design process has the potential to foster empathy and greater engagement, indicating an improved divergent thinking for understanding the users as well as the application field of the desired product. Figure 1.2 shows users experiencing an immersive VR application that is meant to create empathy in the context of public waiting spaces (Stadler et al., 2020a).

1.3.2 Define

The technology of VR has already been used for activities such as creative three-dimensional sketching, brainstorming, and designing mood boards, as well as conducting participatory design workshops. Fromm et al. (2020) conducted a qualitative study consisting of VR brainstorming sessions to examine the effects of the immersive technology on negative group effects.

Figure 1.2 VR experience to create empathy with people at public waiting spaces in terms of room configurations, crowd, interior, and lighting.

The results show the benefits in terms of increased focus on the task as well as providing a relaxing digital environment in which ideas could be freely expressed, which had a positive impact on idea generation. Rieuf and Bouchard (2017) developed a tool for designers for creative drawing and developing mood boards in VR, two essential activities during the *define* phase of the design process. The researchers' findings imply that VR can enhance the emotional component of design activities and can lead to increased engagement of the involved designers. This includes the benefits associated with VR, such as experiencing 3D models and sketches in realistic scales and the ability to experience concepts from different and enhanced perspectives, as well as intuitive and natural interaction with digital content. These findings confirm the conclusions of Keeley (2018), who studied sketching activities in VR. The researcher inferred that VR allows for a greater sense of scales and perspectives.

During the design process and especially in the *define* stage, participatory design approaches are frequently used for defining the design synthesis and also in creative ideation and concept generation. In participatory design activities, designers increasingly cocreate with users, which brings benefits such as a deeper understanding of user needs, greater efficiency in designing products, and the creation of synergies between users and designers (Prahalad and Ramaswamy, 2004). In a co-creative design study, researchers found that the use of VR increased people's motivation to participate and fostered overall engagement. In addition, VR was beneficial in terms of visualizability of design concepts and increased efficiency in terms of time and cost compared to traditional methods. Moreover, the use of VR shifted the role of the involved designers from being creators toward being coordinators and facilitators who helped people express themselves and their needs (Stadler et al., 2020a). In this context, Bruno and Muzzupappa (2010) propose a participatory design approach for evaluating the usability of home appliances that allows users to virtually interact with products. The researchers conclude that VR is "[...] the best tool to satisfy the needs of a participatory design approach [...]" and that the use of VR allows designers to create products with improved usability. In summary, the present research overview shows that VR has the potential to foster not only creative thinking, and also participatory design approaches that retrospectively could lead to increased motivation to take part in the design process as users and also to establish synergies between users and designers. The usage of VR could further facilitate people to express themselves and their needs, resulting in enhanced convergent thinking and an improved design synthesis. Figure 1.3 shows a participatory design workshop in which participants helped the involved designers to derive and understand specific user needs for future public transport in megacities (Stadler et al., 2020c).

1.3.3 Develop

VR has been utilized in the *develop* stage for immersive prototyping and also evaluative activities such as usability testing. Especially in the area of hardware prototyping, VR is already being used to complement and ideally even replace traditional CAD applications such as Rhinoceros[2] and 3ds Max,[3] and research in this field is active to tighten the links between CAD and VR (e.g., Danglade and Guillet, 2022). Many researchers have already investigated the impact of VR and CAD within the design process (e.g., Akca, 2017; Stadler et al., 2020b). Research suggests that the main advantages are visualization and experience of realistic scales, realistic environments, engagement, and immersion. The major disadvantages of VR in this context are the lack of accuracy in developing high-fidelity prototypes, the lack of haptic feedback, and the limited field of view (FOV) for users while being immersed in VR (Stadler et al., 2020b). By comparing commercially

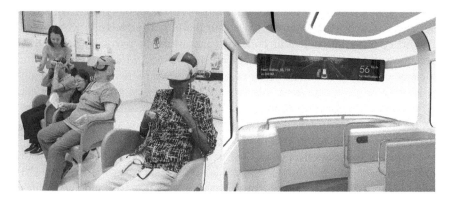

Figure 1.3 Participatory design activities in VR to define user needs for providing information of autonomous vehicles to passengers (e.g., route, velocity, and system confidence).

available CAD applications (desktop-based) with immersive spline and volume creation applications (VR), researchers found that VR-based applications can promote an enhanced sense of scale, improved perspective when experiencing models, and increased usability. In addition, using VR to create models promoted excitement and engagement while designing (based on Stadler et al., 2020b). Beyond that, researchers found that 3D models become considerably easier to understand and experiencing these models becomes less demanding regarding spatial reasoning skills in VR, which significantly reduces learning curves (Coburn et al., 2017). Overall, even though a considerable amount of research is already conducted in the domain of using VR for prototyping, research still needs to expand in order to make VR a considerable tool for day-to-day prototyping.

Furthermore, VR has been used to evaluate design concepts including methods such as usability testing, experience simulation, and user testing (Martin and Hanington, 2012). Especially in application domains in which physical prototyping is time consuming and expensive, VR is often used for evaluation purposes. For example, a number of studies have developed VR simulators to evaluate communication concepts between autonomous vehicles and pedestrians at crosswalks (Stadler et al., 2019). The results indicate advantages of using VR in safety for participants and efficiency in terms of time and cost, as well as laboratorial conditions. Furthermore, scenarios could be visualized that hardly could be recreated in real-life conditions. Still, the VR experiences led participants toward authentic behaviors. In summary, the usage of VR during the *develop* stage has the potential to foster prototyping (e.g., basic CAD works) through the possibility to experience models in realistic scaling, facilitating better understanding of the product to be designed and through improved usability due to natural interactions. In addition, regarding evaluation purposes, VR has the potential to increase efficiency in terms of time and costs, flexibility in evaluating concept variants, and most importantly, ensure safety for participants during evaluative studies. Moreover, the usage of VR evaluations allows data collection in laboratorial environments supporting the collection of valid and reliable data. Figure 1.4 shows a participant during a usability test to evaluate communication cues between pedestrians and autonomous vehicles (Stadler et al., 2019).

1.3.4 Deliver

VR also finds applications in the *deliver* phase of the design process, including activities such as design reviews and immersive presentations. These activities are essential during the design process as vital decisions are made during these activities. Castronovo et al. (2013) evaluated immersive VR systems for design reviews. The researchers concluded that aspects such as immersion and overall value of the VR system were highly rated by reviewers and that using the technology for design reviews allowed users to interact with objects and the virtual environment in real scale and in a very intuitive

Figure 1.4 Usability testing in VR to evaluate explicit human-machine interfaces as communication cues for pedestrians when crossing a road in front of autonomous vehicles.

way. Felip et al. (2020) compared product attributes of furniture presented both in a real environment and in VR, investigating differences as well as equivalences between the respective visualization tools. The researchers concluded that certain product attributes were rated higher when experienced in VR, indicating potential benefits of using VR for presentations and design reviews. De Freitas et al. (2022) found that the immersive technology can be beneficial for design reviews since VR provides the opportunity to experience products out of new and immersive perspectives that could lead to new insights. Furthermore, VR can increase team engagement, improve interaction, and make these interactions more intuitive. VR further offers the potential to increase efficiency in terms of cost and time (e.g., by partly replacing hardware prototypes for design reviews) and also increases safety for participants. Furthermore, the usage of VR for design reviews allows improved communication channels for geographically dispersed team members and allows enhanced data visualizations and interactions (based on Coburn et al., 2017). Limitations of using technology for design reviews include limited realism, latency issues, and potential communication problems between involved team members. In summary, the usage of VR during the *deliver* stage impacts the design process as new channels for communications and discussions are opened up. Furthermore, especially for geographically dispersed teams, the usage of VR for design reviews and presentations offers enhanced communication possibilities and perspectives. Figure 1.5 shows a product presentation in which an immersive VR demonstration was included in order to let the audience see how newly developed products could be used in a range of scenarios (Stadler, 2021).

Figure 1.5 VR–supported product presentation of future guidance systems at transit hubs of autonomous public transport systems (e.g., via AR supported guidance).

1.4 THE IMPACT OF VR ON THE DESIGN PROCESS

As the previous assessment indicates, VR has the potential to impact the design process on several layers: professionals and other stakeholders, users, technology, and design.

1.4.1 The impact of VR on professionals and other stakeholders

On a professional level, past deployment of VR in companies revealed significant profit for many activities, including the development of new products and services, training workers in hazardous situations or on novel manufacturing lines, assisting operators for maintenance activities, healthcare management, or proposing new experiences for customers. VR has shown indeed to facilitate service and product development and its lifecycle management with sped-up yet enhanced decision-making, increased productivity, and reduced production time while reinforcing operators' safety, thus providing significant financial benefits (Balzerkiewitz and Stechert, 2022) (see also for example the report released by Capgemini in 2018[4]). If VR may be considered as a viable tool, it has however not to be forgotten that major technological challenges still need to be overcome (see Section 1.5). It remains also necessary to carefully investigate the actual benefit of the usage of VR in every stage of the design process, to invest rightfully in VR solutions.

1.4.2 The impact of VR on users

On the level of users, the utilization of VR during the design process has several impacts. VR potentially facilitates co-creative activities that involve users in the development, resulting in products that expectedly better fulfill user needs. Especially in this context, research has shown that the usage of VR not only helped users to better express their needs and wants and also fostered motivation of participation in the first place (Stadler et al., 2020a). Surprisingly, this fact not only applies for younger tech-savvy generations and also seniors. Nonetheless, VR also occasionally intimidates people due to bad experiences with lies in the past (e.g., roller coaster ride with a smartphone-based VR application with insufficient frames per second). Thus, it is essential that the technology of VR is made understandable to participants to alleviate the fear of it. Additionally, user-centered interaction techniques and locomotion need to be implemented to ensure successful experiences in co-creative sessions.

Beyond the mentioned impacts for co-creative design activities, the usage of VR during the design process also impacts the users on the level of the products that are designed. First, due to enhanced divergent and convergent thinking, a deeper understanding of the underlying problem as well as user needs can be derived by the designers. Furthermore, during creative activities, innovation can be fostered. And second, during the *develop* stage valid and reliable evaluations can be achieved thanks to VR with increased efficiency in terms of time and costs. Thus, VR could lead to products that better fulfill user needs and that have improved usability. Moreover, product development times could be reduced and product development costs could be decreased, resulting in more affordable products (Stadler, 2021).

1.4.3 The impact of VR on technology

On a technological level, research and development in the field of VR as well as its applications is progressing rapidly. Even though VR may currently be not yet considered a fully mature technology, the present study shows its current potential for professionals. As the technology matures toward an end-user product, more new application areas and use cases emerge, which expectedly could foster further basic research into the technology itself. In this regard, the present study indicates that VR could become a significant technology for conducting experiments and other types of data collection in the future. Thus, VR could have a major impact on scientific endeavors in the future, provided that the visualization technology of head-mounted displays (HMDs) and Cave Automatic Virtual Environments (CAVEs) evolves toward a human-like FOV and resolution. Although research in the field of haptic feedback for VR users is ongoing, it remains uncertain to this day to what extent and when it will be possible to recreate realistic haptic feedback in VR. This fact may limit the use of immersive technology for certain application domains. However, if experiments and further data collections do not require participants to experience haptic feedback (and perhaps a realistic FOV or resolution), VR already has the potential to facilitate the conduct of experiments (e.g., by increasing efficiency and providing novel visualization capabilities).

1.4.4 The impact of VR on design

This chapter demonstrated that VR has the potential to impact the design process, the involved designers and thus, design as a profession as well. It became evident that the usage of VR fosters divergent and convergent thinking, helps to better understand user needs and application fields, offers improved prototyping capabilities, and can be used for time- and cost-efficient evaluations in laboratorial environments, resulting in valid and reliable data collections. Beyond that, thanks to VR, geographically dispersed design teams are offered immersive collaboration and review tools. Due to the range of available hardware, designers have suitable VR devices at hand at any stage of the design process, allowing it to become a strategic tool for them.

The involved designers are impacted by the technology as the way of working and the application of the design activities could be altered. Since the development of VR applications usually requires interdisciplinary teams, the designers become dependent on expertise such as software development. Hence, the tasks for designers frequently shift from being creators toward being project coordinators. Still, designers need to possess increased basic knowledge in professions such as software development to allow effective collaboration with future design teams. Furthermore, during co-creative activities, the role of the involved designers shifts from being concept creators toward being facilitators who help people to express themselves and their needs. Thus, similarly to the introduction of CAD to the profession of design, VR could also be a next game changer for the profession. Its usage during design can foster innovation and allow more efficient ways of working. However, the focus of research and product development, especially in a technology-driven world, should not lie on the usage of particular technologies but on the end-user (i.e., human-centered design) (see Section 1.6). Thus, it is expected that VR could become another strategic tool for designers; however, the immersive technology will not replace conventional design methods. In order to allow a sustainable and effective utilization of VR in design-related professions, the usage of this technology needs to be taught in related professions to allow its usage for future designers.

1.5 LIMITATIONS OF VR

VR, although well disseminated, needs strong attention regarding its limitations. Indeed, its development is still hindered by inherent constraints, which may impact user experience, including for example distance and size perception, known to be usually deformed in VR (Renner et al., 2013), and by extension, lower the acceptance of these technologies. Here we provide several major limitations; however, an extensive list may be considered, for instance through a taxonomy to be formalized linked with the usage of VR and development opportunities.

First limitations are related to technical aspects. Regarding HMDs, most of the devices available on the market have a restricted FOV, around 110°, although recent devices can offer larger FOV. This limitation is compensated by a 360° field of regard. Other immersive displays, such as CAVE systems, can offer a larger FOV, close to the human one, but are limited in the field of regard, as screens have limited physical dimensions. The resolution of the displays may also represent a limitation. Although recent devices can offer up to 4K or even 8K resolutions, the higher the resolution, the higher the need for computational power. Another technical limitation relates to the rendering of stereoscopic images, including for example optical components of the displays, such as the optical lenses embedded in HMDs that usually introduce distortion of the images, or for large immersive displays, stereoscopy technologies, such as active and passive filtering and autostereoscopy.

Apart from technical aspects, other limitations are related to their usability and the well-known cybersickness effect. Regarding usability, as per the ISO 9241-11:2018 norm, VR systems should allow efficiency, effectiveness, and satisfaction (ISO). However, non-expert users often struggle to use VR technologies in each new application, as interaction in and with virtual environments usually requires the manipulation of interaction devices that are not natural by default. An emblematic example is navigation in virtual environments. Immersive displays impose physical constraints (e.g., cables, screen size, tracking area), thus limiting physical displacements. Therefore, natural walking is quickly restricted and must be replaced by unnatural walking, requiring the development of specific techniques, such as teleportation (Prithul et al., 2021) or controller based (e.g., Wang et al., 2019). However, such techniques necessitate optimal parameter tuning that can be time costly and may not fit all users, possibly leading to distraction from the original task, the occurrence of cybersickness effects, or cognitive overload (Xia and Wu, 2021), thus not fulfilling usability criteria. Solutions such as so-called redirected walking techniques, authorizing to physically walk indefinitely in a limited area by deceiving the brain (Fan et al., 2022), or physical devices such as omnidirectional treadmills (Lohman and Turchet, 2022), allow to partly overcome these issues. However, the former again requires fine parameter tuning and the latter demands space and money while not guaranteeing the same sensation of walking as in the real world. Therefore, it is of primary importance to make sure that VR systems do not require long habituation periods to start interacting efficiently, effectively, and satisfactorily within virtual worlds. Last, it is crucial not to overload interaction. Although past work has shown that multisensory feedback (e.g., haptics, sound) may enhance user experience (Wee et al., 2021), available multisensory devices such as haptic gloves can still be limited in terms of interaction accuracy, and may not be relevant to use for all tasks.

Another important aspect is cybersickness effects. There is no doubt now that VR systems may induce sickness effects with very variable levels of criticality (Kemeny et al., 2020). This phenomenon is highly complex to address in the view of effective usage of VR systems, as its mechanism is still debated and its occurrence depends on many parameters, including human-related characteristics, technological aspects, or application scenarization (Kemeny et al., 2020). Mitigation strategies represent a large piece of the literature on cybersickness; however they act more like patches and do not provide definitive strategies to solve this issue. Very recent work shows a tendency to refocus attention on the user and propose solutions to individualize interaction, with the help of artificial intelligence (AI) tools, with promising results (e.g., Wang et al., 2021).

1.6 GUIDELINES FOR USING VR DURING THE DESIGN PROCESS FOR PROFESSIONALS

1.6.1 Consider the actual benefit of the usage of VR

The success of design studies and product development does not solely lie in the usage of VR. At any stage of the design process and for any design activity it has to be considered whether the usage of VR involves specific benefits that outweigh its drawbacks. The development of VR applications involves a certain degree of complexity, usually addressed by interdisciplinary teams. If the usage of VR does not involve significant advantages, its usage might even impair design activities within the respective design process stage, especially considering the fact that conventional design methods already proved their value for design studies. Beyond effectiveness, it has to be considered that the development of VR applications also impacts the efficiency of process stages. Even though the usage of VR for concept evaluations can prove to be time- and cost-efficient, developing complex immersive applications especially in the early stages of the design process might be inefficient in terms of time and money spent compared to conventional design methods.

It is also worth noting that many companies invest in light VR systems, such as HMDs, as being thrilled by such technologies but never use them. A reason often mentioned is that they do not take time to study the usages of VR (i.e., they do not find utility at the moment), therefore, they do not develop internal expertise in VR to run these systems. As a consequence, there is a strong need to be accompanied by external VR experts to help define the usages, train people to develop internal skills, and then deploy VR efficiently according to advantages that could be taken from using VR.

1.6.2 Choose appropriate immersive displays

Once the actual benefit of the usage of VR is determined, setting up a VR system requires technological choices in terms especially of displays. Among existing systems, the most prominent ones are the powerwall, the HMD, and the CAVE. Each system is very different from the other in terms of characteristics and so in terms of price.

HMDs are quite accessible, with prices ranging from around 300€ for entry systems to 30k€ for the most advanced. The choice of the model depends on the activity to achieve. HMDs, as already mentioned in Section 1.5, allow 360° field of regard and fully immerse users, as they shield from reality. This last aspect is important to consider, as by default it prevents users to see themselves and other people, which may be inconvenient for activities for example involving colocalized collaborative work. Embodying users in a virtual avatar is further necessary to maximize presence in virtual environments, representing non-trivial additional work. Nonetheless, HMDs are well suited for activities in which designers can develop and rapidly visualize without the necessary help of coworkers. Thus, the usage of HMDs is especially useful for the early stages of the design process for creative design activities since the setup and usage of these devices involves little complexity and time. Here, depending on the design activity as well as the study context, even budget devices with three degrees of freedom can be sufficient. Alternatively, HMDs with high-resolution displays and six degrees of freedom are frequently used in later stages of the design process for evaluative activities. The advantages of these devices lie in their affordability and low complexity to set up and use. Still, due to their hardware capabilities, high degrees of immersion can be achieved, which can lead to the collection of authentic user behaviors. Moreover, high-performance HMDs are regularly used for design reviews in which one person is immersed in a virtual environment while other reviewers follow interactions via screen mirroring of the VR device. This allows reviewers to focus on discussions and design decisions rather than the interaction with the virtual environment.

CAVE systems are unique systems that are usually not available off-the-shelf but are rather custom made based on specifications. Indeed, contrary to HMDs, CAVE systems are usually made with large screens surrounding the users, of different shapes and sizes, which necessarily limits the space to physically move. A typical shape and size for such a system is a four- or five-sided cube of around three meters length per side. Virtual environments are displayed through video-projectors able to deliver stereoscopic images. Depending on the specifications (e.g., number of sides, screen size and material, projectors' frame rate, resolution, luminance and brightness, stereoscopy type, embedded tracking system), its cost may range between 50k€ and >1M€. Such systems are usually present in large companies or in academic institutions, some of them proposing to make them available to professionals.

Despite a lower field of regard than HMDs, its great advantage lies in its possibility for users to still see themselves and other people, which makes it particularly suitable for colocalized collaborative project review activities or concurrent engineering. This becomes especially interesting for design activities in later stages of the design process such as design reviews and immersive presentations, for instance before production commences, and past studies showed the added value of CAVE systems in design activities (Basset and Noël, 2018). The collaborative nature of CAVE systems in this context allows realistic and immersive experiences of digital content for whole design teams while not impairing communication and discussions. Some existing CAVE systems even allow to render stereoscopic images for several users at the same time with viewpoints adapted to each user. In terms of ergonomics, CAVE systems offer high comfort in usage since users only require to wear light glasses instead of heavy HMDs.

As an alternative, powerwalls, generally composed of either one large screen or several smaller screens put end to end, are less immersive than the previous systems, as the field of regard in the vertical plane is rather limited. However, these systems are well suited to collaborative sessions. Especially for team discussions and design reviews in later stages of the design process, powerwalls constitute an interesting alternative to CAVE systems and HMDs as they are mobile and flexible in use, require little space, and usually are less expensive than a CAVE. Similar to CAVE systems, powerwalls not only allow collaborative sessions between several team members and also allow the possibility to combine digital content with physical objects. Furthermore, since only light glasses are required instead of HMDs, powerwalls offer a high level of comfort while being used, knowing that they can be used in either monoscopic or stereoscopic mode.

In summary, depending on the design process stage and the activity and also aspects such as budget and involvement of team members, each of the three hardware solutions offers its own set of advantages and drawbacks.

1.6.3 Prioritize interactivity over representation

Ensuring a usable application is more important than its visual representation (e.g., by trying to achieve a high degree of realism). Users usually are able to accept a certain degree of abstraction while still experiencing a high degree of immersion. In this context, the term "willing suspension of disbelief" states that users temporarily believe something that is not true in order to enjoy a fiction.[5] This fact is also applicable to VR experiences. Here, users accept certain degrees of abstraction of the visual representations without questioning the whole VR experience, but VR experiences with insufficient usability are rarely successful. This fact shows the importance of user-centered design as well as usability, especially for people who have little to no experience with VR applications.

1.6.4 Choose appropriate interaction techniques

As mentioned previously, interaction (navigation and manipulation) techniques need careful implementation, as the usability of VR systems is at stake. The first aspect to consider is who will use VR and for what purpose. As we demonstrated in Section 1.4, the impact of VR will differ depending on the category of end-users: designers, professionals, stakeholders, and customers will have needs different from each other. Even within a category of users, needs may differ depending on the stage of the design process. If the usage of VR brings benefit (see above), and despite the availability of more and more products on the market, the choice of the technologies and methods relevant to the corresponding activity should be derived from specifications, with a principle that overloading interaction with complex techniques and devices is useless if the activity does not require it. For example, if the activity consists in verifying design elements at some specific locations in a large environment, locomotion in this environment could be performed by teleportation for example, rather than classical controller-based (e.g., joystick) locomotion or using physical devices such as treadmills, simplifying the design of the immersive application and its usage, while ensuring comfort of use. Likewise, if the activity does not require accurate gestures with precise feedback, it may be unnecessary to use complex haptic gloves but rather simply VR controllers or optical finger tracking. Therefore, the simpler, the lighter, the better.

This principle is all the more important to follow as users may not have the same degree of expertise in the use of immersive technologies, the best being to implement interactions adaptive to users and the context, which may require expert skills in VR technology implementation and in fields including artificial intelligence and neuroscience.

To be sure that the system developed answers requirements and fulfills usability, user evaluations may be conducted among a panel of users through subjective and objective means, such as questionnaires (e.g., SUS for usability, SSQ for cybersickness, NASA-TLX for cognitive load), performance measurements (e.g., activity achievement time, error rate), physiological and behavioral measurements (e.g., electrodermal activity measured in real time through wearable sensors,[6] eye gaze through sensors embedded in HMDs,[7] or through observations of users), and oriented or free interviews.

1.6.5 Avoid the exposure of technical limitations of VR

As it was pointed out earlier, the technology of VR involves a set of limitations, mostly of technical nature, such as restricted FOV or display resolution that does not match the human eye. Technical limitations like the aforementioned need to be carefully considered during the development of VR applications. If the designers decide to use VR for evaluative design activities, visualization realism (e.g., size, rendering in terms of color and contrast) needs to be kept in mind. This means that in VR, it could be harder to recognize objects in certain distances than in real life which retrospectively could impair the validity of evaluative data collections. This fact also applies to the FOV. If for instance the usability in aircraft cockpits is evaluated with VR including eye-tracking, it has to be considered that the FOV in VR is different compared to the human eye. Thus, VR experiences that expose such limitations and impair data collections should be avoided.

1.6.6 Minimize cybersickness

We exposed earlier the occurrence of cybersickness as being one major limitation of VR technologies. This phenomenon should particularly be well considered before deploying VR in design processes. Since many factors can influence its occurrence and severity, these should be carefully reviewed, and mitigation strategies be accordingly implemented. From the technological viewpoint, for example:

- ensuring minimal latency in the whole system (between the user command and the response of the system) (Porcino et al., 2017);
- optimizing virtual applications, especially 3D models, to provide at least 60–90 Hz frame rates;[8]
- well-adjusting immersive displays to the eyes, including the position of the device, parallax, and the inter-pupillary distance (physically and by software), which also affects distance perception (Woldegiorgis et al., 2019);
- well designing immersive scenarios (Lo and So, 2001);
- optimizing interaction (i.e., choose appropriate interaction methods and devices – see above – and tune interaction, especially navigation, parameters according to the needs, the context, and users). Particularly for virtual locomotion not based on teleportation, it is advisable to avoid abrupt accelerations and decelerations, keep below specific acceleration thresholds, and maintain navigation speeds close to natural speeds (Terenzi and Zaal, 2020);
- implementing dynamic FOV restriction (Teixeira and Palmisano, 2021) or blur effects (e.g., Chen et al., 2022);
- using salient visual references (e.g., a static grid (Kemeny et al., 2017)); and
- implementing motion platforms (e.g., Plouzeau et al., 2017) or vibratory stimulations (Lucas et al., 2020).

From the human-related viewpoint, for example:

- limiting immersive exposure time, as the longer the exposure, the more likely the occurrence of cybersickness (Garrido et al., 2022). It is often recommended not to exceed 10 minutes of exposure. When a user starts reporting sickness, it is mandatory to immediately quit the VR experience and let him/her rest. It is also advisable after longer exposure to avoid for example driving;

- avoiding repeated exposure in the same day, as cybersickness effects are cumulative;
- avoiding exposure for sensitive users, e.g., pregnant users or suffering from epilepsia;
- considering users' profile (e.g., gender, age, past experience with VR and video games) and individualizing interaction according to the proneness to cybersickness (e.g., Wang et al., 2021); and
- adapting interaction to the real-time user's physiological state (Plouzeau et al., 2018), which requires however to wear physiological measurement devices.

1.7 CONCLUSION

VR technologies, being more and more widely spread in many domains, are changing the way we work. In this chapter, we have shown that the usage of VR has the potential to greatly impact the design process, with tangible advantages and benefits. We also stressed out that despite such enthusiasm, professionals have to consider important limitations still existing, and that challenges need to be overcome for VR to be established as a strategic tool during the design process. We have listed several of importance. However, if these challenges and limitations are taken into account carefully, with clearly identified specifications for the immersive applications, VR can provide with more effectivity and efficiency along design processes. To help professionals overcome such limitations and perform successfully with VR during design processes, we have proposed a general set of guidelines, based on past literature and experience. As a non-exhaustive selection of representative VR case studies was chosen in the present investigation, the generalization of the proposed guidelines is naturally limited. Thus, these guidelines need naturally to constantly be revised and enhanced, as research and development advance in this field, and VR is further adopted on longer periods than those usually described in the literature. To further objectify the investigation and guidelines, the derivation of a taxonomy of using and evaluating VR is planned as a next step.

As these technologies progress, interesting insights may be considered for professionals in the design field. First, considering further human-centered approaches in VR might help designers better appropriate these systems. We have already mentioned recent work proposing to integrate artificial intelligence tools to predict the occurrence and severity of cybersickness; such tools could be used to predict the designers' intentions and help them conduct design activities, the idea not being to replace them but on the contrary to further stimulate them, for example during ideation sessions. Still, similar to one of the proposed guidelines, the usage of AI should result in a significant advantage over conventional methods to justify its usage, and further studies should be conducted to prove its concrete effectiveness. This chapter demonstrated that the immersive technology of VR has the potential to foster divergent and convergent thinking, facilitates co-creative activities, and offers advantages in prototyping and concept evaluation, as well as design reviews and immersive product presentations. With these enhancements, VR has the potential to become the next disruptive game changer for design-related professions by directly impacting the design process and altering the future roles of the involved designers, as well as enhancing the whole profession of design.

NOTES

1 The term "product" in the present chapter includes systems, experiences, and businesses.
2 Rhinoceros (2022), https://www.rhino3d.com/ (Accessed: 25.07.2022).
3 Autodesk, 3ds Max - 3d Modeling and Rendering Software for Design Visualization, Games, and Animation (2022) https://www.autodesk.com/products/3ds-max/overview (Accessed: 25.07.2022).
4 Capgemini, Augmented and Virtual Reality in Operations: A guide for investment (2018), https://www.capgemini.com/us-en/augmented-and-virtual-reality-in-operations (Accessed: 25.07.2022).
5 Oxford Dictionaries, "Suspend Disbelief." https://en.oxforddictionaries.com/definition/suspend_disbelief. (Accessed: 25.07.2022).
6 An example of such device is the Empatica E4 wristband: https://www.empatica.com/en-eu/research/e4/ (Accessed: 25.07.2022).
7 Examples of HMDs integrating eye tracking sensors are the HTC Vive Pro Eye, Varjo's HMDs, the Pico Neo 3 Pro Eye.
8 https://docs.unrealengine.com/5.0/en-US/xr-best-practices-in-unreal-engine/ (Accessed: 25.07.2022).

REFERENCES

Akca, E. (2017). Development of Computer-Aided Industrial Design Technology. *Periodicals of Engineering and Natural Sciences (PEN)*, 5(2), 124–127. doi: 10.21533/pen.v5i2.86
Balzerkiewitz, H.-P., and Stechert, C. (2022). VR in Distributed Product Development – Approach for a Heuristic Profitability Assessment, *Procedia CIRP*, 109, 574–579. doi: 10.1016/j.procir.2022.05.297
Basset, J., and Noël, F. (2018). Added Value of a 3D CAVE within Design Activities. In: Bourdot, P., Cobb, S., Interrante, V., Kato, H., and Stricker, D. (eds), *Virtual Reality and Augmented Reality*. EuroVR 2018. Lecture Notes in Computer Science, 11162, 230–239. Cham: Springer. doi: 10.1007/978-3-030-01790-3_14

British Design Council. (2020). The Double Diamond: A Universally Accepted Depiction of the Design Process. https://www.designcouncil.org.uk/news-opinion/double-diamond-universally-accepted-depiction-design-process   (Accessed: 25.07.2022).

Bruno, F., and Muzzupappa, M. (2010). Product Interface Design: A Participatory Approach Based on Virtual Reality. *International Journal of Human Computer Studies*, 68(5), 254–269. doi: 10.1016/j.ijhcs.2009.12.004

Castronovo, F., Nikolic, D., Liu, Y., and Messner, J. (2013). An Evaluation of Immersive Virtual Reality Systems for Design Reviews. In: *Proceedings of the 13th International Conference on Construction Applications of Virtual Reality*, December 2015, 30–31.

Chen, C. Y., Chuang, C. H., Tsai, T. L., Chen, H. W., and Wu, P. J. (2022). Reducing Cybersickness by Implementing Texture Blur in the Virtual Reality Content. *Virtual Reality*, 26, 789–800. doi: 10.1007/s10055-021-00587-2

Coburn, J. Q., Freeman, I., and Salmon, J. L. (2017). A Review of the Capabilities of Current Low-Cost Virtual Reality Technology and Its Potential to Enhance the Design Process. *Journal of Computing and Information Science in Engineering*, 17(3). doi: 10.1115/1.4036921

Cross, N. (2006). *Designerly Ways of Knowing. Designerly Ways of Knowing*. London: Springer-Verlag London Limited. doi: 10.1007/1-84628-301-9

Cross, N. (2008). *Engineering Design Methods: Strategies for Product Design*. Chichester: John Wiley & Sons Ltd. doi: 10.1016/0261-3069(89)90020-4

Danglade, F., and Guillet, C. (2022). Choice of CAD Model Adaptation Process for Virtual Reality using Classification Techniques. *Computer-Aided Design and Applications*, 19(3), 494–509. doi: 10.14733/cadaps.2022.494-509

Fan, L., Li, H., and Shi, M. (2022). Redirected Walking for Exploring Immersive Virtual Spaces with HMD: A Comprehensive Review and Recent Advances. *IEEE Transactions on Visualization and Computer Graphics*. doi: 10.1109/TVCG.2022.3179269

Felip, F., Galán, J. García-García, C., and Mulet, E. (2020). Influence of Presentation Means on Industrial Product Evaluations with Potential Users: A First Study by Comparing Tangible Virtual Reality and Presenting a Product in a Real Setting. *Virtual Reality*, 24(3), 439–451. doi: 10.1007/s10055-019-00406-9

de Freitas, F., Mendes Gomes, M., and Winkler, I. (2022). Benefits and Challenges of Virtual-Reality-Based Industrial Usability Testing and Design Reviews: A Patents Landscape and Literature Review. *Applied Sciences*, 12(3). doi: 10.3390/app12031755

Frenkler, F. (2020). *The Report. Industrial Design at the Technical University of Munich*. Munich: Technical University of Munich.

Fromm, J., Stieglitz, S., and Mirbabaie, M. (2020). The Effects of Virtual Reality Affordances and Constraints on Negative Group Effects during Brainstorming Sessions. *WI2020 Zentrale Tracks*, 1172–1187. doi: 10.30844/wi_2020_k3-fromm

Garrido, L. E., Frías-Hiciano, M., Moreno-Jiménez, M., Cruz, G. N., García-Batista, Z. E., Guerra-Peña, K., and Medrano, L. A. (2022). Focusing on Cybersickness: Pervasiveness, Latent Trajectories, Susceptibility, and Effects on the Virtual Reality Experience. *Virtual Reality*. doi: 10.1007/s10055-022-00636-4

Gericke, K., and Blessing, L. T. M. (2012). An Analysis of Design Process Models across Disciplines. *Proceedings of International Design Conference, DESIGN DS*, 70, 171–180.

Hauffe, T. (2008). *Design – Ein Schnellkurs [Design – A Crash Course]*. 2nd edition. Köln: DuMont Buchverlag.

ISO (2018). *Usability: Definitions and Concepts*. Standard, International Organization for Standardization.

Keeley, D. (2018). *The Use of Virtual Reality Sketching in the Conceptual Stages of Product Design*. Bournemouth, UK: Bournemouth University.

Kemeny, A., George, P., Mérienne, F., and Colombet, F. (2017). New VR Navigation Techniques to Reduce Cybersickness. In: *IS&T International Symposium on Electronic Imaging: The Engineering Reality of Virtual Reality*, 48–53. doi: 10.2352/ISSN.2470-1173.2017.3.ERVR-097

Kemeny, A., Chardonnet, J.-R., and Colombet, F. (2020). *Getting Rid of Cybersickness: In Virtual Reality, Augmented Reality and Simulators*. Cham, Switzerland: Springer.

Kilteni, K., Bergstrom, I., and Slater, M. (2013). Drumming in Immersive Virtual Reality: The Body Shapes the Way We Play. *IEEE Transactions on Visualization and Computer Graphics*, 19(4), 597–605. doi: 10.1109/TVCG.2013.29

Krauß, V., Nebeling, M., Jasche, F., and Boden, A. (2022). Elements of XR Prototyping: Characterizing the Role and Use of Prototypes in Augmented and Virtual Reality Design. In: *Proceedings of the 2022 CHI Conference on Human Factors in Computing Systems (CHI '22)*, Article 310, 1–18. doi: 10.1145/3491102.3517714

Lo, W.T. and So, R.H.Y. (2001). Cybersickness in the presence of scene rotational movements along different axes. *Applied Ergonomics*, 32(1),1–14 doi:10.1016/S0003-6870(00)00059-4. https://www.sciencedirect.com/science/article/abs/pii/S0003687000000594#preview-section-cited-by

Lohman, J., and Turchet, L. (2022). Evaluating Cybersickness of Walking on an Omnidirectional Treadmill in Virtual Reality. *IEEE Transactions on Human-Machine Systems*. doi:10.1109/THMS.2022.3175407

Lucas, G., Kemeny, A., Paillot, D., and Colombet, F. (2020). A Simulation Sickness Study on a Driving Simulator Equipped with a Vibration Platform. *Transportation Research Part F: Traffic Psychology and Behaviour*, 68, 15–22. doi: 10.1016/j.trf.2019.11.011

Martin, B., and Hanington, B. (2012). *Universal Methods of Design: 100 Ways to Research Complex Problems, Develop Innovative Ideas, and Design Effective Solutions*. Rockport Publishers.

Pahl, G., Beitz, W., Feldhusen, J., and Grote, K.-H. (2007). *Engineering Design – A Systematic Approach*. Springer London.

Plouzeau, J., Chardonnet, J.-R., and Merienne, F. (2017). Dynamic Platform for Virtual Reality Applications. In: *EuroVR*, 2–5.

Plouzeau, J., Chardonnet, J.-R., and Merienne, F. (2018). Using Cybersickness Indicators to Adapt Navigation in Virtual Reality: A Pre-Study. In: *2018 IEEE Conference on Virtual Reality and 3D User Interfaces (VR)*, 661–662. doi: 10.1109/VR.2018.8446192

Porcino, T. M., Clua, E., Trevisan, D., Vasconcelos, C. N., and Valente, L. (2017). Minimizing Cyber Sickness in Head Mounted Display Systems: Design Guidelines and Applications. In: 2017 *IEEE 5th International Conference on Serious Games and Applications for Health (SeGAH)*. IEEE, Perth, Australia, 1–6.

Prahalad, C. K., and Ramaswamy, V. (2004). Co-Creation Experiences: The Next Practice in Value Creation. *Journal of Interactive Marketing*, 18(3), 5–14. doi: 10.1002/dir.20015

Prithul, A., Adhanom, I. B., and Folmer, E. (2021). Teleportation in Virtual Reality; A Mini-Review. *Frontiers in Virtual Reality*, 2, 730792. doi: 10.3389/frvir.2021.730792

Renner, R. S., Velichkovsky, B. M., and Helmert, J. R. (2013). The Perception of Egocentric Distances in Virtual Environments – A Review. *ACM Computing Survey*, 46(2). doi: 10.1145/2543581.2543590

Rieuf, V., and Bouchard, C. (2017). Emotional Activity in Early Immersive Design: Sketches and Moodboards in Virtual Reality. *Design Studies*, 48, 43–75. doi: 10.1016/j.destud.2016.11.001

Schutte, N. S., and Stilinović, E. J. (2017). Facilitating Empathy through Virtual Reality. *Motivation and Emotion*, 41(6), 708–712. doi: 10.1007/s11031-017-9641-7

Stadler, S. (2021). *The Integration of Virtual Reality into the Design Process*. Technical University of Munich. https://mediatum.ub.tum.de/?id=1612177

Stadler, S., Cornet, H., Novaes Theoto, T., and Frenkler, F. (2019). A Tool, Not a Toy: Using Virtual Reality to Evaluate the Communication between Autonomous Vehicles and Pedestrians. In: *Augmented Reality and Virtual Reality*. Cham: Springer Nature Switzerland AG. doi: 10.1007/978-3-030-06246-0_15

Stadler, S., Cornet, H., and Frenkler, F. (2020a). Collecting People's Preferences in Immersive Virtual Reality: A Case Study on Public Spaces in Singapore. In: *Proceedings of the DRS2020*, Brisbane. doi: 10.21606/drs.2020.308

Stadler, S., Cornet, H., Mazeas, D., Chardonnet, J.-R., and Frenkler, F. (2020b). Impro: Immersive Prototyping in Virtual Environments for Industrial Designers. In: *Proceedings of the Design Society: DESIGN Conference*, 1375–1384. doi: 10.1017/dsd.2020.81

Stadler, S., Cornet, H., Huang, D., and Frenkler, F. (2020c). Designing Tomorrow's Human-Machine Interfaces in Autonomous Vehicles: An Exploratory Study in Virtual Reality. In: *Augmented Reality and Virtual Reality*. Cham: Springer Nature Switzerland AG. doi: 10.1007/978-3-030-37869-1_13

Teixeira, J., and Palmisano, S. (2021). Effects of Dynamic Field-of-View Restriction on Cybersickness and Presence in HMD-Based Virtual Reality. *Virtual Reality*, 25, 433–445. doi: 10.1007/s10055-020-00466-2

Terenzi, L., and Zaal, P. (2020). Rotational and Translational Celocity and Acceleration Thresholds for the Onset of Cybersickness in Virtual Reality. In: *AIAA Scitech 2020 Forum*. American Institute of Aeronautics and Astronautics.

Wang, Y., Chardonnet, J.-R., and Merienne, F. (2019). Design of a Semiautomatic Travel Technique in VR Environments. In: *2019 IEEE Conference on Virtual Reality and 3D User Interfaces (VR)*, 1223–1224. doi: 10.1109/vr.2019.8798004

Wang, Y., Chardonnet, J.-R., Merienne, F., and Ovtcharova, J. (2021). Using Fuzzy Logic to Involve Individual Differences for Predicting Cybersickness during VR Navigation. In: *2021 IEEE Virtual Reality and 3D User Interfaces*, 373–381. doi: 10.1109/vr50410.2021.00060

Wee, C., Yap, K. M., and Lim, W. N. (2021). Haptic Interfaces for Virtual Reality: Challenges and Research Directions. *IEEE Access*, 9, 112145–112162. doi: 10.1109/ACCESS.2021.3103598

Woldegiorgis, B. H., Lin, C. J., and Liang, W. Z. (2019). Impact of Parallax and Interpupillary Distance on Size Judgment Performances of Virtual Objects in Stereoscopic Displays. *Ergonomics*, 62(1), 76–87. doi: 10.1080/00140139.2018.1526328

Wynn, D., and Clarkson, J. (2005). Models of Designing. In: Clarkson, J., and Eckert, C. (eds), *Design Process Improvement*, 34–59. London: Springer. doi: 10.1016/j.jvoice.2005.03.006

Xia, X., and Wu, W. (2021). User Experience of Virtual Reality Interfaces Based on Cognitive Load. In: *Advances in Usability, User Experience, Wearable and Assistive Technology*, 340–347. doi:10.1007/978-3-030-80091-8_40

Chapter 2

Revolutionizing computer-aided design with virtual reality

Radu Emanuil Petruse
Lucian Blaga University of Sibiu, Sibiu, Romania

Gerrit Meixner
Heilbronn University, Usability and Interaction Technology Laboratory
(UniTyLab), Heilbronn, Germany

Saša Ćuković
Institute for Artificial Intelligence of Serbia, Novi Sad, Serbia

2.1 INTRODUCTION

Virtual reality (VR) is a simulated experience that allows users to interact with a computer-generated environment. While the technology has advanced significantly in recent years, the idea of virtual reality has been around for several decades. The concept of virtual reality dates back to the 1960s, when Ivan Sutherland, a computer scientist, developed the first head-mounted display (HMD) system. The system was called The Sword of Damocles, and it consisted of a headset that was connected to a computer, and it was able to generate simple 3D images. Although it was a rudimentary system, it was the first step toward creating immersive virtual environments.

During the 1970s and 1980s, research on virtual reality continued, but it was mostly limited to academic and military applications. In the 1980s, Jaron Lanier, a computer scientist, launched the term "virtual reality" and founded VPL Research, a company that produced HMDs and other VR hardware.

The early 1990s saw the emergence of the first consumer VR systems. One of the most popular was the Virtuality arcade machine, which used an HMD and a pair of gloves to create an immersive gaming experience. However, the system was expensive and cumbersome, and it failed to gain widespread adoption.

In the late 1990s, the development of the internet and computer graphics technology led to a renewed interest in virtual reality. In 1995, Nintendo released the Virtual Boy, a portable gaming console that used a red and black HMD to create a 3D experience. However, the console was a commercial failure, and it was discontinued after less than a year on the market.

DOI: 10.1201/9781003306078-3

Despite these setbacks, virtual reality continued to evolve. In the early 2000s, new technologies such as motion tracking and haptic feedback were added to VR systems, making them more immersive and interactive. In the mid-2010s VR really took off, thanks to the development of affordable, high-quality consumer VR systems such as the Oculus Rift and the HTC Vive.

Today, virtual reality is used in a wide range of applications, from gaming and entertainment to education and training. For example, medical students can use VR to simulate surgeries, while architects and engineers can use it to design and test buildings and products. Virtual reality is also being used to treat conditions such as anxiety and phobias, as well as to help patients recover from injuries and illnesses. VR has come a long way since its early beginnings in the 1960s. While it took several decades for the technology to become practical and affordable, it has now become a mainstream technology with countless applications. As VR technology continues to improve and evolve, it will be interesting to see what new possibilities and applications it will enable in the years to come.

2.1.1 Augmented Reality (AR) and Mixed Reality (MR)

VR and AR/MR technologies all emerged from the broader field of computer graphics and computer vision. VR was first developed in the mid-1960s for use in flight simulators, and later expanded into gaming and entertainment applications. AR and MR, on the other hand, emerged from research into computer vision and image processing, which focused on enhancing the interaction between digital content and the physical world. AR and MR can be seen as extensions of VR, as they both involve the use of digital content to augment or enhance the user's perception of reality. However, while VR aims to create a fully immersive digital environment, AR and MR aim to enhance the user's real-world perception by overlaying digital content onto physical objects and spaces. Overall, while AR and MR have some technological roots in VR, they have developed into distinct and separate technologies with their own unique strengths and applications (see Table 2.1).

AR, VR, and MR are all related technologies that offer different experiences and have different advantages and disadvantages. AR is a technology that overlays digital information onto the real world, allowing users to interact with virtual objects and information while still seeing and interacting with their physical surroundings. AR is typically used for applications such as education, gaming, and product visualization. VR, on the other hand, is a completely immersive technology that transports users into a fully digital environment. VR is typically used for gaming, training, and simulation applications. MR, also known as hybrid reality, is a technology that combines elements of both AR and VR. In MR, digital objects are overlaid onto the real world and can interact with physical objects in the user's environment. This allows users to interact with virtual objects in a more natural way than with AR alone.

Table 2.1 Key aspects of VR, AR and MR technologies

Tech.	Hardware	Software	Content	User interface design	Performance
VR	VR requires a device capable of displaying high-quality graphics and tracking the user's movements, such as a PC, game console, or specialized VR headset. The device may also require additional sensors, such as cameras or motion controllers.	VR applications require specialized software that can render high-quality graphics and track the user's movements in real time. This may involve advanced algorithms for rendering and physics simulation, as well as support for motion tracking and input devices.	To create an effective VR experience, digital content such as 3D models, textures, and animations must be designed and optimized specifically for the VR platform. This requires specialized skills and tools, such as 3D modelling software and game engines.	VR applications must have a user-friendly interface that allows users to interact with digital content in a natural and intuitive way. This may involve designing new types of input devices or gestures that are tailored to the specific application.	VR applications require high performance hardware and software to deliver a smooth and immersive experience. This can be a challenge for developers, as the hardware requirements for VR can be demanding and vary depending on the application.
AR	AR requires a device capable of displaying digital content, such as a smartphone, tablet, or specialized AR headset. The device may also require a camera or other sensors to detect and track the user's surroundings.	AR applications require specialized software that can create and display digital content in real time based on the user's surroundings. This may involve computer vision, machine learning, or other advanced algorithms.	To create an effective AR experience, digital content such as 3D models, animations, and interactive elements must be designed and created specifically for the AR platform. This requires specialized skills and tools, such as 3D modelling software and game engines.	AR applications must have a user-friendly interface that allows users to interact with digital content in a natural and intuitive way. This may involve designing gestures, voice commands, or other methods of input that are tailored to the specific application.	In some cases, AR applications may require connectivity to other devices or services, such as cloud-based processing or remote sensors. This requires a stable and fast network connection, which can be a challenge in some environments.

| MR | MR requires a device capable of displaying digital content and tracking the user's movements and surroundings in real time, such as a specialized MR headset. The device may also require cameras, sensors, and other input devices. | MR applications require specialized software that can render digital content in real time and integrate it with the user's surroundings. This may involve advanced computer vision, machine learning, or other algorithms that can accurately detect and track the user's environment. | To create an effective MR experience, digital content such as 3D models, animations, and interactive elements must be designed and optimized specifically for the MR platform. This requires specialized skills and tools, such as 3D modelling software and game engines. | MR applications must have a user-friendly interface that allows users to interact with digital content in a natural and intuitive way. This may involve designing gestures, voice commands, or other methods of input that are tailored to the specific application. | MR applications require high performance hardware and software to deliver a smooth and seamless experience that integrates digital content with the user's surroundings. This can be a challenge for developers, as the hardware requirements for MR can be demanding and vary depending on the application. |

In terms of advantages and disadvantages, AR has the advantage of being able to integrate with the real world, but its visual fidelity may be limited by the technology used to display digital content. VR provides a fully immersive experience, but users are completely cut off from the real world, which can be disorienting and potentially dangerous. MR combines the advantages of both AR and VR, but it is a newer and less mature technology that may have limited availability and higher costs. These technologies have seen a great technological advance over the last decade and the level they have reached today is high enough to be advantageous for industry in terms of saving resources, time, and optimising production processes.

All three technologies, AR, VR, and MR, have potential for industrial applications. However, the most suitable technology would depend on the specific use case and the needs of the industry. AR is particularly well-suited for industrial applications that require workers to access information or instructions while working with their hands, such as assembly or repair tasks. AR can overlay digital information and instructions onto the physical workspace, allowing workers to perform tasks more efficiently and accurately. VR can be useful for industrial applications that require workers to be trained in potentially dangerous or expensive environments, such as hazardous material handling, heavy equipment operation, or emergency response scenarios. VR can provide a safe and controlled environment for workers to practice and learn skills without the risks associated with real-world training. MR, as a combination of AR and VR, has the potential to offer the best of both worlds for industrial applications. MR can overlay digital information onto the physical environment, while also providing an immersive and interactive experience that can improve worker training and productivity. Ultimately, the most suitable technology for industrial applications would depend on the specific needs and requirements of the industry, as well as the available hardware and software solutions.

AR and VR both have potential for CAD (computer-aided design) applications, but each has different strengths and limitations. AR is well-suited for CAD applications that require users to visualize and manipulate digital models in real-world environments. AR can overlay 3D models onto physical objects and spaces, allowing users to see how the model would fit and interact with the real world. This can be particularly useful for design reviews, simulations, and other collaborative workflows. VR, on the other hand, is better suited for CAD applications that require users to fully immerse themselves in a virtual environment to visualize and manipulate complex 3D models. VR can provide an immersive and interactive experience that can enhance spatial understanding and design comprehension, allowing users to explore and manipulate designs from new perspectives.

Both AR and VR can improve the efficiency and accuracy of CAD workflows, allowing users to visualize and manipulate designs in more intuitive and natural ways. The choice between AR and VR would depend on the specific use case and the needs of the CAD workflow, as well as the available hardware and software solutions.

2.1.2 Virtual reality used for computer-aided design

Virtual reality has been used for computer-aided design (CAD) for several years. In fact, one of the earliest applications of virtual reality was in CAD, where designers and engineers could visualize 3D models of products or buildings before they were built.

Using virtual reality in CAD allows designers to view and interact with their designs in a more immersive and realistic way. With a VR headset and controllers, designers can manipulate and explore their designs in 3D, which can lead to more accurate and efficient design iterations. It can also help designers identify potential issues and design flaws before the product or building is built, saving time and money.

Additionally, virtual reality can be used for collaborative design, where multiple designers can work together in a shared virtual environment. This can be particularly useful for large and complex projects where multiple teams are involved. There are already several CAD software programs that incorporate virtual reality, such as Autodesk's VR solutions and SketchUp Viewer for VR. As VR technology continues to improve, we can expect to see even more advanced and sophisticated CAD tools that leverage the benefits of virtual reality.

Here we present several case studies that demonstrate the use of virtual reality in computer-aided design (CAD):

1. Volkswagen: Volkswagen uses virtual reality to aid in their product design process. With VR headsets and controllers, designers can interact with virtual car models and make changes to them in real time. This allows designers to test and refine their designs before the physical prototype is built, resulting in faster and more efficient design iterations. https://www.volkswagen-newsroom.com/en/virtual-reality-3643

2. Siemens: Siemens uses VR in their CAD software, allowing engineers to visualize and manipulate complex 3D designs in a virtual environment. This technology has been particularly useful in designing large industrial machinery and power plants, where a detailed understanding of the product is critical before it is built. https://www.plm.automation.siemens.com/global/en/industries/automotive-transportation/automotive-oems/digital-mockup-virtual-augmented-reality.html

3. HOK: HOK, a global architecture and engineering firm, uses VR to create immersive and interactive virtual environments that allow clients to explore and experience their designs before construction begins. This technology has been particularly useful for large-scale projects, such as sports stadiums and convention centers, where the client needs to visualize the finished product in detail. https://www.hok.com/ideas/research/how-architects-and-designers-can-help-define-the-metaverse/

4. Trimble: Trimble, a provider of technology solutions for the construction industry, uses VR in their SketchUp Viewer software. This allows architects, engineers, and contractors to view and interact with

3D models of buildings and construction sites in a virtual environment. This technology has been particularly useful for planning and coordinating construction projects, as it allows all stakeholders to visualize and understand the project in a more detailed and interactive way. https://www.trimble.com/en/innovation/extended-reality

5. Boeing: Boeing uses virtual reality to visualize and optimize the design of aircraft interiors. With VR headsets and controllers, designers can move around and interact with the virtual cabin, testing different configurations of seats and amenities. This allows designers to make informed decisions about the placement of different components, optimizing space and creating a more comfortable and efficient passenger experience. https://www.boeing.com/company/about-bca/washington/737-max10-virtual-reality-01-28-19.page

6. Ford: Ford uses virtual reality to simulate the assembly line process for their vehicles. With VR headsets and controllers, engineers can test different assembly configurations and identify potential issues before the production line is built. This allows Ford to optimize their production process, reduce costs, and improve quality control. https://www.xrtoday.com/virtual-reality/ford-builds-revolutionary-vr-design-studio/

7. AECOM: AECOM, a global engineering and construction firm, uses VR to create immersive training experiences for their employees. With VR headsets and controllers, employees can simulate complex construction tasks and learn proper safety protocols in a virtual environment. This allows AECOM to train their employees more effectively and efficiently, improving overall safety and productivity on their job sites. https://aecom.com/uk/services/property-solutions/visualisation-and-virtual-reality/

8. ArcelorMittal: ArcelorMittal, a global steel and mining company, uses VR to design and optimize their production facilities. With VR headsets and controllers, engineers can visualize and interact with the virtual plant, testing different layouts and equipment configurations. This allows ArcelorMittal to optimize their production process, reduce costs, and improve efficiency. https://corporate.arcelormittal.com/industries

9. NASA: NASA uses virtual reality to visualize and simulate space missions. With VR headsets and controllers, engineers and astronauts can explore and interact with virtual models of spacecraft, environments, and procedures. This allows NASA to test and refine mission plans before launching into space, reducing risk and improving success rates. https://www.nasa.gov/centers/armstrong/features/interns-design-interactive-virtual-reality-prototype.html

10. Caterpillar: Caterpillar, a manufacturer of heavy equipment, uses virtual reality to train operators and technicians on their products. With VR headsets and controllers, employees can simulate the operation and maintenance of Caterpillar equipment, improving safety and

reducing downtime. https://www.cat.com/en_US/blog/blending-art-engineering.html

11. Gensler: Gensler, an architecture and design firm, uses VR to create immersive design experiences for clients. With VR headsets and controllers, clients can explore and interact with virtual models of their projects, gaining a deeper understanding of the design and providing feedback. This allows Gensler to improve collaboration and communication with their clients, resulting in more successful projects. http://www.gensleron.com/work/tag/virtual-reality

12. Cushman & Wakefield: Cushman & Wakefield, a real estate services company, uses VR to create virtual property tours. With VR equipment, clients can explore and experience properties in a realistic and immersive way, even if they are located far away. This allows Cushman & Wakefield to market their properties more effectively and provide better customer service to their clients. https://www.cushmanwakefield.com/en/spain/industries-and-sectors/tech

13. Thyssenkrupp: Thyssenkrupp, a German engineering conglomerate, uses VR in their elevator design process. With VR designers can test and optimize elevator designs in a virtual environment, identifying potential issues and making necessary adjustments before the elevator is built. This allows Thyssenkrupp to improve the safety and efficiency of their elevators while reducing costs. https://www.thyssenkrupp-steel.com/en/company/digitalization/smart-services/smart-services.html

14. General Electric: General Electric (GE) uses VR in their aviation design process. Engineers can visualize and interact with virtual models of aircraft engines, testing different configurations and identifying potential issues before building physical prototypes. This allows GE to optimize their engine designs and reduce development time and costs. https://www.ge.com/news/taxonomy/term/2708

15. Volvo: Volvo uses VR in their vehicle design process. With VR hardware, designers can interact with virtual car models, testing and refining designs before building physical prototypes. This allows Volvo to improve the safety and efficiency of their vehicles while reducing development time and costs. https://www.media.volvocars.com/global/en-gb/media/pressreleases/253105/volvo-cars-and-varjo-launch-world-first-mixed-reality-application-for-car-development

16. Airbus: Airbus uses virtual reality in conjunction with their CAD software to design and optimize the interiors of their aircraft. Designers can interact with virtual cabin mock-ups and make real-time changes to the design. This allows Airbus to create more comfortable and efficient aircraft interiors, while reducing development costs and improving time-to-market. https://www.airbus.com/en/newsroom/news/2017-09-virtual-reality-with-real-benefits

17. Bombardier: Bombardier, a manufacturer of trains and airplanes, uses virtual reality to simulate and optimize their production processes.

With VR engineers can visualize and interact with virtual models of production lines, testing different configurations and identifying potential issues. This allows Bombardier to optimize their production processes, reduce costs, and improve quality control. https://www.railwaypro. com/wp/bombadier-to-use-virtual-reality-to-accelerate-product-development/

18. TATA Steel: TATA Steel uses virtual reality to design and optimize their steel production facilities. In VR engineers can visualize and interact with virtual models of their production lines, testing different layouts and equipment configurations. This allows TATA Steel to optimize their production processes, reduce costs, and improve safety and efficiency. https://www.controllab.nl/cases/tata-steel/

19. Rolls-Royce: Rolls-Royce uses virtual reality in conjunction with their CAD software to design and test aircraft engines. This allows Rolls-Royce to optimize their engine designs, reduce development costs, and improve safety and reliability. https://www.rolls-royce.com/media/press-releases/2020/13-05-2020-intelligentengine-rr-launches-first-immersive-virtual-reality-training.aspx

Overall, these examples demonstrate the wide range of applications for virtual reality in computer-aided design. By creating more immersive and interactive design experiences, virtual reality is helping companies optimize their processes, reduce costs, and improve quality control. As the technology continues to evolve, we can expect to see even more innovative applications of virtual reality in CAD.

2.1.3 CAD software compatible with VR

Several CAD software packages are compatible with virtual reality (VR) technology allowing users to interact with their designs in a virtual environment. Here are some of them:

- SolidWorks: https://www.solidworks.com/partner-product/demo3dvr-solidworks
- SketchUp: https://vrsketch.eu
- AutoCAD: https://www.autodesk.com/solutions/extended-reality
- PTC Creo: https://www.ptc.com/en/technologies/cad/augmented-reality
- Fusion 360: https://www.plm.automation.siemens.com/global/de/products/mechanical-design/nx-virtual-reality.html
- Rhino 3D: https://mindeskvr.com/rhino/
- Siemens NX: https://www.plm.automation.siemens.com/global/de/products/mechanical-design/nx-virtual-reality.html
- CATIA: https://events.3ds.com/eseminar-virtual-reality-catia-on-3dexperience-platform
- Inventor: https://www.autodesk.com/autodesk-university/class/Virtual-Reality-Inventor-2018

Listed software packages offer a wide range of features and capabilities for designing and prototyping in virtual reality, and can be used in various industries such as architecture, manufacturing, and product design. With the integration of VR technology, CAD software is becoming more immersive and interactive, making the design and prototyping process more efficient and effective.

2.2 APPLICATIONS OF VR IN 3DEXPERIENCE CAD SOFTWARE

The aim of this chapter is to identify and study the advantages and disadvantages of using VR in computer-aided design applications. For this purpose, we chose one of the most popular CAD software, Catia V5, a 3D CAD software widely used in the automotive and aerospace industries and its predecessor, the 3DExperience platform. There are several applications of virtual reality (VR) in CATIA, https://events.3ds.com/eseminar-virtual-reality-catia-on-3dexperience-platform. Here are some examples:

1. Virtual Reality Collaborative Design: CATIA allows designers and engineers to collaborate in a VR environment, enabling them to work on a project simultaneously from different locations. This feature allows for real-time communication and feedback, leading to faster and more efficient design and decision-making.
2. Virtual Assembly: With the help of VR, designers can create and test assembly sequences in a virtual environment, allowing them to identify and solve any potential issues before the physical production of the product. This feature saves time and resources while improving the quality of the final product.
3. Virtual Ergonomics: CATIA also allows designers to test the ergonomics of their designs in a VR environment. With the help of VR, designers can simulate human movements and test the accessibility and comfort of their products before the physical production stage.
4. Virtual Manufacturing: CATIA can simulate the manufacturing process in a VR environment, allowing engineers to identify potential issues and optimize the production process. This feature allows manufacturers to reduce costs, improve quality control, and enhance worker safety.

To use virtual reality (VR) in CAD, the following technological requirements are required:

1. VR Headset: To experience VR, a VR headset, which typically includes a high-resolution display and sensors that track head movements is needed. There are several VR headset options available on the market, such as Oculus Rift, HTC Vive, and Windows Mixed Reality headsets.

2. Powerful Computer: To run CAD software in VR, a powerful computer that can handle the demands of both the software and the VR headset is required. This includes a high-end graphics card, plenty of RAM, and a fast processor.

3. VR-Enabled CAD Software: Not all CAD software is compatible with VR technology. To use VR in CAD, software that supports VR integration should be selected. Some of the popular CAD software that support VR were mentioned earlier (SolidWorks, Autodesk Revit, and CATIA).

4. VR Controllers: In addition to a VR headset, VR controllers that allow to interact with designs in a virtual environment are recommended. These controllers typically include buttons and joysticks that enable selection and manipulation of objects in the virtual space.

5. Tracking System: To ensure accurate movement and positioning in the virtual environment, a tracking system is required. This may involve sensors placed in the room or on the VR headset and controllers.

2.2.1 Case study – VR used with 3DExperience

The computer-aided design (CAD) software used is 3DExperience. It offers compatibility with VR/AR software. 3DExperience is developed by Dassault Systems, developer of CATIA PLM solution. The 3DExperience platform provides a collaborative working environment, with cloud upload options, which facilitates teamwork on the same computer-designed projects, assemblies, or parts. The interface is different from CATIA, therefore it takes some time to adjust with this program. It is also possible to import parts or assemblies of a large number of formats (.step, .stl, .cad, 3dxml etc.) so that one can use the VR/AR module without the reference objects being built on the 3DExperience platform.

The 3DExperience platform does not specify what kind of VR sets it is compatible with and from what will be demonstrated later in this chapter it will be noted that not all VR/AR sets have these capabilities.

2.2.2 Oculus Rift console

The first HMD tested with 3DExperience is the Oculus Rift and here the most important steps are presented. The hardware consists of special glasses with a screen for each eye and motion sensors (HMD), two joysticks and two motion sensors. The motion sensors must be positioned on elevated surfaces, preferably on a higher plane than the user's head, they must be directed toward the user's working perimeter and their sensor-optical angles must intersect. Once the hardware has been installed, connected to the computer and a power source, and the software has been installed, the first steps are to designate a perimeter of movement in the virtual space. This process

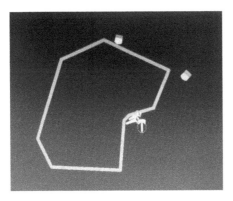

Figure 2.1 Working parameter set, with HMD, sensors, and joysticks visible.

requires moving a joystick around the user to draw the edges of this virtual perimeter within which there are no real-world objects (Figure 2.1).

After selecting the perimeter, user can start using the HMD. To connect the Oculus Rift software with 3DExperience, user needs to enter its advanced settings and allow interaction between it and unknown programs.

After going through these steps, an assembly was loaded into 3DExperience and the VR/AR module was started. Here, before the connection to the HMD can be made, certain parameters need to be selected from the HMD Configuration window (Figure 2.2). Here the program identifies the HMD connected to the computer, lets the user configure the scale at which the 3D aspects appear in the virtual environment and the virtual background. From the "VR Skills" category the user chooses exploration (interacting with 3D objects) or just viewing objects, then under the "Navigation" category the initial movement mode – flying, walking, and teleporting – which can be changed later from the set VR controllers while in use, the movement speed in meters per second, and the surface on which the avatar is placed in the virtual environment. Finally, there is the "Performance and Controls" category where the user chooses how to render images – continuous or interrupted, rendering images viewed in HMD concurrently on a computer desktop window. After setting up the HMD, 3DExperience is ready to launch the simulation projected in the HMD.

In the first attempt to open the assembly with the HMD connected, the assembly was in virtual space, but the user had no ability to move or interact with it. Once immersed in VR, the user always sees the digital version of the joysticks – the Digital Twin. These virtual joysticks may have the same look as the real ones, or, depending on the application used, may have different designs. The position of the joysticks relative to the user's headset can be observed at any time in VR, as long as they are in the field of view, and they mimic real hand movements very well. However, in the 3DExperience program the joysticks were not visible, and therefore had no capabilities to

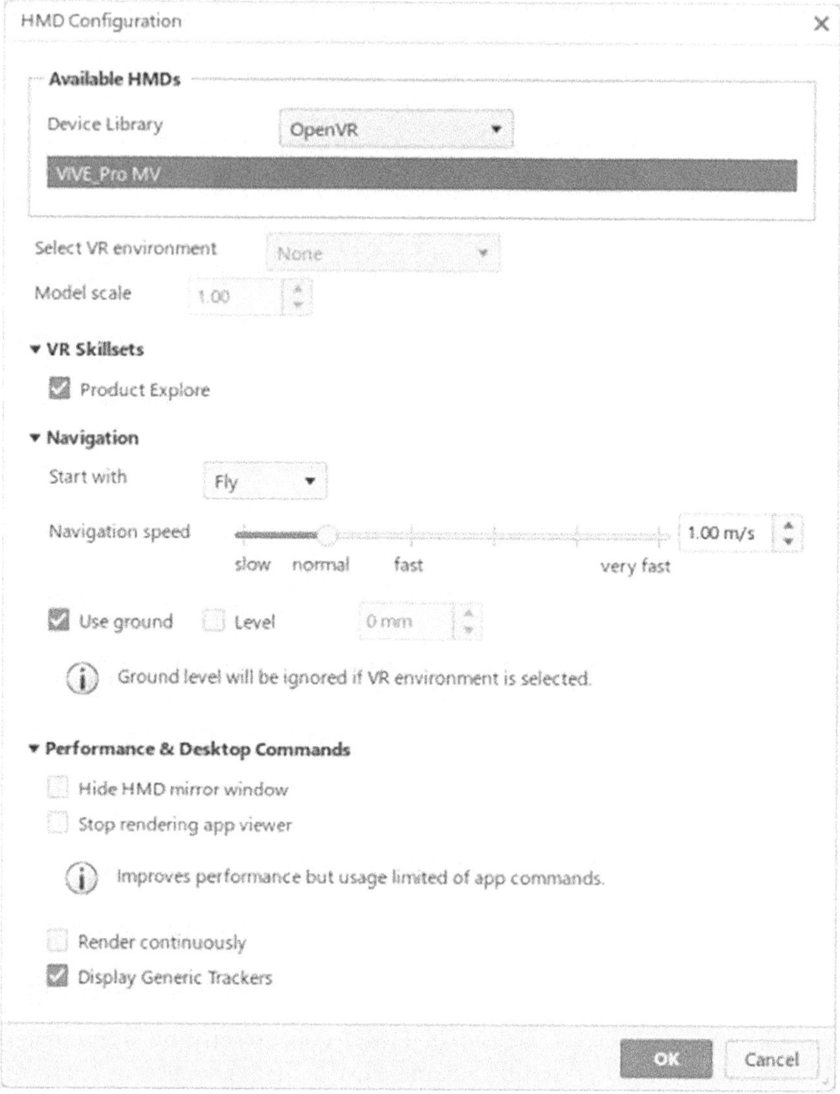

HMD Configuration ✕

Available HMDs

Device Library   OpenVR   ▼

VIVE_Pro MV

Select VR environment   None   ▼

Model scale   1.00   ▲▼

▼ **VR Skillsets**

☑ Product Explore

▼ **Navigation**

Start with   Fly   ▼

Navigation speed   ━━━━●━━━━━━━━━━━━━━━━━   1.00 m/s ▲▼
                        slow   normal   fast   very fast

☑ Use ground   ☐ Level   0 mm   ▲▼

ⓘ Ground level will be ignored if VR environment is selected.

▼ **Performance & Desktop Commands**

☐ Hide HMD mirror window

☐ Stop rendering app viewer

ⓘ Improves performance but usage limited of app commands.

☐ Render continuously
☑ Display Generic Trackers

OK   Cancel

Figure 2.2 HMD Configuration window of the 3D Experience platform.

manipulate 3D objects or move the avatar other than real-world head movements, which were also translated into virtual space. Changes could be made
to the HMD Configuration mode to test whether the Oculus Rift needs
parameters to be adjusted for improved operation. After multiple tweaks it
was concluded that the changes made were to appearance, speed of manipulation, and avatar position adjustment, and no matter how they were configured, the Oculus Rift did not allow interaction in 3DExperience beyond
viewing (from a distance) and simple head movements in the perimeter

designated at the beginning. Joysticks could not be configured to be detected in the 3DExperience virtual space, and therefore had no ability to move or interact with 3D assemblies. On top of this, every time the VR module stopped to change settings, the 3DExperience would shut down and had to be restarted, making working in it more difficult and time consuming. From the preceding observations it was concluded that the Oculus Rift does not have the ability to work optimally with CAD programs, being able to observe CAD parts or assemblies in virtual space, but not having the ability to move or interact in any way with the 3D object, thus making working in this virtual reality console connected to a CAD program useless.

2.2.3 HTC Vive Eye Pro console

Further research revealed that the 3DExperience platform is largely used in conjunction with another HMD that seems to offer greater compatibility: the HTC Vive. The adjustment and calibration part of the HMD consists of locating the position of the monitor in the virtual environment, locating and calibrating the floor by placing the sensing joysticks on it, and finally establishing a virtual working perimeter (Figure 2.3).

After connecting the HMD to the computer, the 3DExperience platform was opened, and in VR/AR mode. An assembly was loaded and the virtual environment view started. First observations are: the Vive Pro's joysticks are

Figure 2.3 User immersed in VR and VR set components.

visible even after linking with 3DExperience, and show more options on them in the virtual space.

2.2.4 Interaction methods virtual reality-CAD

From the right-hand Joystick there is an option to switch between two modes: "Explore" and Navigation. Once the navigation mode is selected, on the left joystick there are three non-navigation modes in the virtual space: "Flight", "Walk", and "Teleport" (Figure 2.4). The functions are used in the following way:

- "Walk": once selected, four arrows will appear on the right controller key, north, west, south, east, and moving the finger on the touch key will move in the desired direction, just in the floor plane, depending on the direction of the user's gaze.
- "Teleport": once selected, the right controller will emit a beam, similar to a laser beam, into the virtual environment. A circle will be placed where it meets the virtual floor, and the avatar will be teleported to the position of that circle.
- "Flight": this function is similar to "Walk" function, the difference is that it provides the ability to move the avatar on all planes, not just the floor. To make this possible, the way the joystick is held acts as a plane on which movement will also take place. For example, if the joystick is held horizontally, and forward motion is chosen, the avatar will move forward; if, on the other hand, the joystick is held vertically and forward motion is chosen, the avatar will move upwards relative to the floor, thus controlling the position of the joystick plane in space, and from this, virtual "Flight" is possible.

These three functions are available in the Navigation mode, which at first glance may seem unnatural to use, but after more work with the headset, the user will get used to it, and intuitively go through movements of any kind with ease. In addition to using the preceding functions for movement, the motion of the user's head is also taken into consideration. All head movements are tracked and translated into the virtual environment, so if the user moves, the avatar will move too. The same goes for head movements like: the user bends, lowers, raises or turns the head in any direction or on any plane.

"Explore" mode has five specific functions, which will appear like the navigation functions when the user holds down the grab button on the right hand. On the left hand the five functions that allow interaction with 3D objects appear inside the virtual joystick. These functions are: "Explode", "Section", "Transparency", "Measure", and "Hide/Show". Each of these functions allows the user the option to interact with the assembly, and they have the same characteristics as in CATIA, but the way of using differs. In "Explore" mode the user always has the list of functions on the left joystick,

Figure 2.4 The functions that provide movement in the virtual environment: walking, flying and teleporting.

from which he can easily select one, and from the trigger key of the right joystick he can use the function (for Explode both triggers will be used).

With the "Explode" function the user can hold down both triggers as if they were clenching both fists. When the fists are moved away from each other, and depending on the distance between the fists, all the pieces of the assembly will be exploded at a distance in direct proportion to the distance of the fists, so we can move the pieces away from each other by any desired distance, unlike CATIA where the pieces are automatically moved apart (Figure 2.5).

Figure 2.5 Industrial equipment with Explode function applied.

In "Section" function the user will see a virtual laser beam coming from the right controller; when the trigger is pulled this beam will be activated and the user can move it through the material – through part of the assembly. When the trigger is released, a sectioning plane will be created and the part of the assembly passing through this plane will be hidden (Figure 2.6).

Figure 2.6 Sectioned workbench.

In "Measure" function the user can position a point placed on the studied assembly. When releasing the trigger, the point is fixed in position; repeating the procedure will create a second point and the distance between these will be displayed above the distance and on the right controller (Figure 2.7).

"Hide/Show" and "Transparency" functions have the same mode of operation. In that case, once selected, the user will be able to point the joystick straight at a piece in the assembly, and when the trigger is pulled this piece will be hidden (for the Hide/Show function) or shown as transparent, respectively, with only its edges remaining visible in the Transparency function (Figure 2.8).

Figure 2.7 Plotting two points between which to make the measurement.

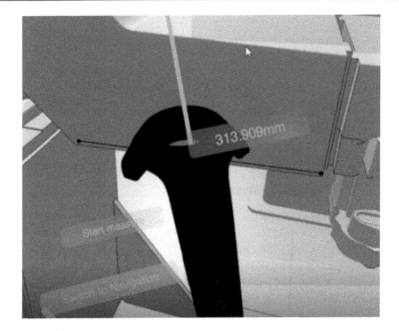

Figure 2.7 (Continued)

Figure 2.8 Transparency function.

Figure 2.8 (Continued)

Pressing the no.1 key on the left joystick will open a list with two options: to delete any changes previously made by the Explore functions, and to change the view of the loaded assembly (Figure 2.9).

In order to study the applicability of VR in industry, using the 3DExperience platform, several trials were made. A few assemblies were opened, most of them entire production or assembly lines; that is, all the

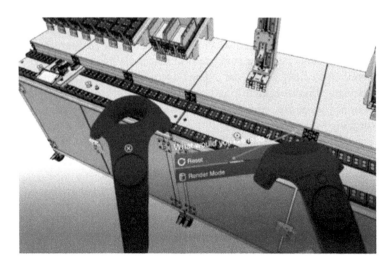

Figure 2.9 Changing rendering modes.

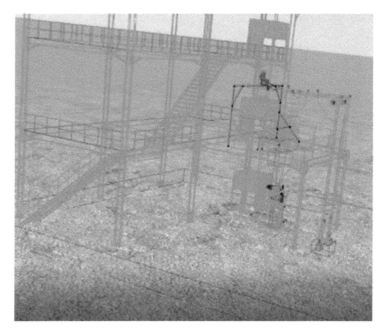

Figure 2.9 (Continued)

VR set functions were tested one by one, observing their accuracy, ease of use, and applicability.

2.3 RESULTS AND DISCUSSIONS

To obtain a virtual workspace, compatible with HTC Vive Eye Pro console, several CAD models and assemblies were tested (a bicycle assembly line, a modular workbench, a construction materials production line, a shaft parts production line, and a car). The 3D models were manipulated and explored using the aforementioned options. In addition to working in the 3DExperience program, various VR applications for 3D design, modelling, and sketching were also tested. The following section presents the results, outlining the main ideas, advantages, disadvantages, and directions for improvement and optimization considering various areas of applicability of VR technologies in the engineering industry such as:

- Visualization of parts, assemblies, and processes – quality inspection in a virtual environment,
- Manipulating of 3D objects – collaborative working,
- Creating 3D models/sketches using VR,
- Studying the ergonomics of a 3D workspace,
- Training in the virtual environment.

2.3.1 Visualisation of parts, assemblies, and processes – virtual engineering control

VR technology has proven to be optimal in terms of 3D models visualization and inspection in several aspects; these will be outlined in the following. After experimenting with walking through a scaled production line in the virtual environment it is found that the sensation of viewing objects at a 1:1 scale is pleasant, natural, and very close to reality, with the user feeling completely immersed in the environment. Thus, a high-quality technical inspection of 3D models can be undertaken before their physical production.

Good immersion and closeness to a real environment makes virtual technical inspection of 3D models easy, and with better results than inspecting 3D objects on a screen monitor. This mode of visualization is a major advantage for the industry as it allows the user to control and improve assemblies at the design stage without actually building them thus minimizing mistakes before they are physically built. This will reduce the costs that may arise later by fixing design issues. The 3DExperience's Explode and Transparency features also help the user to visualise the assembly for a more detailed view (Figure 2.10).

In the automotive industry, where the prototype of a new car is created from wax or similar materials, VR allows designers to inspect the car to real scale and make various modifications. This design inspection and modifications that can be achieved using VR technology bring a numerous advantage in cost, time, and material reduction (Figure 2.11).

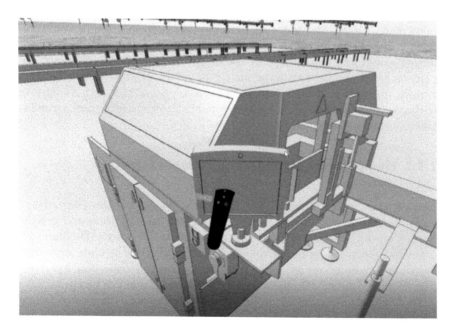

Figure 2.10 View of the equipment of a production line.

Figure 2.11 Use of HMD for the purpose of studying virtual technical inspection.

Due to the development of technology resulting in increasingly better immersion, some users may experience dizziness, headaches, or confusion when using HMD. This is however not a big disadvantage, occurring mainly during games and less during the use of the CAD modules. Moreover, the percentage of people who have such experiences is small. There are also various methods by which these symptoms are prevented, such as starting with shorter exposure times, wearing the HMD properly, setting a conducive environment, etc. (Middler 2022).

2.3.2 Manipulating 3D objects – collaborative working

The VR experience combined with the 3DExperience platform has advantages and disadvantages in terms of 3D object manipulation and collaborative work, the latter being more prevalent in this case. 3DExperience offers five functions for interacting with virtual objects. The Hide/Show and Transparency functions are useful for visualization and inspection, but those that help manipulate 3D objects have shortcomings that can be optimized.

The Explode function is useful when studying an assembly to better observe its individual parts and their position. Using this function is easy, intuitive, and more helpful to the user, as it is used in VR not in traditional

CAD programs. However, this function becomes almost useless once the user is immersed in a large assembly such as a production line. Using Explode function, all parts will be pushed into space in all directions relative to the center of the assembly; so, if the user wants to study a CNC machine that is not in the center of the assembly, it will be moved outward from the whole assembly, making studying it with the Explode function difficult or even impossible. One way to improve this is to be able to detach sub-assemblies which can be then modified, with the rest of the loaded parts remaining intact. The user can choose the desired sub-assembly directly in VR by selecting the parts included in the assembly, or from the model tree structure of the whole assembly.

Working on user-selected sub-assemblies can also be implemented in the Cut function, where currently, once the cutting plane is selected, it will cut the entire assembly. The user can also orient the sectioning plane to any position in space but cannot choose which part will be hidden and which part will remain visible. To optimize this process, after positioning the sectioning plane, the user should have the option to choose which part remains visible.

The Measure function is easy to use but does not provide sufficient accuracy when measuring. General measurements can be made, indicating lengths to the nearest micron, but the positioning of the points between which the measurement is to be made is too imprecise (Figure 2.12).

Thus, the user can make measurements that give him information about distances around him, but he cannot position points with a high precision and has no way of finding precise distances of edges or surfaces. There is no way to measure angles or to find areas. One way to improve this measuring tool would be to implement a "snap" function. Also, for measuring angles, areas, volumes, or other parameters, a list of options could be introduced to be accessed while using the HMD.

As mentioned earlier, the introduction of a list of options would bring many benefits, it could include a multitude of tools, from the tree structure present in CAD programs to options for editing, sketching, finding information about the 3D object, measuring, and manipulating objects in the virtual environment (Figure 2.13). These kinds of virtual tool menus are already implemented in other 3D modelling apps available for the HTC Vive (Figure 2.14).

Manipulating 3D objects is not currently possible in 3DExperience, any more than modifying them via Cut, Transparency, Hide/Show, and Explode. HTC Vive Eye Pro allows manipulation of objects similar to holding an object in user's hand in reality, with an optimization that makes the experience close to the reality. In 3DExperience, however, it is not possible to move the position of a part that belongs to an assembly or on its own.

Experiments have been made in collaborative work where one user carries the HMD, and another operates 3DExperience from the computer. 3DExperience does not allow changes to be made to the 3D model on the

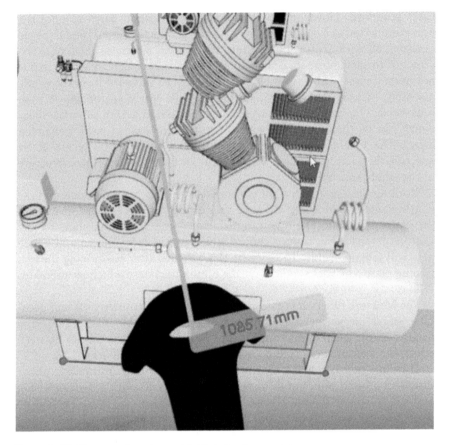

Figure 2.12 Measure function – highlighting imprecision.

computer while the HMD is connected in VR mode. The only options allowed here are to change view modes, change opacity, or start the kinematic simulation – the options that are not of great interest.

2.3.3 Training in the virtual environment

The VR/AR module in 3DExperience allows the loading of 3D models with an assigned kinematics, thus it is possible to view moving 3D objects in the virtual environment and therefore allows users to perform staff training for a certain pre-created scenario. The kinematics of the assembly should be created in the Mechanical Systems Design module, then Mechanical Systems Experience to run the simulation in 3DExperience and then to be opened in VR. This gives a major advantage, allowing to proceed with the training process before having the equipment on site (e.g., the training is done before the equipment is delivered to the company), or with less energy

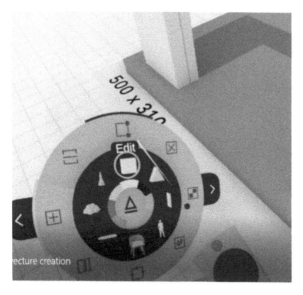

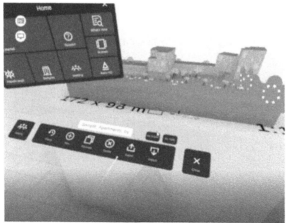

Figure 2.13 Menu available in Arkio.

consumption, as the equipment is not put into operation. Also, by doing the training virtually, the risk of injury to the trainees and the risk of machinery breakdown when used by inexperienced people is excluded. Avoiding such risks that cause material damage to the company, and as a method of saving working time, this module is one of the most advantageous aspects of working with VR technology in companies in the industry (Figure 2.15).

Moreover, viewing an assembly with assigned kinematics gives the user an ease of full-scale visualization of the created assembly, thus allowing the improvement of design process.

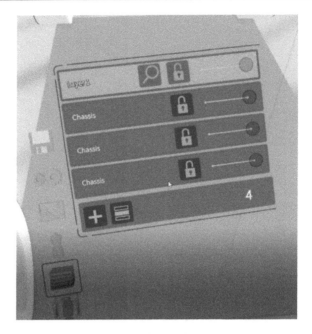

Figure 2.14 Menu available in Gravity Sketch.

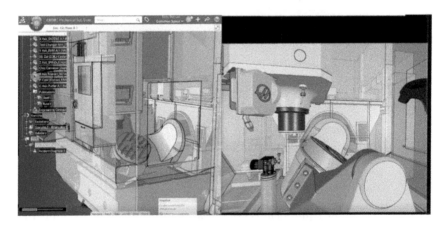

Figure 2.15 Testing a Haas CNC machine for virtual training.

2.3.4 Studying the ergonomics of a 3D object

Creating the kinematics of assemblies and visualising it in the virtual environment also helps to study the ergonomics of a workstation straight from the design phase. To respect the ergonomics standards, the worker's position should be natural with plenty of room to move while working (Figure 2.16).

Figure 2.16 Studying ergonomics in the virtual environment.

Once the 3D model of the workplace is uploaded into the virtual environment with the technological process information, ergonomics can be easily tested for optimal workspace design with minimal subsequent modifications that would incur costs.

2.3.5 Creating 3D models/sketches using VR

3DExperience does not allow 3D parts to be created in the VR module, but various 3D design software have been tested, including Arkio, Strata, Calc Flow, Gravity Sketch inStudio VR SE. Arkio is a VR CAD software designed to develop architectural structures. This software allows the user to create and subsequently modify almost any geometrical shape. The cursor has a snap function (Figure 2.17) on the edges and corners of the created objects; also dimensions are shown from the current cursor position to the sides of the surface on which it is placed.

It uses an extensive menu designed to choose shape types, change, measure, and edit them; viewing mode; virtual background; and more, as depicted in Figure 2.17. Having this wide set of construction options, a user-friendly interface, and the option to be immersed in the same environment with the 3D model that the user created, the VR offers a better overview of the 3D model, a unique experience, and a perfect working environment in which one can remain immersed for long periods of time. Immersion during creation offers a whole new experience, far superior to that of computer design, where designers can create models and sketches quickly or load existing ones to display to clients.

Gravity Sketch is another 3D sketching and modelling program tested, aimed at creating artistic and technical models, with the possibility to load parts built in CAD programs and modify them later as shown in Figure 2.18. It also offers an extensive menu with very good options, immersion, optimization, and

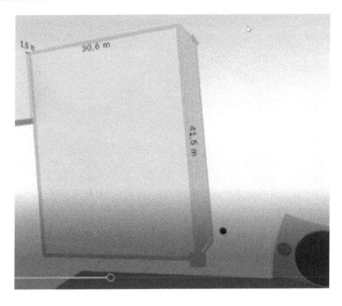

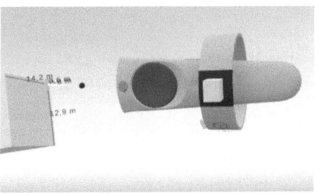

Figure 2.17 Creating 3D objects in Arkio.

working environment that gives the user a good working experience. It allows the creation of various shapes such as sheet metal surfaces, parts with complex, rotational, or prismatic geometries, as well as selection of the material they are made of, choosing the opacity and colour, and so on.

A Vive-owned comapny, Mindesk is investing in the development of a special VR platform for CAD designers, a real-time CAD collaboration platform that allows multiple users to review, create, and edit 3D CAD models immersed in virtual reality.

In the past designers spent hours exporting their CAD model into the third-party programming engines, consuming a lot of time and making their

Figure 2.18 3D Sketch module.

work more cumbersome. On the new Vive platform, it will be possible to go directly into VR without the need to prepare or export the model. The company's clients are mainly in the fields of architecture, naval design, industrial product design, and creative arts where time is of the key importance. Today, architects create physical prototypes of CAD models to show them to clients, which is time-consuming and consumes materials that will later be discarded, so designing or uploading the model directly to VR makes their job much easier. Mindesk also offers the collaborative option of designing in computer CAD at the same time as VR (Team, VIVE 2019).

2.3.6 Continuous development and optimisation

During the time of this work the CAD 3DExperience software has gone through several updates, the latest of which also brought changes to the VR/AR module. The changes were primarily of a *visual nature*: different menu configuration, better view of the text, and also of a *functional nature*: a new function was introduced – the VR Viewpoints function (Figure 2.19). This newly introduced function allows the user to save certain viewpoints in the VR environment, which can be returned to at any time and from any position by selecting the desired point from the menu. With this function, a designer presenting, for example, his project to clients can save certain viewpoints to show them the 3D object of interest at a glance.

The implementation of this feature also shows that the CAD platform is in continuous development and although various drawbacks of the platform could be listed, the team behind it is working on constantly optimizing it to provide a suitable workspace for designers in the virtual environment.

Figure 2.19 VR Viewpoints function – newly implemented.

2.4 CONCLUSIONS

The main conclusions that can be drawn from this work are the following:

- Virtual reality technology is advantageous in the field of technical inspection due to its good immersion and closeness to reality, which provides a suitable working environment. With the implementation of inspection in a virtual environment, a company using such technology benefits from the reduction of errors already at the design stage, which entails subsequent cost savings, reduction of the time allocated to the technical inspection process, and touching up any non-conformities virtually with the design, rather than physically on the ready-made part or assembly.
- Manipulating the 3D objects included in an assembly is not possible in the virtual environment. Also, the 3DExperience modelling platform lacks more functions than available in CAD programs that would be beneficial for designing or modifying parts and assemblies in VR. However, existing VR consoles on the market show that they can work with complex programs, and the 3DExperience platform is constantly being improved by adding new functions so that they can be implemented in various areas of engineering work.
- Training in VR is superior to that currently practiced, especially in areas with a high risk of injury of employees using specialized equipment or through the training required to learn the work processes.

Training in a VR environment removes the risk of employees' injuries, reduces energy consumption as equipment is not operated during training on resource-intensive equipment, excludes the risk of equipment failure, and can save time and costs.

- 3D sketching and modelling in VR are beneficial for designers and architects to reduce design time, building mock-ups for clients, building and inspecting prototypes, and re-designing them. VR technology provides a much better perspective of the objects created at any scale than on a computer screens.

ACKNOWLEDGEMENTS

Part of this work has been researched by Eng. Oprea-Ștef Robert during his bachelor thesis.

BIBLIOGRAPHY

AECOM – Integrated Services, Accessed May 11, 2023. https://aecom.com/uk/services/property-solutions/visualisation-and-virtual-reality/

Bombadier to use virtual reality to accelerate product development, Accessed May 11, 2023. https://www.railwaypro.com/wp/bombadier-to-use-virtual-reality-to-accelerate-product-development/

Creo AR Design Share, Accessed May 11, 2023. https://www.ptc.com/en/technologies/cad/augmented-reality

Design inside virtual reality, Accessed May 13, 2023. https://vrsketch.eu

Digital Mockup, Virtual & Augmented Reality, Accessed May 11, 2023. https://www.plm.automation.siemens.com/global/en/industries/automotive-transportation/automotive-oems/digital-mockup-virtual-augmented-reality.html

Digital Transformation: Using Augmented Reality to Experience Design, Accessed May 11, 2023. http://www.gensleron.com/work/tag/virtual-reality

Employees use virtual reality to figure out best way to build 737 MAX 10, Accessed May 11, 2023. https://www.boeing.com/company/about-bca/washington/737-max10-virtual-reality-01-28-19.page

Extended reality: Virtual, augmented, and mixed, Accessed May 11, 2023. https://www.autodesk.com/solutions/extended-reality

Ford Builds Revolutionary VR Design Studio, Accessed May 11, 2023. https://www.xrtoday.com/virtual-reality/ford-builds-revolutionary-vr-design-studio/

HOK design and technology leaders share their thoughts on navigating the metaverse, Accessed May 11, 2023. https://www.hok.com/ideas/research/how-architects-and-designers-can-help-define-the-metaverse/

Middler, Jordan. 2022. What causes motion sickness in VR and what can you do to avoid it? April 13. Accessed June 12, 2022. https://www.livescience.com/what-causes-motion-sickness-in-vr

NASA Interns Design Interactive Virtual Reality Prototype, Accessed May 11, 2023. https://www.nasa.gov/centers/armstrong/features/interns-design-interactive-virtual-reality-prototype.html

NX Virtual Reality, Accessed May 11, 2023. https://www.plm.automation.siemens. com/global/de/products/mechanical-design/nx-virtual-reality.html

Rhinoceros in Virtual Reality, Accessed May 11, 2023. https://mindeskvr.com/rhino/

Rolls-Royce launches first immersive virtual reality training for business aviation customers, Accessed May 11, 2023. https://www.rolls-royce.com/media/press-releases/2020/13-05-2020-intelligentengine-rr-launches-first-immersive-virtual-reality-training.aspx

Smarter steels for people and planet, Accessed May 11, 2023. https://corporate. arcelormittal.com/industries

Step into the new reality of work, Accessed May 11, 2023. https://www.trimble.com/ en/innovation/extended-reality

Tata Steel Port Talbot – VR Training Simulator, Accessed May 11, 2023. https:// www.controllab.nl/cases/tata-steel/

Team, VIVE. 2019. VIVE X company, Mindesk, secures $900k to bring CAD designers into Virtual Reality. March 11. Accessed June 17, 2022. https://blog.vive.com/ us/vive-x-company-mindesk-secures-900k-bring-cad-designers-virtual-reality/

The Blending of Art and Engineering, Accessed May 11, 2023. https://www.cat.com/ en_US/blog/blending-art-engineering.html

Viewing Fusion 360 designs in VR, Accessed May 11, 2023. https://forums.autodesk. com/t5/fusion-360-ideastation-archived/vr-support-for-fusion-360/idi-p/7335824

Virtual Engineering – an instrument of the digital transformation, Accessed May 11, 2023. https://www.thyssenkrupp-steel.com/en/company/digitalization/smart-services/smart-services.html

Virtual Reality Bites: 6 ways industry is harnessing the power of VR And AR, Accessed 05 11, 2023. https://www.ge.com/news/taxonomy/term/2708

Virtual reality in the real estate sector, Accessed May 11, 2023. https://www. cushmanwakefield.com/en/spain/industries-and-sectors/tech

Virtual Reality with CATIA on the 3DEXPERIENCE platform, Accessed May 11, 2023. https://events.3ds.com/eseminar-virtual-reality-catia-on-3dexperience-platform

Virtual Reality with Inventor, Accessed May 11, 2023. https://www.autodesk.com/ autodesk-university/class/Virtual-Reality-Inventor-2018

Virtual reality with real benefits, Accessed May 11, 2023. https://www.airbus.com/ en/newsroom/news/2017-09-virtual-reality-with-real-benefits

Volvo Cars and Varjo launch world-first mixed reality application for car development, Accessed May 11, 2023. https://www.media.volvocars.com/global/en-gb/ media/pressreleases/253105/volvo-cars-and-varjo-launch-world-first-mixed-reality-application-for-car-development

VR in SolidWorks, Accessed May 13, 2023. https://www.solidworks.com/partner-product/demo3dvr-solidworks

VR in Volkswagen, Accessed May 11, 2023. https://www.volkswagen-newsroom. com/en/virtual-reality-3643

Chapter 3

Innovations in healthcare product development

Exploring AR/VR/MR technologies

Muhammad Mohsin, Zartasha Mustansar,
Rehan Zafar Paracha, Maheera Amjad
and Rida Ayub Chaudary
School of Interdisciplinary Engineering & Sciences (SINES) National
University of Sciences & Technology (NUST), Islamabad, Pakistan

Jamil Ahmad
Department of Computer Science and Information Technology,
University of Malakand, Chakdara, Dir Lower, Khyber Pakhtunkhwa,
Pakistan

Umer Asgher
SMME, National University of Sciences & Technology (NUST), Islamabad,
Pakistan

3.1 INTRODUCTION

Before we delve into the discussion about augmented reality (AR), virtual reality (VR), and mixed reality and their scope in the medical field, it is essential to reiterate the basic definition of reality as compared to AR/VR/ MR and their state of pertinent technologies. To answer the first question of what constitutes reality, let's take help from an example: six blind men who had never seen an elephant before in life decided to see (feel) how an elephant looks (feels) like. Upon the first interaction with an elephant, and clearly not being able to use their visual sense, they decided to use their sense of touch as a tool to feel the elephant. All men approached the elephant from different directions, and after the encounter, each man alleged something as: "The elephant is like a great mud wall baked hard in the sun", "he is exactly like a spear", "The elephant is very much like a rope", "This elephant much resembles a serpent", and so on (see Figure 3.1).

The idea here is that we make our perception of reality based on what we can feel/sense/touch. Our reality in essence is what we know and that is where augmented/mixed and virtual reality technologies come into action.

DOI: 10.1201/9781003306078-4

Figure 3.1 Blind men and the elephant parable.

AR/VR/MR are ways to enhance existing physical reality with the help of digital tools targeting our visual, auditory, and other senses. It is also important to differentiate between AR, VR, and MR. To put it simply:

- AR allows superposition digital experience on top of the real world. (Least immersive). Example: Pokemon Go game (Figure 3.2).
- MR not only allows the superposition of digital elements but also allows to interact with those digital elements. Example: Applications using Microsoft Hololens (Figure 3.3).
- VR creates a digital experience that is completely separated from the real world. (Most immersive). Example: Applications such as VR glasses such as Meta Quest Pro or others (Figure 3.4).

The basic differences among these technologies can be derived from the type of technology used, level of immersion, and type of applications created using these technologies.

AR/VR/MR is used in vast applications from gaming to entertainment. AR/VR/MR is now being deployed to develop applications and solutions to cater to the needs of the medical industry. It is very easy to adopt AR/VR/MR in smaller portable hardware like mobile phones and wearables; it could be your smart watch, too. Now it is possible to utilize AR/VR/MR in understanding medical procedures in much better and immersive real-life ways than ever possible. In this chapter, we will talk about some of the examples of the application of AR/VR/MR in healthcare, followed by a discussion of the merits and drawbacks of the technology. For ease of understanding, we will divide AR/VR/MR in healthcare into five categories as shown in Figure 3.5.

Figure 3.2 Digital experience with least immersive (Pokemon Go game).

Figure 3.3 Applications based on Microsoft Hololens.

Figure 3.4 Example using VR glasses such as Meta Quest Pro or others.

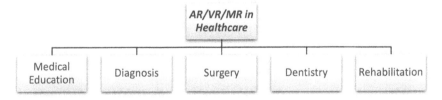

Figure 3.5 Categorization of applications of AR/VR in the field of healthcare.

3.2 MEDICAL AND HEALTHCARE EDUCATION

Learning any field requires proficiency and supremacy of skills for better performance that comes through repeated practice, especially in the medical domain where the doctors/practitioners are required to complete a certain number of hours under guided supervision. Medical training can be time-consuming and expensive (sometimes at the cost of human life). Also, safety and ethical concerns are repeatedly raised over medical training. Use of AR, VR, and MR technologies for healthcare training can be useful in learning and attaining clinical excellence. As an example, lets discuss how AR/VR/MR can be used in conjunction with human anatomy (Kamphuis et al., 2014).

3.2.1 Human anatomy using AR

One of the most crucial subjects for students of the healthcare domain remains to be human anatomy. In traditional methods, anatomy is taught through dissecting cadavers. To visualize healthy and diseased organs, dissection is performed. This practice is not only expensive but also has been called out repeated times for being unethical (Winkelmann, 2007). Using the existing information and knowledge, AR technology can provide enhanced solutions for teaching/learning anatomy (Kamphuis et al., 2014).

Example of existing AR technologies for teaching/learning of the anatomy is Bangor Augmented Reality Education Tool for Anatomy (BARETA). BARETTA is more effective and ethical as compared to the traditional method of teaching/learning on cadavers. It combines rapid prototyping technology with AR and provides learners with visuals and touch options for detailed inspections and understanding of each organ in a healthy state (Thomas, William John, and Delieu, 2010).

3.2.2 Human anatomy using MR

As discussed, MR not only allows the superposition of digital elements but also supports interaction. MR becomes a very effective tool when it comes to interacting with the human body (in a mixed reality setting), as students/practitioners can not only see a human body from the inside but interact and choose the best course of action. Also, MR can be useful to preplan a surgery or any other medical procedure.

A study (Stojanovska et al., 2020) discusses that as the medical curriculum increases, there are less and less time and resources available for students to practice anatomy, hence the use of MR in teaching/learning anatomy can be effective. The same study with the help of randomized controlled trials showed that there is no statistical difference between the cadaver-based and MR-based teaching/learning and exams. Results indicate that medical students, regardless of the study modality, performed similarly on the MR and the cadaver practical exams.

An example of practical solutions for MR in anatomy would be by a company named HoloAnatomy® Software, which claims to allow:

- Customizable shared view with detailed illustrations of human systems.
- Side-by-side differences between female and male anatomy.
- Automatic labels or custom labels and the ability to isolate particular structures.
- Help in understanding the position of body (prone, supine, or others).

3.2.3 Human anatomy using VR

VR allows the most immersive experience; VR gives users a different perspective when it comes to learning anatomy. For many years VR has been used in medical teaching/learning. For example, VR-based classes allow students to gain rich experience of the human body and help in developing treatments for diseases without subjecting the practitioners to the risk of infection.

A meta-analysis (Zhao et al., 2020) of 15 randomized controlled trials from 1990 to 2019 concluded that VR improves test scores (on teaching outcomes) moderately compared with other traditional approaches. The study suggests that VR acts as an efficient way to improve the student/user's level of knowledge of anatomy.

An example of VR in medical education would be that of American company Automage. Anatomage specializes in the visualization of the anatomy of the human body. The company claims to have anatomically correct 3D models that show human organs as well as fully interconnected venous, vascular, and arterial structures. Automage is available as a VR app on the Meta Quest 2 by the company Meta (formerly known as Facebook) for medical facilities.

3.3 DIAGNOSTICS

AR/VR/MR solutions in clinical diagnosis can improve procedural and diagnostic accuracy. AR/VR/MR technology can bring accurate psychological experiences through immersive simulations in a risk-free environment. The use of AR/VR/MR enables multiple tasks, including but not limited to

- Diagnosing and treating dementia, depression, PTSD, phobias, and other physical disorders and pathologies.
- Faster and more effective remote diagnostics and surgery.
- Training medical personnel.
- Exposing patients to information they need to learn faster and more effectively.

Medical practitioners along with engineers have tested various technologies and instruments that can help in the accurate diagnosis of medical conditions. Various AR/VR/MR technologies are currently used in the medical sector (Ma et al., 2022).

3.4 SURGERY

Modern-day surgeons are heavily dependent on technologies to assist them in operating rooms. Immersive technologies such as AR/VR/MR can enhance the performance of surgeons and assist them in doing difficult procedures requiring higher precision. Immersive technologies help in navigation during surgical procedures, helping surgeons to visualize damaged organs, which are not easily observable by the naked eye. This visual information can also be shared with surgeons, medical students, nurses, residents, and other relevant stakeholders (Okamoto et al., 2015).

AR-based navigation systems are already available and have become essential for orthopedics, otolaryngology, neurosurgery, and maxillofacial surgery surgeries. Surgeons can now overlay real-time patient data and 3D anatomical models onto their field of vision, enhancing precision and reducing errors. This AR-driven approach improves surgical planning and navigation, ultimately leading to safer and more efficient procedures. The type of image generated using an AR-based navigation system is an important part that depends on the shape, color, and location of the target organ. Images generated with an AR-based navigation system are displayed as volume-rendering or surface-rendering images. *Volume-rendered* images are considered inappropriate due to their poor contrast and inadequacy caused by the details of organs displayed over the target region. *Surface-rendered* images are more appropriate and accessible. They also provide various color options depending on the target organ. Although volume-rendered images also provide color selection options, the process is not as fast as required during surgery in real time (Okamoto et al., 2015). Overlaid images on target organs can be visualized in three different ways:

A. Images can be directly projected on the target organ. These projected images can be effectively used during laparoscopic surgery (Sugimoto et al., 2010). In some cases, this projection-based AR display can be interrupted by any hindrance or moving object, such as the body of the surgeon or any other staff member, which makes such a projection system more accessible to flat surfaces of organs. However, this system has been improved by using a portable projection device.

B. A monitor-based system can also allow the surgeon to examine organs during video-assisted surgery (Okamoto et al., 2013).

C. To visualize AR-based images, a glass-like transparent monitor allows surgeons to examine the superimposed image using a relatively smaller region of a glass plate. Such systems with a narrow field of view do not assist the surgeon during abdominal surgery but are more accessible during neurosurgery. Furthermore, a head-mounted optical system based on mixed reality (MR) has been developed, which allows surgeons and physicians to visualize images from the perspective of the patient (Ferrari et al., 2009).

Augmented reality specifically in biomechanics as well allows researchers to create immersive simulations of human movement and biomechanical processes. This technology helps analyze and optimize athletic performance, design ergonomic products, and develop more effective rehabilitation methods by providing real-time, interactive insights into how the body moves and functions.

3.4.1 Examining complex dynamics using AR

AR has been used to visualize complex dynamic structures of the human body. An example of that would be as described in Hamza-Lup et al., (2007): 3D dynamics of the lungs can be superimposed directly on the patient during surgery using a real-time visualization system. High-resolution tomography (HRCT) is combined with a lung model. A surgeon can visualize and examine any malformation and imperfection in 3D lung dynamics. Several lung emergencies, including lung surgeries, closed pneumothorax, lung infections, lung transplants, lung cancer surgery, and others, can be examined using this prototype.

3.4.2 VR in surgery

Virtual reality (VR) is an interactive real-time environment created from images generated by computer simulation. 3D technology based on VR provides a first-person view while performing surgery. These 3D technologies surpass the current 2D video learning and training processes by providing a true-to-life experience. MOVEO Foundation uses the Oculus Rift platform to provide learners and trainees with head-mounted VR devices with a virtual, seemingly original operating surgeon experience (Al-Qattan and Al-Turaiki, 2009).

3.4.3 Broadcasting and recording VR surgery

A live broadcast at the Royal London Hospital provided a full 360° view of the operating room from a patient's point of view. Such broadcasts are proposed to be a significant part of healthcare education. The use of AR can be cost effective with the use of devices like Google Cardboard (Khor et al., 2016). VIPAR has also generated a system allowing a remote surgeon to help in other surgeries. This remote assistance can be done by augmenting

Table 3.1 List of most popular AR and VR devices used in healthcare and surgery

AR devices	VR device
Microsoft HoloLens	Oculus Rift
Sony Smart Eyeglass	Sony PlayStation VR
Epson Moverio BT-20	HTC Vive
Google Glass	Samsung Gear VR
Vuzix M100 Smart Glasses	Fove VR
Recon Jet	Avegant Glyph
Optinvent Ora-1	

Data from Khor et al., (2016)

their hands into the display of the actual surgeon who is performing surgeries while wearing a headset. Table 3.1 provides a comprehensive list of AR and VR devices popular among the healthcare community.

Table 3.1. List of most popular AR and VR devices used in healthcare and surgery (data from Khor et al., 2016).

3.5 DENTISTRY

With the development of the healthcare technologies sector, dentistry has also had its share of upgradation. Instruments used in surgery, imaging, and scans of oral cavities and teeth have improved experience during dental care/surgeries. The use of image guidance during dental implants can significantly improve accuracy as compared to manual implantation. This image guidance can be in 3D overlaid images or infrared tracking cameras (Brief et al., 2005).

The use of AR/VR devices in dentistry is a complex process as it depends on various aspects, including but not limited to a variety of tissues in the oral cavity and the complexity seen in the types of equipment used. Various tissues present in the oral cavity include multi-layer teeth, bone, and gingiva. The complexity of equipment varies depending on its shape, formation, movement, and speed (Raja'a and Farid, 2016).

The stylus is used during the simulation of tooth reduction in a virtual environment. This stylus appears on a 3D stereoscopic monitor and is seen as the instrument used during surgery with the help of special goggles. During the procedure, computerized oral cavity tissues and equipment models demonstrate tooth reduction assisted by advanced visual applications and software. Unlike standard training systems where resin models are used, VR systems can display various layers of teeth, including enamel, dentin, and dental pulp. This visual depiction can be easily used to avoid unnecessary dental pulp exposure during clinical procedures (Mallikarjun et al., 2014).

3.6 AR-BASED TECHNOLOGIES TO IMPROVE PHYSICAL REHABILITATION

Physical rehabilitation is needed to improve normal physical motion/function lost because of any medical condition. Rehabilitation sessions can be long, tiring, and costly. AR-based sensors acquire data from patients during gamified sessions composed of various physical exercises. Inertial movement unit (IMU) sensors are used to identify limb motion with the equilibrium of the body, electrocardiogram (ECG) sensors are used to monitor cardiac activity, and electromyograph (EMG) sensors are used to assess muscle health (relaxation and contraction) (Monge and Postolache, 2018).

An example is applying an adaptive mixed-reality training system for patients suffering from hemiparesis. This system provides real-time, customizable, adaptive, and multimodal feedback generated from the affected region (such as the arm or torso) of patients. These feedback reports are generated in the visual or musical form (Duff et al., 2010). These gamified sessions provide patients with engaging activities, and reports generated as output are then used to identify the underlying cause of the disease. The system also measures the extent of disease with the help of scoring points generated during exercises. This is extremely transformational in the field of research and development.

Another example of AR in rehabilitation is presented by Baldominos, Saez, and del Pozo, (2015), where using Unity3D, a prototype was generated for rehabilitating the rotator cuff of the right shoulder. In this model, the user plays the role of a goalkeeper in the soccer game. The movement and posture of the patient are analyzed during the session. During the game, the score is directly proportional to the movement of the patient. The player must move their arm completely to stop the ball and get the maximum score.

Briefly, there are numerous models of reliable and portable AR/VR systems nowadays. A variety of them can be used for different rehabilitation therapies. These systems have common components like sensor, camera, monitor, and VR programs or software, and all of them can be deployed to improve methods of rehabilitation therapies in future and effectively configure them for improved clinical applications.

3.7 DISCUSSION (CHALLENGES AND FUTURE OF AR IN HEALTHCARE)

Looking at what we have discussed in this chapter, it would not be wrong to think healthcare stakeholders are paying great attention to the field of AR and its applications, not just from the technical perspective but also from ethical, financial, and practical use case scenarios. As we speak of the applications, we must realize how big companies like Facebook, Apple, and ScienceSoft have invested large sums of capital in developing AR hardware.

At this stage, it is safe to say that AR/VR/MR is not just another unantici-pated development of the modern world but an actual future technology (Zhu et al., 2014). AR/VR/MR empower medical professionals with immer-sive training and surgical planning tools, improve patient engagement and education through realistic simulations, and enable remote consultations. These technologies also aid in rehabilitation, pain management, and phar-maceutical research. By enhancing data visualization, fostering global col-laboration, and advancing medical research, AR and VR hold tremendous potential to transform healthcare, although cost and accessibility challenges must be addressed for widespread adoption.

This practice of inferring from the research is crucial to comprehend the trends of how widely and rapidly people are adapting AR in healthcare, despite all the exposures involved. Such deep dives into scientific and practi-cal life literature give the reader a broad perspective of challenges and potential future applications of the technology being discussed. Speaking of challenges, a few are highlighted in this chapter:

A. Displaying 3D images: It highly depends on displaying technolo-gies and techniques. The accuracy of real and virtual spaces requires knowledge of the characteristics of both real and virtual cameras. Camera calibration is eliminated for see-through systems, but they still require tracking and optimized head and eye movements from various perspectives. This optimization can introduce several errors, so there is a need for detailed calibration (Tuceryan, Genc, and Navab, 2002).

B. Projecting 2D images on 3D planes does cause inaccuracy due to incon-sistency of perceived spatial orientations and unidentified objects lying in mid of the projection. In operating rooms where instruments are present across the operating table, it can cause inaccuracy of the pro-jected image. AR windows must be placed at an appropriate distance and location from the target. For various endovascular and other sur-geries where the actual target location is distant from the manipu-lation site, AR windows must be placed at an appropriate distance (Guha et al., 2017).

C. Obstruction caused by the operator's or surgeon's hands: Obstructions can lead to misinterpretation of the projected image, especially in the case of overlaying virtual images. In cases with rapid perspective change, an additional challenge of temporal synchronization of virtual and real environments exists. It exists in optical see-through systems, where a little delay in projecting virtual images can be distracting and problematic for surgeons.

When considering challenges, it is essential to discuss the potential and future applications of the technology. AR/VR/MR holds excellent benefits, and it would be complicated to put them all in one place, but here are some:

- Financial and monetary values.
- Improved medical/healthcare learning.
- Cheaper medical education and training sources.
- More accessible and relatable healthcare awareness.
- Timely and more accurate diagnosis.

REFERENCES

Al-Qattan, M M, and T M Al-Turaiki. 2009. "Flexor Tendon Repair in Zone 2 Using a Six-Strand 'Figure of Eight' Suture." *Journal of Hand Surgery (European Volume)* 34 (3): 322–328.

Baldominos, Alejandro, Yago Saez, and Cristina Garcia del Pozo. 2015. "An Approach to Physical Rehabilitation Using State-of-the-Art Virtual Reality and Motion Tracking Technologies." *Procedia Computer Science* 64: 10–16.

Brief, Jakob, Dieter Edinger, Stefan Hassfeld, and Georg Eggers. 2005. "Accuracy of Image-Guided Implantology." *Clinical Oral Implants Research* 16 (4): 495–501.

Duff, Margaret, Yinpeng Chen, Suneth Attygalle, Janice Herman, Hari Sundaram, Gang Qian, Jiping He, and Thanassis Rikakis. 2010. "An Adaptive Mixed Reality Training System for Stroke Rehabilitation." *IEEE Transactions on Neural Systems and Rehabilitation Engineering* 18 (5): 531–541.

Ferrari, Vincenzo, Giuseppe Megali, Elena Troia, Andrea Pietrabissa, and Franco Mosca. 2009. "A 3-D Mixed-Reality System for Stereoscopic Visualization of Medical Dataset." *IEEE Transactions on Biomedical Engineering* 56 (11): 2627–2633.

Guha, Daipayan, Naif M Alotaibi, Nhu Nguyen, Shaurya Gupta, Christopher McFaul, and Victor X D Yang. 2017. "Augmented Reality in Neurosurgery: A Review of Current Concepts and Emerging Applications." *Canadian Journal of Neurological Sciences* 44 (3): 235–245.

Hamza-Lup, Felix G, Anand P Santhanam, Celina Imielinska, Sanford L Meeks, and Jannick P Rolland. 2007. "Distributed Augmented Reality with 3-D Lung Dynamics—A Planning Tool Concept." *IEEE Transactions on Information Technology in Biomedicine* 11 (1): 40–46.

Kamphuis, Carolien, Esther Barsom, Marlies Schijven, and Noor Christoph. 2014. "Augmented Reality in Medical Education?" *Perspectives on Medical Education* 3 (4): 300–311.

Khor, Wee Sim, Benjamin Baker, Kavit Amin, Adrian Chan, Ketan Patel, and Jason Wong. 2016. "Augmented and Virtual Reality in Surgery—The Digital Surgical Environment: Applications, Limitations and Legal Pitfalls." *Annals of Translational Medicine* 4 (23): 454. https://doi.org/10.21037/atm.2016.12.23

Ma, Marco King In, Chinmoy Saha, Stephanie Hiu Ling Poon, Rachel Sze Wan Yiu, Kendrick Co Shih, and Yau Kei Chan. 2022. "Virtual Reality and Augmented Reality—Emerging Screening and Diagnostic Techniques in Ophthalmology: A Systematic Review." *Survey of Ophthalmology* 67 (5): 1516–1530.

Mallikarjun, Savita Abdulpur, Superna Tiwari, Sunil Sathyanarayana, and Pheiroijam Romibala Devi. 2014. "Haptics in Periodontics." *Journal of Indian Society of Periodontology* 18 (1): 112.

Monge, João, and Octavian Postolache. 2018. "Augmented Reality and Smart Sensors for Physical Rehabilitation." In *2018 International Conference and Exposition on Electrical and Power Engineering (EPE)*, Lasi, Romania 1010–1014. https://doi.org/10.1109/ICEPE.2018.8559935

Okamoto, Tomoyoshi, Shinji Onda, Michinori Matsumoto, Takeshi Gocho, Yasuro Futagawa, Shuichi Fujioka, Katsuhiko Yanaga, Naoki Suzuki, and Asaki Hattori. 2013. "Utility of Augmented Reality System in Hepatobiliary Surgery." *Journal of Hepato-Biliary-Pancreatic Sciences* 20 (2): 249–253.

Okamoto, Tomoyoshi, Shinji Onda, Katsuhiko Yanaga, Naoki Suzuki, and Asaki Hattori. 2015. "Clinical Application of Navigation Surgery Using Augmented Reality in the Abdominal Field." *Surgery Today* 45 (4): 397–406.

Raja'a, M, and Farzaneh Farid. 2016. "Computer-Based Technologies in Dentistry: Types and Applications." *Journal of Dentistry (Tehran, Iran)* 13 (3): 215.

Stojanovska, M, G Tingle, L Tan, L Ulrey, S Simonson-Shick, J Mlakar, H Eastman, et al. 2020. "Mixed Reality Anatomy Using Microsoft HoloLens and Cadaveric Dissection: A Comparative Effectiveness Study." *Medical Science Educator* 30 (1): 173–178. https://doi.org/10.1007/s40670-019-00834-x

Sugimoto, Maki, Hideki Yasuda, Keiji Koda, Masato Suzuki, Masato Yamazaki, Tohru Tezuka, Chihiro Kosugi, et al. 2010. "Image Overlay Navigation by Markerless Surface Registration in Gastrointestinal, Hepatobiliary and Pancreatic Surgery." *Journal of Hepato-Biliary-Pancreatic Sciences* 17 (5): 629–636.

Thomas, Rhys Gethin, Nigel William John, and John Michael Delieu. 2010. "Augmented Reality for Anatomical Education." *Journal of Visual Communication in Medicine* 33 (1): 6–15.

Tuceryan, Mihran, Yakup Genc, and Nassir Navab. 2002. "Single-Point Active Alignment Method (SPAAM) for Optical See-through HMD Calibration for Augmented Reality." *Presence: Teleoperators & Virtual Environments* 11 (3): 259–276.

Winkelmann, Andreas. 2007. "Anatomical Dissection as a Teaching Method in Medical School: A Review of the Evidence." *Medical Education* 41 (1): 15–22.

Zhao, Jingjie, Xinliang Xu, Hualin Jiang, and Yi Ding. 2020. "The Effectiveness of Virtual Reality-Based Technology on Anatomy Teaching: A Meta-Analysis of Randomized Controlled Studies." *BMC Medical Education* 20 (1): 127. https://doi.org/10.1186/s12909-020-1994-z

Zhu, Egui, Arash Hadadgar, Italo Masiello, and Nabil Zary. 2014. "Augmented Reality in Healthcare Education: An Integrative Review." *PeerJ* 2: e469.

Part 2

Enhancing manufacturing with virtual, augmented, and mixed reality

Chapter 4

Transforming manufacturing with digital twins and metrology in VR

Slavenko Stojadinovic
University of Belgrade, Faculty of Mechanical Engineering, Department
for Production Engineering, Belgrade, Serbia

4.1 INTRODUCTION

Virtual reality (VR) plays an important role in the era of digital production control. In addition to managing production and control processes, it also serves for visual monitoring of production, identification of bottlenecks, simulation, and collision avoidance.

In the metrological sense, most often VR, augmented reality (AR) and mixed reality (MR) are today united in the concept of digital twin (DT) which enables both the control of the measurement process and the simulation and verification of the measurement process.

Digital measuring twin (DMT) presents a mirror between the physical and virtual measuring world. As such, DMT has significant impact on measurement planning through increased efficiency, optimization of the measurement process by reducing the throughput times, and real-time status of the physical components of the measurement system and working conditions (Stojadinovic et al., 2021a). According to Boschert et al. (2018, 209), "one of the main benefits of the Digital Twin for mechatronic and cyber-physical systems is to provide the information created during design and engineering also at the operation of the system".

Depending on the level of application or the need for application, DT can be with bi-directional information flow and one-directional information flow. One example of DT with one-directional information flow is shown in Stojadinovic et al. (2021a). It is based on the STEP-NC processing and measurement planning methodology and uses STEP-NC Machine software to simulate and verify measurement protocols.

In the context of manufacturing metrology, DT partially or fully provides the following:

- VR: A true virtual environment of measuring process that operators can access to use measuring data and reports.
- AR: Uses overlap nominal and real value of tolerance on the measuring process that we observe.
- MR: Presents the real measuring parts to the virtual digital parts, allowing real operators to interact with them.

DOI: 10.1201/9781003306078-6

4.1.1 Background and driving forces

Virtual metrology (VM) monitors quality characteristics in the production process in real time or off-line mode. According to Cheng et al. (2012) VM is a method to conjecture manufacturing quality of a process tool based on data sensed from the process tool and without physical metrology operations. Automatic virtual metrology (AVM) implies that the processes of data collection from sensors, their processing, and data analysis are automated. The paper by Cheng et al. (2012) defines the VM automation levels, proposes the concept of automatic virtual metrology (AVM), and develops an AVM system for automatic and fab-wide VM deployment. The example of automatic VM model refreshing for chemical vapor deposition tools is also illustrated in this paper.

In recent years, more and more high-tech manufacturing plants have used VM technology to monitor the production quality of machines and processes (Th et al., 2020). According to Th et al. (2020) the principle of VM operation consists of two phases:

- The off-line modeling stage: various calculation methods are used (such as neural networks, regression techniques, etc.) to build a virtual metrology model, and
- The on-line conjecture stage: the established virtual metrology model can be used to instantly estimate the manufacturing quality of the workpiece or the health of the machine.

Therefore, the VM can solve the measurement delay problem without increasing the measurement cost and achieve the full inspection realm that the quality of each production workpiece can be monitored online and immediately. According to Th et al. (2020), Microsoft Azure Machine Learning Studio (AMLS) is a cloud machine learning service developed by Microsoft. It integrates the tools needed for machine learning on a cloud platform and uses drag and drop to analyse machine learning related data, model building, performance testing, and service building, which greatly reduce the threshold for learning. For providing factory-wide manufacturing service, research presented in Th et al. (2020) used AMLS machine learning services to construct a virtual metrology cloud platform so that all production machines have the virtual metrology capability with a highly integration solution. Finally, according to Th et al. (2020), the actual production data of the factory was used to conduct the integration test and performance evaluation of the system to verify the availability and industrial utilization of the research.

The traditional virtual metrology method cannot satisfy the demand of the manufacturing process (Chen et al., 2013). In order to get the real time measurement for the high-mix manufacturing process, a new VM algorithm that combines the advantage of both standard statistical methods and time serial analysis is proposed in Chen et al. (2013). According to Chen et al. (2013) the VM algorithm consists of three stages:

1. Key variables are selected, which contain important information regarding the source of variation of the current process condition.
2. The statistical MANCOVA technique is adopted to build conjecture models for products with different specifications considering the product effects.
3. The time serial, that is, the IMA(1,1), is integrated into virtual metrology approach, which reflects the current unmeasured information of the process, and thus the accuracy of the virtual metrology model is substantially improved.

The purpose of the paper (Tieng et al., 2015) is trying to apply VM presented in Cheng et al. (2011, 2015) for measuring machining precision of machine tools. Authors of the paper (Tieng et al., 2015) emphasize that besides embedding essential sensors on the machine tool effectively, the challenges are:

- Segmentation: to accurately segment essential parts of the raw process data from the original NC file,
- Data Cleaning: to effectively handle raw process/sensor data with low S/N ratios, and
- Feature Extraction: to properly extract significant features from the segmented raw process data.

The development of a virtual metrological computed tomography (CT) for numerical measurement uncertainty determination at the Institute of Manufacturing Metrology (Friedrich-Alexander-University Erlangen-Nuremberg (FAU), Germany) using the software aRTist 2 by the BAM German Federal Institute for Materials Research and Testing is described (Wohlgemuth et al., 2018). The virtual metrological CT presented in Wohlgemuth et al. (2018) uses a Monte-Carlo approach for numerical measurement uncertainty determination. Results of the paper (Wohlgemuth et al., 2018) demonstrating that numerical uncertainty determination according to GUM Supplement 1 and in accordance with uncertainty determination according to guideline VDI/VDE 2630 Part 2.1 is possible for selected measurement tasks are presented.

To inspect and qualify complex internal geometries that are not accessible with an external probe, parts are typically scanned with computed tomography (CT) and manually compared to the computer-aided design (CAD) model using visual inspections (Klacansky et al., 2022). Matching the CAD model to the 3D reconstructed object is challenging in a traditional desktop environment due to the lack of depth perception and 3D interaction. An additional challenge comes from the geometric complexity of CAD meshes and large-scale CT scans. Authors of the paper (Klacansky et al., 2022) present a VR system for manual qualification, providing a new defect visualization method. Describing the VR system presented in Klacansky et al. (2022):

- First, we describe a semiautomatic CAD-to-Scan Registration approach in VR using a finite element mesh.
- Second, we introduce the Defect Box, which enables full-resolution inspection for massive scans and CAD-CT comparison of local defect regions.
- Finally, the VR system includes intuitive 3D Metrology methods that enable natural interactions for the measurement of features and defects in VR.

According to Lynn et al. (2012), VM is the estimation of metrology variables that may be expensive or difficult to measure using readily available process information. These authors investigate the application of global and local VM schemes to a data set recorded from an industrial plasma etch chamber. Authors of the paper (Lynn et al., 2012) investigated partial least-squares regression, artificial neural networks, and Gaussian process regression as candidate modelling techniques, with windowed Gaussian process regression models providing the most accurate results for the data set investigated.

The presented approach to development of DT in this chapter includes four levels: (i) mathematical modeling: model of the measuring sensor path; (ii) data modeling: generating the needed set of information to integrate the given tolerances and geometry of the parts by ISO 1101 standard and developed ontological knowledge base; (iii) application of artificial intelligence techniques to optimize the measurement path, numbers of measuring part setup and configuration of the measuring probes; and (iv) simulation of measurement path for a collision check by generated algorithms and simulating them.

VR reflects in simulation of the measurement path and visual checks of collisions, the path sequences are generated in the control data list and measuring protocol for appropriate coordinate measuring machine (CMM). The advantage of this VR approach is its suitability for monitoring and digitalization of the measurement process planning, simulation carried out and measurement verification based on CMM, reduction of the overall measurement time as early as in the inspection planning phase, and minimizing human involvement or human errors through intelligent planning, which directly influences increased production efficiency, competitiveness, and productivity of enterprises. VR in manufacturing metrology contents enables digital measurement twin and monitoring the measuring operation of a real CMM based on a virtual one. The measuring experiment was performed using two machined prismatic workpieces.

4.2 ONTOLOGICAL MODELING OF GEOMETRY

In order to develop one DT it is necessary to create the necessary set of data. Since this is a measurement of one class of mechanical parts, which are prismatic, the primary data set is the geometry of these parts. Engineering ontology (EO) is used to model this type of data. As one of the techniques of artificial intelligence, it goes far beyond the framework needed to model geometry data, so it is also used to classify and reuse knowledge in one area. All three possibilities of application (modeling, classification, and reuse) are used for the domain of coordinate metrology, that is, virtual measurement on CMM.

According to Stojadinovic and Majstorovic (2014) the term ontology is known in philosophy where it's "defined as a branch of metaphysics that studies the nature of being" (Swartout and Tate 1999) or of the "species kinds of things that exist" (Chandrasekaran et al., 1999). In engineering this term is primarily designed for knowledge representation of some area, for example manufacturing metrology. In artificial intelligence and knowledge representation research, the term ontology links for reuse and sharing of a field of knowledge, pointing out that the main purpose of EO is the transfer and exchange of knowledge (Stojadinovic and Majstorovic, 2014). On the other hand, for one of the authors, arguing that it is the basic logical structure around which a knowledge base will be built, the ontology connects to the knowledge base (Swartout and Tate, 1999). However, one thing is certain, "the ontology has found its place in areas where is the semantics of the base of communication between people and systems" (Uschold and Gruninger, 2004). According to Stojadinovic and Majstorovic (2014), some of the reasons that stimulate the development of methodologies for the development of EO are:

- Today's engineers rarely make the effort to find engineering content outside the search via key words (McMahon et al., 2004), ignoring the reuse knowledge, because the appropriate tools to search information engineering are not enough developed.
- In the industrial sector, design engineers spend 20–30% of their time communicating and assuming information (Court et al., 1998).

4.2.1 Geometrical features and parameters

Geometric features and metrological features make up a basis for the analysis of the measurement sensor probes' accessibility, measurement sensor configuring, path planning, and generation of the measuring protocol for input measuring requirements (Stojadinovic and Majstorovic, 2019).

Each geometric feature is unambiguously determined by a set of parameters relative to the local coordinate system (O_F, X_F, Y_F, Z_F) and measurement coordinate system of the measurement part (O_W, X_W, Y_W, Z_W). According to Stojadinovic and Majstorovic (2019) and Stojadinovic et al. (2016), the parameters can be of the following types: coordinates (X, Y, Z), diameter (D, D_1), height (H, H_1), width (a), length (b), feature vector $(\mathbf{n})$, feature fullness vector $(\mathbf{n_p})$.

Stojadinovic and Majstorovic (2019) described parameters as following: (i) vector $\mathbf{n}$ determines feature orientation across space, (ii) feature position is determined by coordinates (X_0, Y_0, Z_0) or (X_P, Y_P, Z_P), and (iii) fullness vector $\mathbf{n_p}$ and feature vector $\mathbf{n}$ define approach direction of the measurement sensor probe, whereas (iv) $\mathbf{n_G}$ and $\mathbf{n_L}$, respectively, represent the global approach direction for the feature and the local approach direction for the measuring point.

All mentioned vectors for basic geometrical features are shown in Table 4.1.

Table 4.1 Geometrical features and their parameters

No	Name	Feature	Parameters
1	Point		Coordinates: X_P [mm] Y_P [mm] Z_P [mm]
2	Plane		Coordinates: X_0 [mm] Y_0 [mm] Z_0 [mm] Dimensions: a [mm] b [mm] Normal vector: $\mathbf{n}$
3	Circle		Coordinates: X_0 [mm] Y_0 [mm] Z_0 [mm] Dimensions: D [mm] Normal vector: $\mathbf{n}$ Fullness vector: $\mathbf{n_p}$

(Continued)

Table 4.1 (Continued)

No	Name	Feature	Parameters
4	Cylinder		Coordinates: X_O [mm] Y_O [mm] Z_O [mm] Dimensions: D [mm] H [mm] Normal vector: **n** Fullness vector: $\mathbf{n_p}$
5	Truncated cone		Coordinates: X_O [mm] Y_O [mm] Z_O [mm] Dimensions: D [mm] D_1 [mm] H [mm] H_1 [mm] Normal vector: **n** Fullness vector: $\mathbf{n_p}$
6	Truncated hemisphere		Coordinates: X_O [mm] Y_O [mm] Z_O [mm] Dimensions: D [mm] H_1 [mm] Normal vector: **n** Fullness vector: $\mathbf{n_p}$

Adapted from Stojadinovic and Majstorovic (2019)

4.2.2 EO and CAD geometry

The proposed ontological development in engineering can be categorized according to what is intended. According to Zhanjun et al. (2009) it has three purposes: a high level of specification of knowledge domains, system interoperability, and exchange of knowledge as well as its reuse of knowledge. The developed ontology is implemented in Protégé software. Software is a free, open-source ontology editor and knowledge-based framework, based on Java. According to developer (Stanford University), Protégé implements a set of knowledge-modeling structures and actions that support the creation, visualization, and manipulation of ontologies in various representation formats. It used OWL editor that supports the Web Ontology Language, as the most recent development in standard ontology language. OWL ontology includes description of classes, properties, and instances.

In this subchapter will be performed implementation of the proposed method of ontological modeling of metrology features, which is given in the previous subchapter, according to the modeling principles set out in Matthew et al. (2011) and Noy and McGuinness (2001). The implementation of metrology features in Protégé includes modeling:

- classes and class hierarchy,
- individuals,
- properties of classes and individuals.

According to Stojadinovic and Majstorovic (2011) classes represent metrological features, which are organized in a hierarchy while individuals are represented in Protégé as a specific class. The notation for the classes is K_i, where i = 1,2,3,..., n and denotes the ordinal number of features such as point, line, cylinder, and so on. The notation for subclasses is K_ij, where j = 1,2,3,..., m and indicates the ordinal number of the subclass. Finally, the notation for an individual is K_ij_Ik, where k = 1,2,3,... and denotes the ordinal number of the individual that makes up the subscript within a given class. As can be seen the affiliation of the subclass to the class, as well as the individual subclass is described by the underscore (_). For example (Figure 4.1), K_1 class of point consists of subclasses K_14, K_17, K_18, K_19 and as a result of that individuals point (K_1j_Ik) take part in the description of other classes such as K_4, K_7, K_8 and K_9. In Figure 4.1 are shown

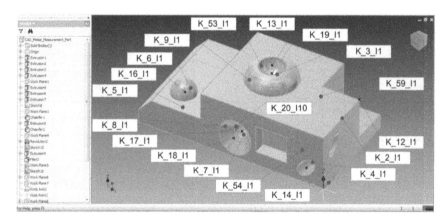

Figure 4.1 CAD representation metrological and geometrical features as classes, subclasses, and individuals of EO.

examples of classes, subclasses, and individual for one representative prismatic machine part from the point of view of its CAD geometry.

The advantage of defined class hierarchy, for the case to describing the geometry which consists of basic metrology features, is that the methodology is the same for all prismatic parts (Stojadinovic and Majstorovic, 2011).

4.3 MEASURING PATH MODELING

Visualization of the measuring path during the measurement includes the most important part of the measurement planning process. In addition, other elements of the measuring system, such as CMM and the environment, also are visualized. In terms of hardware, the measuring system for measuring the CMM generally consists of a measuring machine, a sensor (probe), a measuring part, and clamping accessories. In order to determine the position and orientation of these components in relation to the coordinate system of the machine, it is necessary to define a mathematical model.

4.3.1 Mathematical modeling of initial measuring path

The indirect goal of the mathematical model is to eliminate the collision between the measuring sensor (star probe configuration and head) and the measuring part. In other words, its role is to define a collision-free point-to-point path for pre-known positioning of the measuring part and selected and installed clamping accessories, as well as selected, known, configuration of the measuring sensor. Its primary role is to establish links between coordinate systems and generate an initial (point-to-point) measurement path that will be later optimized in purpose to shorten length of path and traveling time of the measurement probe (Stojadinovic and Majstorovic, 2019; Stojadinovic et al., 2016, 2021b, 2021c). The basic equation of the model is:

$$^{M}r_{P_i} = {}^{M}r_W + {}^{W}r_F + {}^{F}r_{P_i} = {}^{M}r_F + {}^{F}r_{P_i}$$

According to Stojadinovic and Majstorovic (2019) and Stojadinovic et al. (2016) generating point-to-point measurement path defines distribution of two sets of points:

- set of measuring points,
- set of nodes points.

Distribution of measuring points for different geometric features such as plane, circle, hemisphere, cylinder, and so on is obtained by modifying Hamersley (Lazzari et al., 2017) sequences. An example of formulas for calculation of measuring points coordinates $P_i(s_i, t_i, w_i)$ in *Cartesian* coordinate system for a plane according to Stojadinovic and Majstorovic (2019) and Stojadinovic et al. (2016) is given as follows:

$$s_i = \frac{i}{N} \cdot a$$

$$t_i = \left(\sum_{j=0}^{k-1} \left(\left\lfloor \frac{i}{2^j} \right\rfloor \bmod 2 \right) \cdot 2^{-(j+1)} \right) \cdot b$$

$$w_i = 0$$

where: a[mm]– x-axis constraint value; b[mm]– y-axis constraint value.

According to Stojadinovic and Majstorovic (2019) and Stojadinovic et al. (2016), set of node points implies two sets $P_{i1}(s_{i1}, t_{i1}, w_{i1})$ and $P_{i2}(s_{i2}, t_{i2}, w_{i2})$, where is i = 0, 1, 2, ..., (N − 1) and N – number of measuring points. Sub-set $P_{i1}(x_{i1}, y_{i1}, z_{i1})$ presents points for the transition from fast to slow feed. The distance between points $P_{i1}(x_{i1}, y_{i1}, z_{i1})$ and $P_i(x_i, y_i, z_i)$ is presented (Figure 4.2) by d_1– slow feed probe path, and the distance between points $P_{i2}(x_{i2}, y_{i2}, z_{i2})$ and $P_{i1}(x_{i1}, y_{i1}, z_{i1})$ is d_2– rapid feed probe path.

According to Ana et al. (2021) and Sander and Norbert (2020), coordinates of the nodal points $P_{i1}(x_{i1}, y_{i1}, z_{i1})$ and $P_{i2}(x_{i2}, y_{i2}, z_{i2})$ are defined from:

$$x_{i1} = x_{P_iP_{i1}} + x_i, y_{i1} = y_{P_iP_{i1}} + y_i, z_{i1} = z_{P_iP_{i1}} + z_i,$$

$$x_{i2} = x_{P_iP_{i2}} + x_i, y_{i2} = y_{P_iP_{i2}} + y_i, z_{i2} = z_{P_iP_{i2}} + z_i.$$

where coordinates x_i = s, y_i = t, z_i = w_i are actually coordinates of the measuring point $P_i(s_i, t_i, w_i)$, while other unknown coordinates are determined from the expression:

$$\overrightarrow{P_iP_{i1}} = \overrightarrow{n_{pi}} \cdot d_1 = x_{P_iP_{i1}}\vec{i} + y_{P_iP_{i1}}\vec{j} + z_{P_iP_{i1}}\vec{k}$$

$$\overrightarrow{P_iP_{i2}} = \overrightarrow{n_{pi}} \cdot (d_2 + d_1) = x_{P_iP_{i2}}\vec{i} + y_{P_iP_{i2}}\vec{j} + z_{P_iP_{i2}}\vec{k}$$

where $\overrightarrow{n_{pi}}$ is the vector of fullness of GF.

The equation for calculation distributed measuring points for other GF is presented in Stojadinovic and Majstorovic (2019). An example of calculated coordinates of the distributed measuring points for two types of GF is shown in Table 4.2.

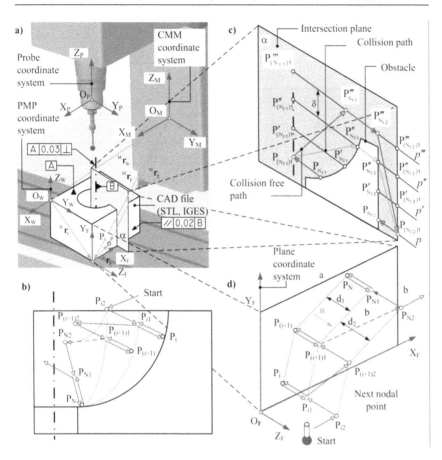

Figure 4.2 Mathematical model: a) a PW and its tolerances, b) initial measuring path for truncated sphere, c) collision free path, and d) initial measuring path for plane.

(Source: Stojadinovic et al., 2021b.)

4.3.2 Collision avoidance principle

Based on STL model for the presentation of workpiece geometry, the tolerances of workpiece, the coordinates of the last point $P_{(N_{F1})1}$ of a feature truncated hemisphere, and the coordinates of the first point $P_{(N_{F2})1}$ of a feature plane, the simplified principle of collision avoidance between PW and probe is shown in Figure 4.2c (Stojadinovic et al., 2021b). An obstacle to be overcome by the principle of collision avoidance is represented in the intersection plane α and refers to parallelism tolerance designated in Figure 4.2a.

According to (Stojadinovic et al., 2021b) "the principle is iterative and consists of moving line p for distance δ until the line became collision free (line segment p)".

Table 4.2 Coordinates of distributed measuring; initial path in point-to-point form

			Unit GF			
		Plane			Cylinder	
Points and No.	X [mm]	Y [mm]	Z [mm]	X [mm]	Y [mm]	Z [mm]
P_i 1	0,0000	0,0000	0,0000	0,0031	−0,5000	0,0000
2	0,1000	0.6641	0,0000	−0,2939	−0,4045	0,6640
3	0,2000	0.3281	0,0000	−0,4755	−0,1545	0,3281
4	0,3000	0.9922	0,0000	−0,4755	0,1545	0,9921
5	0,4000	0.1563	0,0000	−0,2939	0,4045	0,1562
6	0,5000	0.8203	0,0000	−0,0092	0,5000	0,8203
7	0,6000	0.4844	0,0000	0,2939	0,4045	0,4843
8	0,7000	0.1484	0,0000	0,4755	0,1545	0,1484
9	0,8000	0.0625	0,0000	0,4755	−0,1545	0,0625
10	0,9000	0.7266	0,0000	0,2939	−0,4045	0,7265
P_{i1} 1	0,0000	0,0000	0,3333	0,0028	−0,4600	0,0000
2	0,1000	0.6641	0,3333	−0,2704	−0,3721	0,6641
3	0,2000	0.3281	0,3333	−0,4375	−0,1421	0,3281
4	0,3000	0.9922	0,3333	−0,4375	0,1421	0,9922
5	0,4000	0.1563	0,3333	−0,2704	0,3721	0,1563
6	0,5000	0.8203	0,3333	−0,0085	0,4600	0,8203
7	0,6000	0.4844	0,3333	0,2704	0,3721	0,4844
8	0,7000	0.1484	0,3333	0,4375	0,1421	0,1484
9	0,8000	0.0625	0,3333	0,4375	−0,1421	0,0625
10	0,9000	0.7266	0,3333	0,2704	−0,3721	0,7266
P_{i2} 1	0,0000	0,0000	1.0000	0,0018	−0,3000	0,0000
2	0,1000	0.6641	1.0000	−0,1763	−0,2427	0,6641
3	0,2000	0.3281	1.0000	−0,2853	−0,0927	0,3281
4	0,3000	0.9922	1.0000	−0,2853	0,0927	0,9922
5	0,4000	0.1563	1.0000	-0,1763	0,2427	0,1563
6	0,5000	0.8203	1.0000	−0,0055	0,3000	0,8203
7	0,6000	0.4844	1.0000	0,1763	0,2427	0,4844
8	0,7000	0.1484	1.0000	0,2853	0,0927	0,1484
9	0,8000	0.0625	1.0000	0,2853	−0,0927	0,0625
10	0,9000	0.7266	1.0000	0,1763	−0,2427	0,7266

Data from Stojadinovic et al. (2021b)

4.3.3 PW setup and probe configuration

According to Stojadinovic et al. (2020a, 2020b) inspection on three-axis CMM can be performed from six directions corresponding to the axes of the machine +X, −X, +Y, −Y, +Z and −Z. Authors define feature approach direction (FAD) from the standpoint of access to the feature, while it defines probe approach direction (PAD) from the standpoint probes. The FADs are shown in Figure 4.3b. They also define possible directions of access to the features and are used to analyze the setup of the measuring part. PADs are shown in Figure 4.3a. They define the possible directions of access of the probe and are oriented opposite to the FAD (Stojadinovic et al., 2020a, 2020b).

According to Stojadinovic et al. (2020a, 2020b) in order to apply GA, it is necessary to define the Boolean matrices:

- Setup S: the elements of the matrix S links to the FADs and can be 0 or 1. For example, according to fig. 4.3c the element of the matrix S (C, F#1) takes value 1 because the cylinder C can be accessed from FAD#1.
- Configuration C: the element of the matrix S (F, F#4) takes the value 0 because the cylinder C cannot be accessed from the FAD # 4. Analogous to the filling of elements of the matrix S, the configuration matrix C is also filled to use PADs.

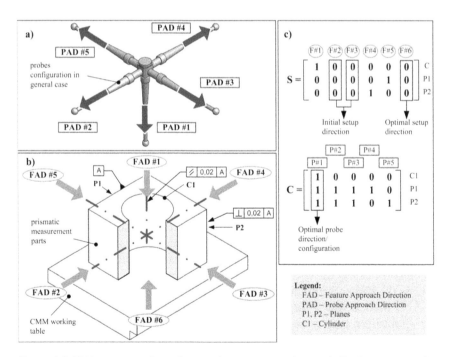

Figure 4.3 PW setup and probe configuration analysis: a) Probes approach directions, b) Features approach directions, c) Setup and configuration matrices.

It should be noted that the number of rows of both matrices is equal to the number of features creating tolerances. In the case shown on the Figure 4.3, it is two types of tolerance and three features.

Optimal solutions for the case of measuring parts setup are obtained by GA model (Stojadinovic and Majstorovic, 2019) and are represented by zero-columns. Optimal solutions for the case of probe configuring (measuring heads) are also obtained by mentioned GA model but represented by the unit-column.

4.3.4 Initial measuring path

According to Stojadinovic and Majstorovic (2019) Stojadinovic et al. (2021b) overall travelled path by a measuring probe in the inspection in N measuring points represents an initial measuring path of a measuring sensor and can be calculated as

$$
D_{tot} = \sum_{i=0}^{N-1} \left(\left| \overrightarrow{P_{i2}P_{i1}} \right| + 2 \cdot \left| \overrightarrow{P_{i1}P_i} \right| + \left| \overrightarrow{P_{i1}P_{(i+1)2}} \right| \right) +
$$

$$
+ \sum_{i=1}^{P} \left(\left| \overrightarrow{P_{NF_i}P_{(NF_i)1}} \right| + \left| \overrightarrow{P_{(NF_i)1}P_{NF_i}'''} \right| + \left| \overrightarrow{P_{NF_i}'''P_{NF_2}'''} \right| + \left| \overrightarrow{P_{(NF_2)1}P_{NF_2}} \right| \right)
$$

where: P – number of obstacles (transitions from one feature to another), $\left| \overrightarrow{P_{i2}P_{i1}} \right|$ – rapid feed rate and $2 \cdot \left| \overrightarrow{P_{i1}P_i} \right|$ double travelled slow feed rate for the i-th point, and $\left| \overrightarrow{P_{i1}P_{(i+1)2}} \right|$ – length of distance in probe's transition from previous i-th point to the next (i+1) nodal point.

4.3.5 Optimal measuring path

In the CMM inspection planning process, three processes are dominant in terms of decision-making and optimization. The first is the process of generating the optimal path of the measuring sensor, the second is deciding on the placement of the part and the configuration of the measuring sensor. These three decision-making processes can be optimized by applying the appropriate artificial intelligence technique. For the measurement path it turns out to be good to use the Ants Colony Optimization (ACO) method, while for setting the PW and configuring the measurement sensors genetic algorithms (GA) is used. Selected methods of artificial intelligence are not mandatory for application (others can be used as well), but they provide a number of facilitations for application and good results at the output.

As stated, the ACO method is used to optimize the measurement path. The input data are potential paths generated in the form of point-to-point, that is, the initial measurement path described in the previous subchapter.

Table 4.3 Results of comparison of the three paths

No.	Name of path/impact	Feature	
		Plane	Cylinder
I	PTC Creo MP* (D_C) [mm]	202.6522	228.9870
2	Online progammed MP (D_S) [mm]	203.3896	290.9837
3	Optimized MP by ACO (D_O) [mm]	159.4604	172.2142
4	$I_C = 100 - D_O/D_C$ [%]	21.31	24.80
5	$I_S = 100 - D_O/D_S$ [%]	21,60	40,81

Data from Stojadinovic et al. (2021b)
* Note: MP – measuring path

In order to compare the optimal paths, two more new paths were generated for the same feature types. The first path is generated on CMM by manual programming, and the second is automatically generated in Pro/ENGINEER software. According to Stojadinovic et al. (2021b) the results of comparison based on this optimization model for three paths and two GFs is given in Table 4.3. The value of optimal path saving is shown in rows 4 and 5.

4.4 SIMULATION MODELS

Modeling and simulation in PTC Creo and DMIS software aim at visualization and collision verification and measurement paths, as well as generation of output (so-called CL – cutter location) files for further use and realistic measurements, primarily in the VR, AR, and MR as well as I4.0 concept. The simulation in MatLab software aims to visualize the path and calculate different types of measurement paths for comparison purposes and also as input for data parsing, and create a control data list for the control unit of some of the CMMs.

Simulation constraints are primarily related to the geometry of the parts. Namely, the simulation presented in the paper is applied only to prismatic parts or machine parts consisting of basic geometric features such as planes, cylinders, cones, spheres, and so on. Developed simulation models cannot be assigned a free form surface because it is limited only to basic geometric features.

4.4.I PTC Creo

The simulation in PTC Creo environment is based on the already created CAD model measuring system consisting of workpiece, fixture clamps, and CMM. The software offers the option of using its CMM so that the CAD model CMM does not have to be created except in cases of visualization of the existing one. According to Stojadinovic et al. (2021a, 2021b, 2022b) the modeling and simulation procedure is as follows:

- Modeling of the 3D PW;
- Import of the modeled 3D PW into the CMM module (manufacturing module);
- Setting up the CMM process, includes three processes:
  - Defining CMM workcell;
  - Defining probes or measuring heads;
  - Defining fixtures.
- Setting operations: defined the initial coordinate system of CMM;
- Defining steps of the operations or more specific operations;
- Creating DMIS (.ncl) code and post processing.

In addition to the distributed measuring points by features, in order to create a collision-free path, it is necessary to define auxiliary points. These points represent collision-free points when moving from one feature to another.

As can be seen from the described simulation procedure, the creation of DMIS code is the last operation aimed at preparing data for input into the CMM control unit. Probe Path is a command used to display the path of the measuring sensor and generate DMIS code. Figure 4.4 shows a measuring path for cylinder with generated DMIS code for cylinder.

According to Stojadinovic et al. (2022) this code contains information on the movement along the CMM axes, the coordinates of the measuring path points and other necessary information. Specifically, this code was generated for CMM DEA-IOTA 2203. For real measurement on this machine, it was necessary to correct the code and adjust it to the conditions of PW alignment on the CMM table, that is, determining the position and orientation of the PW coordinate system in relation to the CMM coordinate system (Stojadinovic et al., 2022b).

4.4.2 PC-DMIS

PC-DMIS software enables simulation and real-time measurement, that is, is in communication with CMM and performs statistical data processing based on the acquisition of measuring points and thus generates measurement results (Stojadinovic et al., 2022b). Part of the DMIS code as well as a graphical representation of the measurement results is given in Figure 4.5.

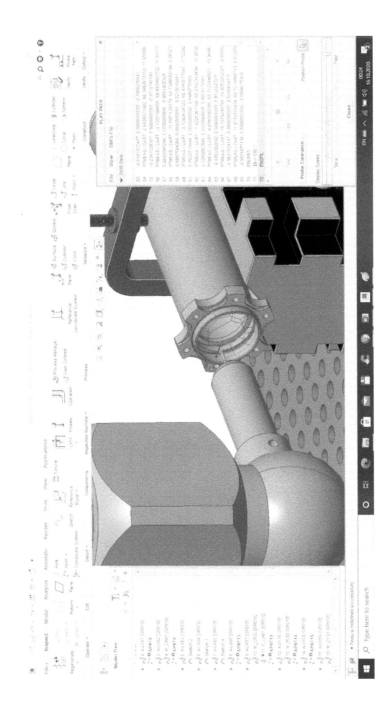

Figure 4.4 Defining the measuring path for a cylinder with generated DMIS code.

Figure 4.5 PC-DMIS simulation view.

4.5 DIGITAL MEASURING TWIN

DMT consists of a physical twin and its digital replica virtual twin. The model of DEA-IOTA 2203 machine was created in PTC Creo and PC-DMIS software was used as a virtual twin. The created DT is shown in Figure 4.6. Figure 4.5a shows the virtual twin in PTC Creo software, while the real process is shown in Figure 4.6. It is noted that the developed DT has a one-way flow of information from the virtual to the physical CMM model (Stojadinovic et al., 2022a). As a result, it is impossible to update the data in the opposite direction, that is, from physical to virtual twin. Given that inspection planning is a one-way process (unrepeatable once completed) this is considered acceptable, and therefore a two-way flow of information within the two basic components of DT is not necessary (Stojadinovic et al., 2022a).

In order to realize DT, it is necessary to harmonize the output-input. According Stojadinovic et al. (2022a), the PC-DMIS software allows the import of a .ncl (DMIS) file, previously generated and tested in the PTC Creo software using the standard import → DMIS command block.

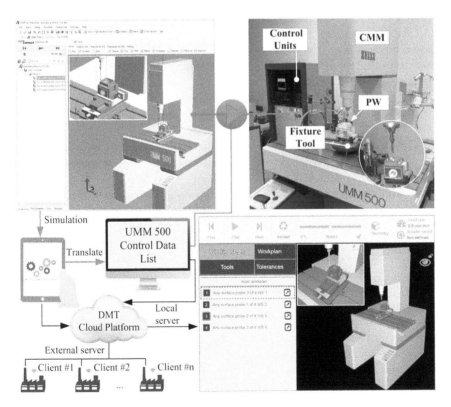

Figure 4.6 DT based on CMM.

(Source: Stojadinovic et al., 2021c.)

Previously, a .ncl (DMIS) file was generated in PTC Creo to verify the inspection plan procedure on the virtual CMM. The machine in the functional sense completely coincides with the real measuring machine DEA-IOTA 2203, on which the plan of inspection of the PW was performed.

4.6 CONCLUSIONS

This chapter presents an approach to the development of DT with main purposes: (i) to support the measurement process monitor by VR, (ii) verify the quality of manufacturing by tolerance inspection, (iii) ensure accuracy of dimensions and roughness of surfaces, and thus (iv) reduce production costs.

DT includes the verification of measurements on a virtual measuring machine and a physical CMM with a defined information exchange protocol. The novelty of the research is application into today's trend of industry 4.0 of its production and manufacturing metrology.

Besides developed off-line DT, future research will also include DT development with bi-directional data flow between physical and virtual CMMs. One of the future development directions will be extension of this concept to CMMs of various manufacturers (software). Also, on the basis of proposed methodology, the directions of future research would embrace extension to non-prismatic machine parts and development of digital thread for measurements on a CMM.

The flexibility of the exposed measurement methodology dominates for prismatic measuring parts in the following segments:

- Automatic measurement and monitoring of series of the same parts and groups of metrologically similar parts as well as metrologically completely different parts.
- Apply as an on-machine measurement system where the CNC machine is also a CMM machine (with the addition of a measuring head to the main spindle of the CNC machine).
- Application and measurement in pre-process, process, and post-process stages of processing.

Modeling and simulation, in PTC Creo and DMIS software, aim at visualization and collision verification and measurement paths, as well as generation of output (so-called CL – cutter location) files for further use and realistic measurements, primarily in the VR, AR, and MR as well as I4.0 concept. Generating this file and developing the appropriate postprocessor leaves the possibility to create a control data list for programming CMMs different producers. As is known, CMMs are programmed in the language of their producer, therefore the proposed concept of this simulation and its output (file) could be useful in terms of the unification format of CMM programming languages and software.

ACKNOWLEDGEMENTS

The presented research was supported by the Project of the Ministry of Education, Science and Technological Development of the Republic of Serbia.

REFERENCES

Ana, P. C. M., Horacio, A. G., Darío, G. L., Maria, F. M. A., Pedro, D. U. C., Pedro, A. O. C., Thomas, R. K., Emilio, G. C. (2021). Connectivity as a Design Feature for Industry 4.0 Production Equipment: Application for the Development of an In-Line Metrology System. *Applied Sciences*, 11, 1312.

Boschert, S., Heinrich, C., Rosen, R. (2018). Next Generation Digital Twin. In *Proceedings of TMCE 2018*, Las Palmas de Gran Canaria, Spain, 7–11 May.

Chandrasekaran, B., Josephson, J. R., Benjamins, V. R. (1999). What Are Ontologies, and Why Do We Need Them? *IEEE Intelligent Systems*, 14 (1), 20–26.

Chen, S., Sheng, B., Pan, T. (2013). Development of virtual metrology algorithm for the high mixed manufacturing process. In *Proceedings of the 32nd Chinese Control Conference*, 1783–1786.

Cheng, F. T., Jonathan, Y. C. C., Hsien-Cheng, H., Chi-An, K., Ying-Lin, C., Ju-Lei, P. (2011). Benefit Model of Virtual Metrology and Integrating AVM into MES, *IEEE Transactions on Semiconductor Manufacturing*, 24, 261–272.

Cheng, T. F., Huang, C. H., Kao, A. C. (2012). Developing an Automatic Virtual Metrology System, *IEEE Transactions on Automation Science and Engineering*, 9 (1), 181–188.

Cheng, F. T., Chi-An, K., Chun, F. C. Wen, H. T. (2015). Tutorial on Applying the VM Technology for TFT-LCD Manufacturing. *IEEE Transactions on Semiconductor Manufacturing*, 28, 55–69.

Court, A. W., Ullman, D. G., Culley, S. J. (1998). A Comparison between the Provision of Information to Engineering Designers in the UK and the US. *International Journal Information Management*, 18 (6), 409–425.

Klacansky, P., et al. (2022). Virtual Inspection of Additively Manufactured Parts. In *Proceedings IEEE 15th Pacific Visualization Symposium (PacificVis)*, 81–90.

Lazzari, A., Pou, J. M., Dubois, C., Leblond, L. (2017). Smart Metrology: The Importance of Metrology of Decisions in the Big Data Era. *IEEE Instrumentation & Measurement Magazine*, 20, 22–29.

Lynn, A. S., Ringwood, J., MacGearailt, N. (2012). Global and Local Virtual Metrology Models for a Plasma Etch Process. *IEEE Transactions on Semiconductor Manufacturing*, 25, (1), 94–103.

Matthew, H., et al. (2011). *A Practical Guide to Building OWL Ontologies Using Protégé 4 and CO-DE Tools*. University of Manchester, Manchester, UK.

McMahon, C. A., Lowe, A., Culley, S., Corderoy, M., Crossland, R., Shah, T., Stewart, D. (2004). Waypoint: An Integrated Search and Retrieval System for Engineering Documents. *ASME Journal of Computing and Information Science in Engineering*, 4 (4) 329–338.

Noy, N. F., McGuinness, D. L. (2001). Ontology Development 101: A Guide to Creating Your First Ontology, Stanford University, Knowledge Systems Laboratory Technical Report KSL-01-05 and Stanford Medical Informatics Technical Report SMI-2001-0880.

Sander, L., Norbert, G. (2020). A Factory Operating System for Extending Existing Factories to Industry 4.0. *Computers in Industry*, 115, 103128.

Stojadinovic, S., Majstorovic, D. M. (2011). Metrological primitives in production metrology – ontological approach. In *Proceedings 34th International Conference on Production Engineering*, 29.–30. September 2011, Niš, Serbia University of Niš, Faculty of Mechanical Engineering.

Stojadinovic, S., Majstorovic, V. (2014). Developing Engineering Ontology for Domain Coordinate Metrology. *FME Transactions*, 42 (3), 249–255.

Stojadinovic, S., Majstorovic, V. (2019). *An Intelligent Inspection Planning System for Prismatic Parts on CMMs*. Springer International Publishing, Switzerland.

Stojadinovic, S., Majstorovic, V., Durakbasa, N., Šibalija, T. (2016) Towards an Intelligent Approach for CMM Inspection Planning of Prismatic Parts. *Measurement*, 92, 326–339.

Stojadinovic, S., Majstorovic, V., Durakbasa, N. (2020a). Toward a Cyber-Physical Manufacturing Metrology Model for Industry 4.0. *Artificial Intelligence for Engineering Design, Analysis and Manufacturing*, 35 (1), 1–17.

Stojadinovic, S., Majstorovic, V., Djurdjanovic, D., Zivkovic, S. (2020b). An Approach of Development Smart Manufacturing Metrology Model as Support Industry 4.0, In: Wang, L., Majstorovic, V., Mourtzis, D., Carpanzano, E., Moroni, G., Galantucci, L. (eds) *Proceedings of 5th International Conference on the Industry 4.0 Model for Advanced Manufacturing*. Lecture Notes in Mechanical Engineering. Springer, Cham.

Stojadinovic, S., Majstorovic, V., Durakbasa, N. (2021a). An Approach to Development of the Digital Inspection Twin Based on CMM. *Measurement: Sensors*, 18, 100300.

Stojadinovic, S. M., Majstorovic, V. D., Gąska, A., Sładek, J., Durakbasa, N. M. (2021b). Development of a Coordinate Measuring Machine—Based Inspection Planning System for Industry 4.0. *Applied Sciences 11*, 8411.

Stojadinovic, M. S., Zivanovic, S., Slavkovic, N., Durakbasa, M. N. (2021c). Digital Measurement Twin for CMM Inspection Based on STEP-NC. *International Journal of Computer Integrated Manufacturing*, 34 (12), 1327–1347.

Stojadinovic, S., Majstorovic, V., Zivkovic, S., Kasalica, V., Stanic, D. (2022a). An Approach of Development Digital Twin Based on CMM as Support Industry 4.0. *International Scientific Journal INDUSTRU 4.0*, 2, 50–53.

Stojadinovic, S., Majstorovic, V., Durakbasa, N., Stanic, D. (2022b). Contribution to the Development of a Digital Twin Based on CMM to Support the Inspection Process. *Measurement: Sensors*, 22, 2022, 100372.

Swartout, W. R., Tate, A. (1999). Guest Editors' Introduction: Ontologies. *IEEE Intelligent Systems*, 14 (1), 18–19.

Th, O., Hung, M. H., Lin, Y. C., Chen, C. C. (2020). Construction of Virtual Metrology Cloud Platform with Machine Learning Tools for Providing Factory-Wide Manufacturing Service. In: Sitek, P., Pietranik, M., Krótkiewicz, M., Srinilta, C. (eds) *Intelligent Information and Database Systems. ACIIDS 2020. Communications in Computer and Information Science*, vol 1178. Springer, Singapore.

Tieng, H., Yang, C. H., Cheng, T. F. (2015). Total precision inspection of machine tools with virtual metrology. In: *IEEE International Conference on Automation Science and Engineering (CASE)*, Gothenburg, Sweden, 1446–1447.

Uschold, M., Gruninger, M. (2004) Ontologies and Semantics for Seamless Connectivity. *SIGMOD Record*, 33 (4), 58–64.

Wohlgemuth, F. M., Andreas, M., Hausotte, T. (2018). Development of a Virtual Metrological CT for Numerical Measurement Uncertainty Determination Using aRTist 2: Monte-Carlo Based Numerical Measurement Uncertainty Determination for CT Measurements According to GUM Aupplement 1. *tm – Technisches Messen*, 85 (12), 728–737.

Zhanjun, L., Maria, C., Karthik, R. (2009). A Methodology for Engineering Ontology Acquisition and Validation. *Artificial Intelligence for Engineering Design, Analysis and Manufacturing*, 23 (1), 37–51.

Chapter 5

Enhancing human-robot collaboration

Augmented reality interfaces for smarter path planning

Federico Manuri and Andrea Sanna
Politecnico di Torino, Torino, Italy

Francesco De Pace
TU Wien, Wien, Austria

Valerio Belcamino and Paolo Forteleoni
Politecnico di Torino, Torino, Italy

5.1 INTRODUCTION

The fourth industrial revolution is changing the way industries adopt novel technologies in their manufacturing processes, with the goal of creating smart factories that are supposed to be fully autonomous and intelligent (Kagermann et al., 2013). The term Industry 4.0, coined by the German government, describes an ambitious plan aimed at enhancing manufacturing industries through the adoption of innovative, high-tech solutions, technologies, and approaches (Hofmann & Rüsch, 2017). The nine pillars of Industry 4.0 represent technological innovations, such as the Internet of Things or Cyber-Physical Systems, which factories are encouraged to embrace with the goal of enhancing all aspects of the manufacturing process (Erboz, 2017).

Among the innovative approaches, the idea of a collaborative and shared space where robots and humans work together toward a common goal introduced a novel challenge: the creation of effective interfaces for highly automated and (possibly) artificial intelligence (AI)–driven collaborative robots (De Pace et al., 2020). One of the key innovations that can successfully help industries to address this challenge is augmented reality (AR): it has been deployed in a great variety of industrial tasks in the last decades and is considered one of the major Industry 4.0 foundations (De Pace et al., 2018). Another crucial technology is represented by autonomous robots, which are robots that act without the need for human control, exploiting many types of sensors to perceive the surrounding environments and AI approaches to define their behavior and improve their adaptability to

DOI: 10.1201/9781003306078-7

ever-changing conditions, thus working side-by-side with the human operators. Industrial robots have been traditionally deployed in well-defined
areas, completely separated by human operators to reduce the risk of hazards. However, international standards such as the ISO 10218 define rules
and requirements to define collaborative robots (cobots) as robots that can
work in collaboration with humans (Vaidya et al., 2018). Cobots' safety
regulations rely on sensors to perceive the position of humans in proximity,
as well as lightweight construction materials, limitations of speed and force,
and rounded edges. However, these safety techniques do not usually provide
proper feedback to the user, who may suffer trust issues toward the robot.
On the other hand, AR interfaces offer novel forms of interaction that can
clarify the robot's intentions and behavior to the human operator, improving the trust among parts and the perceived safety near the robot. Moreover,
AR interfaces provide innovative interaction paradigms to control the
robots effectively and easily. Human operators and cobots are expected to
share their workspace even more in the future, as the number of robots
employed in industries is steadily increasing, changing the approach to production lines, and leading to novel forms of interaction (Gaz et al., 2018).
Thus, investigating and developing innovative interfaces that can enhance
human-robot collaboration (HRC) while guaranteeing the safety of human
workers is nowadays of primary importance.

This chapter is organized as follows: Section 1.2 provides an overview of
human-robot interaction and, more specifically, path planning tasks, whereas
Section 1.3 explores the usage of AR for HRC. Section 1.4 focuses on AR
interfaces for path planning, describing a possible system architecture and
the differences between a handheld user interface and a head-mounted one.
Section 1.5 describes the usability analysis of the two proposed interfaces,
whereas Section 1.6 depicts the conclusions.

5.2 RESEARCH METHOD

5.2.1 Human-robot interaction

Human-robot interaction (HRI) is a branch of the Human–Machine
Interaction research area that focuses on the process of designing communication between humans and robots, providing an easy way to address two
challenges: conveying the user's intentions into a sequence of input for the
robot, complying with the robot's capabilities and the task at hand, and
displaying effective feedback on the robot's internal status, operations, and
behavior. The definition of usable interaction methodologies and interfaces
for HRI has been both a challenging issue and a fundamental goal in the
robotic research field to improve the adoption of robotics assistants that can
support humans in different crucial activities. Robots can be classified into
two general categories, namely, service and industrial robots. Even if the proposed architecture can be exploited both for service and industrial robots,

the focus of this paper is on industrial robotic manipulators. Nowadays, industrial robots are invaluable components in manufacturing systems, due to their capability of precision, repeatability, reliability, and predictability. They have been successfully employed in a wide variety of applications, environments, and tasks, including but not limited to material handling, assembly, welding, and painting.

5.2.2 Path planning

Once programmed properly to perform specific operations, robots have been proven to increase both productivity and efficiency. There exist two programming approaches to define the behavior of a robot in an industrial task; interested readers can refer to Pan et al. (2012) and Ong et al. (2020):

1. online programming methods;
2. offline programming methods.

Online methods require the user to interact with an operating robot, usually in its working environment, thus leading to possible security issues if the robot does not comply with the collaborative specifications. Offline programming methods require the user to interact with a virtual counterpart of the real robot. Even if these methods reduce the user's need for manually writing programming code, they are still time-consuming, especially for complicated tasks. The most common programming interface for industrial robots is the teach pendant, a handheld device that allows the users to move the robot with a joystick and record the path traveled by the robot. However, joysticks do not provide a complete transposition of a robot's movement capabilities since a robot has more degrees of freedom. Another option is to specify the point of interest through Cartesian coordinates, with the coordinate system aligned to an element of choice in the working environment.

Kinesthetic teaching is an approach to providing demonstrations to a robot in learning from demonstration whereby a human physically guides a robot to perform a skill: the user can move the robot and record the desired path to reach points of interest. Even if this approach is faster and more intuitive, it may not be feasible depending on the robot's dimensions or position, or due to security concerns.

Furthermore, programming by demonstration (PbD) exploits the user's expertise in demonstrating a task manually while the robot observes, follows, or replicates the task in real time. However, the demonstration may not be correct in terms of speed or accuracy with respect to the robot's capabilities; thus, it may be difficult for the robot to properly replicate the proposed trajectory. PbD requires the robot to observe the user and their interactions with the environment through the usage of sensors and artificial intelligence systems to elaborate these inputs. From the robot point of view, PbD can help robots to overcome the challenges related to dynamic environments and HRC.

On the contrary, the offline programming approach consists of programming the robot through a digital twin in a virtual environment (VE) without the need for the real robot. In the VE it is possible to perform teaching and simulation tasks employing advanced path planning and optimization algorithms with collision avoidance, thus reducing the effort required by the user and improving the robot's performance. Offline programming requires accurate virtualization of both the robot and the environment in terms of 3D models; thus, a priori knowledge of all the workpieces and the working area is needed, which is not always possible. Moreover, the kinematic engine of the real robot should be available in the VE to develop realistic simulations. Creating the digital twin of a robot is a time-consuming task and the resulting simulation module must be tested on the real one to verify the correctness of the simulated behavior.

Overall, programming and re-programming robots is a time-consuming, complex task: this problem represents a limiting factor in the widespread application of robots by small and medium enterprises. For this reason, the research and development of usable, effective interfaces that can simplify robot path-planning tasks is a challenging issue in the robotic domain.

5.2.3 Augmented reality for human-robot collaboration

The foundations for an effective HRC should be speed, easiness, security, and reliability. The introduction of a "robotic collaborator" should not slow down the user task, thus the interface should be easy to use and responsive. On the other end, user-perceived security is the most crucial feature to obtaining an effective collaboration with the robot. The security specifications that are required to define a robot as 'collaborative' are not enough to this end: the robotic system should also provide the user with a clear understanding of its intentions in order to adequately promote trust between the parts. To address this challenge, AR has been effectively used in recent years to provide the user with useful information about the system status and intention in HRC. AR enables the user to experience a view of the real world enriched by digital content, such as textual information, 3D models, animations, videos, and audio. All these assets are specifically related to the view framed by the user. AR systems rely upon a camera framing the environment; computer vision algorithms capable to identify and track meaningful references in the framed view, such as specific objects or other visual clues (a texture, an image, a QR code, etc.); and a display to show the user digital contents aligned with the real world.

Nowadays, there are three possible visualization approaches available to the user: (i) video see-through devices are screens displaying both the image framed by an RGB camera and the digital assets; (ii) optical see-through devices using semi-transparent lenses that let the user see the real world directly and miniaturized projectors that can display the digital content on the lenses; and (iii) projected solutions use projectors to display the digital content directly on physical surfaces. However, since the most relevant challenge in the industry domain is to provide digital content from a point of view that is as aligned as possible with the user view, the most common solutions are handheld or wearable devices. Hand-held solutions, such as smartphones and tablets, require the user to grasp the device with one or both hands. Wearable devices are represented by head-mounted displays like the Microsoft Hololens or the Epson Moverio, which free the user's hands but may be more cumbersome.

The state of the art provides many works and projects involving AR and cobots, however, evaluations of the effectiveness of AR interfaces in this research domain are quite uncommon, as often occur in the human-machine interaction domain, especially from a user-centered perspective. AR interfaces have been deployed in the HRC area to address three main needs: providing information pertaining to the current task or the robot itself (informative interfaces), displaying virtual feedback from the robot control system (control feedback interfaces), and visualizing the robot workspace (workspace interfaces). Interested readers are encouraged to refer to De Pace et al. (2020) for a complete review of the main uses of the AR interfaces in the HRC domain.

AR interfaces pertaining to the control feedback category are commonly used to provide feedback over the user's input itself and to visualize and manipulate the virtual robot paths. A comparison between an AR gaze-based interface and a gesture-based one is proposed in Krupke et al. (2018). The motion of a digital twin of a robotic arm provides the user feedback on the robot's behavior, whereas the user input consists in selecting the real objects that should be manipulated by the robot. A Wiimote controller has been effectively used as a physical control for a wearable AR device to interact with a virtual robot in Araque et al. (2011) and Sita et al. (2017). AR interfaces can be used not only to point out the motion of the robot through its digital counterpart but also to highlight objects of interest in the real world using virtual metaphors. An AR interface to control a robotic arm for a pick-and-place scenario has been proposed by Frank et al. (2016), exploiting the camera stream of the device to let the user select the object of interest by taping it on the touchscreen, and superimposing the virtual representation of the object over the real one to provide visual feedback of the user's input. The same task has been addressed by Hügle et al. (2017) using the camera of a handheld device to recognize hand gestures that are then translated into robot instructions by the system. The proposed solution has been compared by the authors with a kinesthetic approach and with an offline programming approach. Overall, the tests' results showed that the AR interface greatly lowered the task time, and it was more appreciated by the users. The camera of handheld devices can also be used to automatically recognize in the real world the objects of interest that should be manipulated by robotic arms, as shown in Gradmann et al. (2018): the authors of this research proved that the proposed object detection algorithm is reliable enough to ensure an effective programming interface for the real manipulator.

5.3 IMPLEMENTATIONS AND RESULTS

5.3.1 Augmented reality interfaces for path planning

Desktop AR interfaces have been employed in several works to define and modify the virtual paths of robotic manipulators. Ideally, a virtual path is a virtual representation of the path that the physical robot will travel during its task. Since path programming requires the user to define one or more points of interest that the robot should reach with a specific orientation of the end-effector, a virtual path could be defined as a set of 3D points defined by the user. The spline that connects each point in the desired sequence is computed by the robot inverse kinematic (IK) solver. In Chong et al. (2009), the users can add, remove, and modify the points of a virtual path using a flat image-based stylus tracked by an external camera. If a virtual point is not reachable by the real manipulator, its color is changed to red to warn the user. In Fang et al. (2012) the accuracy of a desktop AR interface for path planning has been evaluated. Results show that the system can achieve an accuracy of 11 mm by employing a camera placed at 1.5 m from the workspace. Other projects involving AR desktop interfaces to manipulate robot paths can be found in Fang et al. (2014) and Pai et al. (2015). Projected and wearable interfaces have been also employed to define virtual robot paths: Zaeh and Vogle (2006) developed an interactive AR projected interface to define the path of industrial robots. The users can define a set of virtual points using a tracked stylus, then the resulting path is traveled by the real manipulator. The proposed system has been proven to greatly reduce the task time with respect to a kinesthetic approach, also achieving a system accuracy of 0.5 mm. Similarly, in Veiga et al. (2013) the projected AR interface allows the users to control a manipulator during the grinding processes of ceramic parts: results confirm the outcomes of the interface proposed in Zaeh and Vogle (2006), with a considerable reduction in the task time. Regarding wearable devices, in (Kyjanek et al., 2019) the users can manipulate the virtual path by exploiting the gesture recognition capabilities of the adopted device, whereas the torques of each joint are displayed in the real environment. Quintero et al. (2018) compared an AR interface based on gesture and speech recognition commands with a traditional kinesthetic programming method. Despite the AR interface requiring less time to program the robot compared to the kinesthetic approach, high levels of mental loads have been detected, since users have to memorize and remember all the available voice commands. In Ong et al. (2020) a tracked stylus is used in combination with a wearable device to manipulate virtual paths: as seen in other similar works, the proposed interface greatly reduced the execution time for welding and pick-and-place tasks. Other research projects involving the use of wearable AR interfaces in the HRC domain can be found in Guan et al. (2019) and Manring et al. (2020). To the best of the authors' knowledge, only two works analyze the effectiveness of an AR handheld interface to manipulate virtual robot paths. The first one (Chacko, 2020) proposes a handheld solution based on a smartphone device: the interface has been assessed considering both objective and subjective parameters. However, it presents the following limitations: (i) the creation of the virtual path is limited to 2D planar surfaces, and (ii) the interface has been evaluated by only one user. Another work (De Pace et al., 2021) extends the analysis done in Chacko (2020) by evaluating more challenging tasks, considering both 2D and 3D paths, and assessing the interface accuracy by considering several users. In this chapter, two different AR interfaces are considered, one based on a handheld device, and the other one based on a wearable device. The two interfaces are analyzed from the user's point of view and a usability assessment with the System Usability Scale is performed.

5.3.2 System architecture

An AR system that enables users to perform path-planning activities should rely at least on two physical counterparts: the collaborative robot and the AR device. However, a valuable feature for a path planning application should be the capability to provide a virtual preview of the robot's motion. This enables the user to see through AR the digital twin of the real robot traveling the planned path and verify that, given a set of points of interest to travel through, the robot is capable of planning a path and traveling it without problems. Thus, it becomes relevant to understand the capabilities of the robot control workstation, which is a computer specifically designed to handle the robot algorithms and its capabilities to deal with possible inputs and to produce outputs. Eventually, the robot control workstation may not be able to provide the robot simulated path as an output or to convey the output to the AR device in a compatible format. In such cases, it may be necessary to deploy another workstation with the role of either forwarding the data between the robot and the device and/or providing missing data through a virtual simulation.

To effectively provide path planning capabilities, the AR device should be able to perform the following tasks: tracking the robot in the real environment, displaying AR contents, and providing an easy way for the user to insert, modify or remove traveling points to define the path. Moreover, it should be possible to specify for each point the pose of the end-effector. Tracking the robot in the real world may rely upon existing libraries such as Vuforia (https://developer.vuforia.com/downloads/sdk) or creating a proprietary object tracking module based on computer vision libraries such as OpenCV (https://opencv.org). The tracking system may identify a 2D feature in the environment, such as an image or a QR code, or rely on the

3D model of the physical robot. When the system obtains a precise correspondence between the real world and the virtual one, it is possible to display AR content accurately aligned with respect to the real environment. Thus, when defining the path for the robot through control points, the user would be able to observe these points and evaluate their correspondence with respect to real-world coordinates. When the user adds a point, the system should be able to provide fast feedback about its reachability, which means the robot is capable to reach the given point or not. Reachability depends not only on the working area of the robot but also on the capability of the inverse kinematic engine to avoid singularities that are point coordinates the system is not able to reach from a given pose even if they are inside the robot's working area (usually, the IK solver cannot resolve the analytic function to compute the proper joints' rotations). If the system can reach a given point and more than one point is available, the system should be able to show a spline representing the path that the robot would travel when moving from one point to another. Then, when the user completes the path, it should be possible to preview the robot's movements to assess the correctness of the given trajectory. This feature can be particularly useful if the system does not provide an automatic obstacle avoidance algorithm. Finally, the user should be able to start the physical robot movement to verify the correctness of the simulation.

Figure 5.1 shows an example of the proposed system architecture. It is possible to identify three distinct elements: (i) an AR device, (ii) a remote personal computer (PC), and (iii) a real robotic manipulator. The AR device displays an interface for path planning developed with the Unity 3D game engine (https://unity.com/). The Vuforia SDK has been integrated to carry out the tracking of the real world, to obtain a common reference system between the tablet and the manipulator. The tracking methodology adopted is image-based, with a target positioned at a known location with respect to the real robot basis. The remote PC, which runs the Ubuntu 20.04.2.05 distribution (http://www.releases.ubuntu.com/20.04/) and the robot operating system (ROS) Melodic (https://wiki.ros.org/melodic), computes the virtual robot path, exchanging data with the AR device. The robotic arm is represented by the COMAU e.DO (https://www.comau.com/en/our-competences/robotics/edo), a six degrees-of-freedom (DOF) ROS-based manipulator equipped with a gripper end-effector. A local area network (LAN) enables the AR device, the PC, and the robotic arm to effectively exchange data. Since the IK solver is decentralized with respect to the real manipulator, the proposed architecture could be extended to other robotic arms, simply adapting the data transfer protocol and deploying the appropriate IK solver. The system works as follows: when a new virtual point is added by the user through the AR interface, the point position and orientation are sent through a TCP socket connection to the PC. Then, the PC computes a possible path using the IK algorithm provided by the MoveIt ROS package (https://moveit.ros.org/). The resulting path is sent back to the Unity

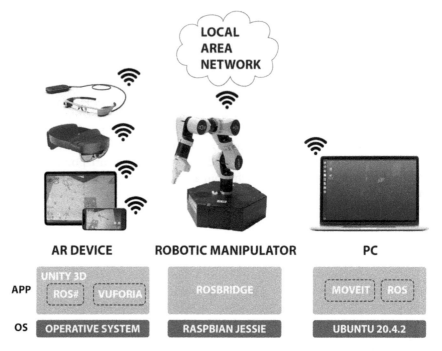

Figure 5.1 The hardware and software architecture of the proposed system.

3D application, and it is displayed in AR to provide a preview correctly aligned to the real environment. Finally, when the user is pleased with the path traveled by the virtual robot, the motion of the real robot can start by sending the acquired path to the real manipulator. In the following sections, a detailed description of two possible handheld AR interfaces is presented, explaining the mechanism of virtual path creation and modification.

5.3.3 Interfaces for handheld devices

Handheld devices can show the view framed by the camera on the touchscreen, thus, it is sufficient to display buttons or info on top of the camera view to provide the user with a proper user interface. Moreover, thanks to the touchscreen and the tracking system, the user should be able to tap on the screen to select a 3D coordinate. Overall, the handheld interface should provide two relevant functionalities: adding one or more virtual points to the real scene and visualizing a preview of the virtual robot path. When the user frames the image target, a virtual representation of the robotic manipulator is superimposed on its real counterpart. It is possible to display only the end-effector in the AR interface to reduce the negative effects of possible occlusions. The user can add a new virtual point (VP) to the real scene by touching the tablet surface at the desired location. A virtual point should be represented by a 3D element small enough to provide a high level of precision in terms of coordinates, but big enough to be easily selectable with the touch display. To ease the VP addition, it is possible to define a virtual bounding box to limit the available area for placing VP to prevent the user from adding a point outside of its working range or inside a known obstacle in range to avoid collisions, for example, below the robot workbench (if any). A virtual sphere may effectively represent the VP, carrying both the positional and rotational information required by the IK solver to compute the end-effector pose. Moreover, when a new VP is rendered into the scene, it is instantiated with a default orientation, for instance, with the forward vector parallel to the surface's normal direction. To modify a VP position, the user selects one and the three local axes may be displayed to enable an easy drag and drop towards a new location constraining the movement along one axis at a time. Changing the modifying modality from position to rotation, a virtual gimbal is rendered over the VP and it can be used to change its orientation around its local axes.

To improve the user's perception of the final pose of the end-effector, the AR interface can display a 3D model of the end-effector at the VP location, mapping the VP's transformations directly to the virtual end-effector, as shown in Figure 5.2.

When the user adds a new point to the scene, it is added sequentially to a point list, since a new VP is inserted by default as the last element of the current path. However, if many points are visible in the scene, it may be difficult to select the right one at a given time depending on their proximity. To

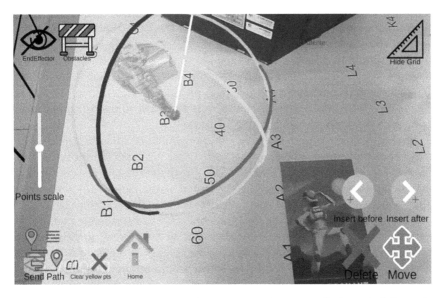

Figure 5.2 Changing the rotation of a given virtual point with the aid of the end-effector preview.

simplify the selection step, a button-enable selection system should be available through the AR interface, for example., a couple of arrow buttons that enable the user to move backward and forward along the VP list. This VP selection option also provides the user with the ability to add a VP between two other existing VPs. Moreover, as for the virtual row and column spreadsheet, two more buttons may allow the user to select if the new point should be added before or after the current one. However, if two points are too close to each other, the system should prevent the user from adding a new point between them. A simple algorithm to check this condition may verify that when the user wants to add a new VP at the left side of P1, $D > s$, with D being the distance between two VP and s being the VP diameter, respectively. In case the condition is verified, a new VP of diameter s is rendered at $D/2$ (and the new VP is added to the point list at the specified position); otherwise, the dimension of the VPs is iteratively reduced until a suitable position is found. The reduction is constrained by $s > s_{min}$ to ensure a clear visualization of the VPs (the s_{min} value has to be experimentally computed). If the constraint is violated, a message should inform the user that it is not possible to add the VP in the desired position.

As the users add more and more points to the path, they may be interested in viewing a real-time preview of the resulting path. However, the robot path may not be computed in real-time (i.e., when a new point is added or modified) due to the time complexity of the IK solver. To solve this problem, a Catmull-Rom virtual spline can be first displayed starting from the current position of the robot end-effector and passing through the VP added by the user, repeating this process every time a new VP is added to the scene. Even if this spline provides only an approximation of the real robot path, it should be enough to improve the user's perception of the VP sequence.

Conversely, once the user wants a precise preview of the real robot path, the user should be able to send this request to the remote PC. Since each VP describes the position and orientation of the end-effector along the path, the IK solver tries to calculate a suitable path passing through all the VPs added by the user. When the path is computed it is sent back to the AR application to replace the approximated Catmull-Rom spline.

After updating the path preview, the user should be able to start the virtual robot movement, allowing the user to pre-visualize the movement of the real robot. Finally, if the user is satisfied with the virtual preview, the real manipulator can move along the computed path. Figure 5.3 shows the approximated (left) and real robot (right) virtual paths, respectively.

It would be possible for the user to define a VP not reachable by the real manipulator: this may happen because it may be difficult to anticipate if the robot may reach a point with a given pose, even if it is inside the robot's working area. In such a case, the IK solver would fail in computing a suitable path, and the PC should send an error message to the AR application, which may color in red the unreachable VP to inform the user. A VP is considered unreachable if the end-effector cannot reach its spatial coordinate

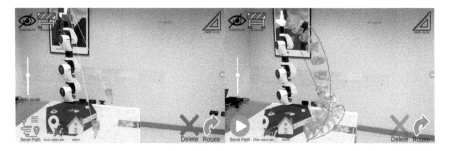

Figure 5.3 The approximated robot path (on the left) and the same line modified according to the real path (on the right).

position or it cannot reach the VP position with the orientation specified by the user. Hence, the user has to modify the position and/or orientation of the VP to complete the path creation, sending it back again to the remote PC.

Moreover, if the VE contains a virtual representation of possible physical obstacles in the working area, then the AR interface may provide a collision detection capability: the system can change a VP color to red if the spline of one of the VP intersects a virtual obstacle, highlighting a possible collision between the object and the end-effector.

Finally, the interface should provide the user the ability to delete one VP, for example, by selecting it and by pressing a "Delete" button. Eventually, the system may provide a shortcut to delete all the VPs at the same time. A video showing the main functionalities of the proposed AR interface can be found at https://youtu.be/DkYMzhNnwf0.

5.3.4 Interfaces for head-mounted devices

Head-mounted devices provide different challenges in terms of interface creation with respect to handheld ones. The most important ones are the reduced field of view (FOV) and the lack of a physical display to touch. The first challenge is mitigated by placing both the elements of the user interface as virtual elements in the virtual space, instead of the classical 2D layer on top of the camera view, thus extending the available area for the UI elements. The second challenge is overcome by providing different interaction paradigms, such as gestures, gaze tracking, or eye tracking. For example, in developing an AR interface for the Microsoft Hololens 2, it is possible to provide a user experience very similar to the one described for the handheld device: virtual buttons positioned near the robot list all the commands available to the user, as shown in Figure 5.4, whereas performing the grasping gesture in front of the Hololens 2 camera will mimic the tap on the tablet's touchscreen.

One of the main advantages of a head-mounted solution is the chance to provide a hand-free interaction, thus allowing the user to hold working

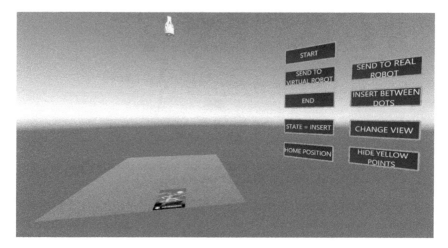

Figure 5.4 Virtual buttons displaying the available commands in AR.

tools. Gaze tracking interfaces display a virtual pointer at the median point of the eyes: moving the head will change the pointer position, thus enabling the user to select different elements in the space. Eye-tracking interfaces can detect the eye direction even when the head is still, thus providing even greater simplicity in the interaction than gaze-tracking solutions. However, to detect a 3D point in the physical space, the system needs a reference to detect the proper depth with respect to the user's point of view. When a gesture interaction system is employed, the hand represents that reference; when using a gaze or eye-tracking system, a depth reference is missing, thus, these types of interfaces are more suited to 2D path planning activities than 3D ones. Otherwise, the system should always display a novel VP at a pre-defined depth and the interface should provide buttons to move the VP to the desired position.

5.4 ASSESSING THE USABILITY OF AR INTERFACES FOR PATH PLANNING

To evaluate an AR interface for path planning, the following methodology should be adopted: (1) developing an AR interface that provides the user with at least two functionalities, adding one or more virtual points to the real scene, and visualizing a preview of the virtual robot path; (2) defining a sequence of tasks to evaluate the proposed AR interface; (3) defining a proper metric to measure the accuracy of the AR interface; (4) choosing an appropriate questionnaire (or more than one) to measure both the interface usability and workload.

Whereas the first point has been thoroughly discussed in the previous sections, the second point is highly dependent on the robot type, the working environment, and the real user case; the tasks chosen for the evaluation step should be both representatives of the AR interface usage in real conditions and allow the users to test all the functionalities provided by the interface. Furthermore, depending on the real task, some metrics may be more relevant than others to assess the interface; typical metrics may include but are not limited to completion time, number of errors, number of false positive and false negative interactions with the interface, and completion rate. Finally, a questionnaire such as the one provided by the System Usability Scale (Brooke, 1996) may be useful to evaluate the usability of the interface.

5.4.1 Usability evaluation

To assess the effectiveness of the proposed solution, 19 users have been involved in a user study. The proposed tasks required the users to create a virtual path, composed of two or more distinct VPs, using 3D-printed objects as references for the target poses of the robot's end-effector in the real environment. Figure 5.5 shows an example of physical target poses, with the sticks' inclination representing the end-effector rotation.

The tasks have been designed to encourage the users to apply translational and rotational actions, thus improving their knowledge of the interface. One group performed the tasks with the handheld device, whereas the other group used the head-mounted device. The interfaces' usability has been assessed with the System Usability Scale (SUS) questionnaire (Brooke, 1996), which the users filled out after completing the tasks. Table 5.1 shows the SUS score for each interface. Overall, these preliminary results prove that both interfaces are deemed sufficiently appropriate to generate the virtual robot path, with a preference for the wearable device over the handheld one. However, performing the t-test on the two groups resulted in a p-value

Figure 5.5 3D printed objects used as references for the target poses.

Table 5.1 SUS scores, average scores, and standard deviations for the head-mounted and handheld interfaces

	Head-mounted		Handheld	
	SUS SCORE		SUS SCORE	
U1	80		82,5	U1
U2	92,5		50	U2
U3	67,5		87,5	U3
U4	77,5		82,5	U4
U5	97,5		72,5	U5
U6	90		67,5	U6
U7	87,5		57,5	U7
			97,5	U8
			77,5	U9
			60	U10
			75	U11
			77,5	U12
	84,64	AVG SUS SCORE	73,96	
	10,25	STD DEVIATION	13,46	

of 0,088 which is greater than 0,05, thus it is not possible to reject the null hypothesis. Further usability tests may prove if one of the two interfaces is better than the other.

5.5 CONCLUSIONS

The fourth industrial revolution is changing the way industries adopt novel technologies in their manufacturing processes, and the idea of a collaborative, shared space where robots and humans work together toward a common goal introduced a novel challenge: the creation of functional interfaces to interact with highly automated, AI–driven collaborative robots. AR is one of the key innovations that can successfully help industries to address this challenge, whereas path planning is one of the most significant activities involving humans and robots in the same physical space. After exploring the state-of-the-art pertaining AR interfaces for path planning, the proposed work provides a description of a possible system architecture for creating such interfaces. The most important functionalities that these systems should provide are further discussed, considering two different AR interfaces, one based on a handheld device and the other one based on a wearable device. The two interfaces are analyzed from the user's point of view and a usability assessment with the System Usability Scale is performed.

Overall, the preliminary results prove that both interfaces are deemed sufficiently appropriate to generate the virtual robot path, with a preference for the wearable device over the handheld one. However, due to the t-test result, further tests should be held in the future to prove if one of the two interfaces is better than the other.

REFERENCES

Araque, D., R. Díaz, B. Pérez-Gutiérrez, and A.J. Uribe (2011). Augmented reality motion-based robotics off-line programming. In *2011 IEEE Virtual Reality Conference*, pp. 191–192, IEEE.

Brooke, J. (1996). Sus: A "quick and dirty" usability. *Usability Evaluation in Industry*, 3, p. 189.

Chacko, S.M., A. Granado, and V. Kapila (2020). An augmented reality framework for robotic tool-path teaching. *Procedia CIRP*, 93, pp. 1218–1223.

Chong, J.W.S., S.K. Ong, A.Y.C. Nee, and K.B. Youcef-Youmi (2009). Robot programming using augmented reality: An interactive method for planning collision-free paths. *Robotics and Computer-Integrated Manufacturing*, 25, pp. 689–701.

De Pace, F., F. Manuri, and A. Sanna (2018). Augmented reality in industry 4.0. *American Journal of Computer Science and Information Technology*, 6, pp. 1–7.

De Pace, F., F. Manuri, A. Sanna, and C. Fornaro (2020). A systematic review of augmented eality interfaces for collaborative industrial robots. *Computers & Industrial Engineering*, 149, pp. 1–19.

De Pace, F., A. Sanna, F. Manuri, D. Oriti, S. Panicucci, and V. Belcamino (2021). Assessing the effectiveness of augmented reality handheld interfaces for robot path programming. In *International Conference on Intelligent Technologies for Interactive Entertainment*, pp. 336–352, Springer, Cham.

Erboz, G. (2017). How to define industry 4.0: Main pillars of industry 4.0. In *Managerial Trends in the Development of Enterprises in Globalization Era: 7th International Conference on Management (ICoM 2017)*, pp. 761–767.

Fang, H.C., S.K. Ong, and A.Y.C. Nee (2012). Interactive robot trajectory planning and simulation using augmented reality. *Robotics and Computer-Integrated Manufacturing*, 28, pp. 227–237.

Fang, H.C., S.K. Ong, and A.Y.C. Nee (2014). Novel AR-based interface for human-robot interaction and visualization. *Advances in Manufacturing*, 2, pp. 275–288.

Frank, J.A., M. Moorhead, and V. Kapila (2016). Realizing mixed-reality environments with tablets for intuitive human-robot collaboration for object manipulation tasks. In *2016 25th IEEE International Symposium on Robot and Human Interactive Communication (RO-MAN)*, pp. 302–307, IEEE.

Gaz, C., E. Magrini, and A. De Luca (2018). A model-based residual approach for human-robot collaboration during manual polishing operations. *Mechatronics*, 55, pp. 234–247.

Gradmann, M., E.M. Orendt, E. Schmidt, S. Schweizer, and D. Henrich (2018). Augmented reality robot operation interface with Google tango. In *ISR 2018 50th International Symposium on Robotics*, pp. 1–8, VDE.

Guan, Z., Y. Liu, Y. Li, X. Hong, B. Hu, and C. Xu (2019). A novel robot teaching system based on augmented reality. In *2019 International Conference on Image and Video Processing, and Artificial Intelligence*, 11321, SPIE.

Hofmann, E., and M. Rüsch (2017). Industry 4.0 and the current status as well as future prospects on logistics. *Computers in Industry*, 89, pp. 23–34.

Hügle, J., J. Lambrecht, and J. Krüger (2017). An integrated approach for industrial robot control and programming combining haptic and non-haptic gestures. In *2017 26th IEEE International Symposium on Robot and Human Interactive Communication (RO-MAN)*, pp. 851–857, IEEE.

Kagermann, H., W. Wahlster, and J. Helbig (2013). *Recommendations for Implementing the Strategic Initiative Industrie 4.0: Final Report of the Industrie 4.0 Working Group*. Forschungsunion, Berlin, Germany.

Krupke, D., F. Steinicke, P. Lubos, Y. Jonetzko, M. Görner, and J. Zhang (2018). Comparison of multimodal heading and pointing gestures for co-located mixed reality human-robot interaction. In *2018 IEEE/RSJ International Conference on Intelligent Robots and Systems (IROS)*, pp. 1–9, IEEE.

Kyjanek, O., B. Al Bahar, L. Vasey, B. Wannemacher, and A. Menges (2019). Implementation of an augmented reality AR workflow for human robot collaboration in timber prefabrication. In *Proceedings of the 36th International Symposium on Automation and Robotics in Construction, ISARC*, pp. 1223–1230, International Association for Automation and Robotics in Construction (IAARC) Banff, Canada.

Manring, L., J. Pederson, D. Potts, B. Boardman, D. Mascarenas, T. Harden, and A. Cattaneo (2020). Augmented reality for interactive robot control. In *Special Topics in Structural Dynamics & Experimental Techniques*, 5, pp. 11–18. Springer, Cham.

Ong, S.K., A.W.W. Yew, N.K. Thanigaivel, and A.Y.C. Nee (2020). Augmented reality-assisted robot programming system for industrial applications. *Robotics and Computer-Integrated Manufacturing*, 61, pp. 1–7.

Pai, Y.S., H.J. Yap, and R. Singh (2015). Augmented reality-based programming, planning and simulation of a robotic work cell. Proceedings of the Institution of Mechanical Engineers, *Journal of Engineering Manufacture*, 229, pp. 1029–1045.

Pan, Z., J. Polden, N. Larkin, S. Van Duin, and J. Norrish (2012). Recent progress on programming methods for industrial robots. *Robotics and Computer-Integrated Manufacturing*, 28, pp. 87–94.

Quintero, C.P., S. Li, M. K.X.J. Pan, W.P. Chan, H.F.M. Van der Loos, and E. Croft (2018). Robot programming through augmented trajectories in augmented reality. In *2018 IEEE/RSJ International Conference on Intelligent Robots and Systems (IROS)*, pp. 1838–1844. IEEE.

Sita, E., M. Studley, F. Dailami, A. Pipe, and T. Thomessen (2017). Towards multimodal interactions: Robot jogging in mixed reality. In *Proceedings of the 23rd ACM Symposium on Virtual Reality Software and Technology*, pp. 1–2.

Vaidya, S., P. Ambad, and S. Bhosle (2018). Industry 4.0 – A glimpse. *Procedia Manufacturing*, 20, pp. 233–238.

Veiga, G., P. Malaca, and R. Cancela (2013). Interactive industrial robot programming for the ceramic industry. *International Journal of Advanced Robotic Systems*, 10, pp. 1–8.

Zaeh, M.F., and W. Vogl (2006). Interactive laser-projection for programming industrial robots. In *2006 IEEE/ACM International Symposium on Mixed and Augmented Reality*, pp. 125–128, IEEE.

Part 3

Crafting the future

System design and applications

Chapter 6

Unveiling the future of medical imaging

Scan to VR pipeline for visualization

Saadia Talay and Zartasha Mustansar

Department of Engineering, School of Interdisciplinary Engineering
& Sciences (SINES) National University of Sciences and Technology
(NUST), Islamabad, Pakistan

*Huda Al-Mubarak, Amjad Aldarwish, Fatimah Alhamoud,
Noor Aljabr, Kamran Hameed Khawaja
and Mahbubunnabi Tamal*

Imam Abdulrahman Bin Faisal University, Dammam, Kingdom of Saudi
Arabia(KSA)

6.1 INTRODUCTION

The incorporation of advanced technologies, such as virtual and augmented
reality, in medical imaging is a crucial need in the present era. These techniques provide a more natural and intuitive way for medical professionals to
interact with medical images, enabling the conversion of medical scans into
3D models that can be viewed and manipulated in a realistic and immersive
manner. This facilitates the diagnosis, treatment planning, and patient education processes. Immersive technology offers an interactive approach for
comprehending medical images, which can lead to a more efficient learning
process for medical professionals and enhanced patient outcomes. However,
the use of immersive technology with low-resolution images presents certain
challenges that can affect the accuracy of 3D models and user experience.
The integration of immersive technology in medical imaging is a promising field that holds significant potential for revolutionizing the way medical
professionals interpret medical images.

In the clinical industry, virtual reality (VR) has the potential to be a powerful tool. Diagnosing medical conditions based on 2D images can be challenging and often requires extensive training and experience for accurate
interpretation. Modern CT and MRI software allow for the generation of
3D models from 2D image datasets, which can be displayed on computer
monitors and manipulated with mice or keyboards. However, these traditional methods still lack an intuitive interface for model manipulation.

VR is an advanced technology that creates an artificial, three-dimensional, computer-generated environment, allowing users to experience a virtual world. VR offers a more intuitive way of interaction and enables easier perception of complex data by providing a sense of presence in the virtual environment. This immersive effect cannot be achieved with still pictures or animations, no matter how realistic they may be. Therefore, VR has the potential to revolutionize the way medical professionals interact with 3D medical imaging and provide a more accurate diagnosis.

Immersive virtual reality technology creates an environment in which users can interact with and manipulate their surroundings. A typical VR system depends on user inputs to engage with the virtual environment, hardware outputs to generate a sense of immersion, and software to ensure proper control and synchronization of the entire system (Mazuryk & Gervautz, 1999).

Achieving an immersive experience in virtual reality is made possible through the use of various hardware components, such as a stereoscopic head-mounted display (HMD), a haptic feedback device, and realistic sound effects. The HMD tracks the position and orientation of the user's head and displays the virtual environment accordingly, providing a fully immersive visual experience. Meanwhile, the haptic feedback device, which is most commonly hand controllers, enables users to interact with the virtual environment by allowing them to "touch," move, pick up, and drop objects and materials from the surroundings. These devices create a sense of physical presence and enable a more intuitive way of interacting with the virtual environment.

Recent applications of VR in the medical field include surgery training, diagnostic imaging, and examination of pathology slides. Dargar et al. (2015) discussed the use of immersive virtual environments for training of complex tasks such as surgery. The environment is meant to mimic the actual clinical setting and train students using high-fidelity visuals and other sensory feedback. Farahani et al. (2016) explored the possibility of viewing and studying pathology slides using VR. They compared the concordance of the final diagnosis of pathology slides with the time taken to examine them on a conventional 5K monitor as well as in VR using the Oculus Rift. King (King, 2015) developed an immersive VR environment for diagnostic medical imaging. It utilized the Oculus Rift to display multiple image slices data with the help of Unity and 3D Slicer. Egger et al. (2017) developed an interface between HTC Vive and MeVisLab via OpenVR for medical applications. This included integrating the OpenVR library in the MeVisLab platform, which enabled a simple approach to view medical image data inside the HTC Vive for immersive three-dimensional VR examination. VR exposure prior to endoscopic treatments had a likelihood in relieving their anxiety during the procedure and improved satisfaction with sedation of endoscopic procedures (Kim et al., 2023). VR–based surgical training simulators in laparoscopic surgery demonstrated effectiveness to explicit the surgeons' training status (Lee et al., 2023).

Through virtual reality visualization, medical specialists are able to manipulate the 3D model of a specific organ or organ system using hand-held controllers, which closely mimics natural movement and facilitates the interpretation of imaging scans. This allows for a detailed examination of the area of interest, and trial-and-error procedures can be performed to determine the optimal method for prognosis and treatment. Additionally, this technology can be utilized by surgeons for surgical planning, and by students to practice real-life situations without risking harm to an actual patient.

Putting everything in perspective, VR technology has seen significant growth in recent years, with research focusing on various applications such as education, gaming, and healthcare. VR can be used for immersive medical training, allowing medical students and professionals to experience simulated scenarios and acquire practical skills. Use of VR is very prominent in cognitive training, showing promising results in improving cognitive function in older adults. In the gaming industry, VR has also been used to enhance the player experience, with research showing that it can improve immersion and engagement in games. These trends suggest that VR has significant potential in various industries and can continue to revolutionize the way we experience the world around us.

6.2 CASE STUDY

Several processes need to take place to translate medical images from the imaging modality into virtual space. The pipeline is summarized in the Figure 6.1. An example is a study of the coronary artery. A number of cardiovascular diseases (CVDs) are due to the build-up of plaque inside the coronary artery, or atherosclerosis. This reduces or even prevents the blood flow to the myocardium thereby reducing the oxygen and nutrients supply resulting in myocardial damage and consequently partial or complete heart failure.

To prevent atherosclerotic coronary artery disease, it is crucial to diagnose the extent of the atherosclerosis and to provide timely treatment. Ideally, diagnostic procedures should be non-invasive, painless, harmless, and should provide specific and accurate results.

It is a challenge to reproduce the concealed anatomy and pathology in sufficient detail with techniques that rely solely on indirect measures. Presently, a variety of techniques are used to detect the presence and degree of atherosclerosis depending on the area being scanned, and the amount of information and degree of accuracy required.

With time, it has become apparent that while the type and characteristics of the imaging system are important to take into consideration, the methods

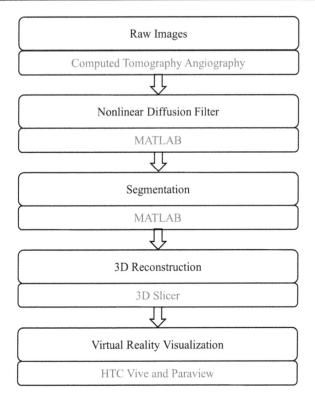

Figure 6.1 Summary of the pipeline to visualize medical images in virtual reality.

of processing, visualizing, and interpreting these medical images plays a great role in the diagnosis and prognosis of any disease that may be present.

The coronary arteries extend from the aorta and branch out as they progress down towards the bottom of the heart. As they branch further, their diameter decreases in size with the smallest branch's diameter reaching 1.5 mm (Dodge et al., 1992). These miniscule branches are difficult to discern directly from medical images without post processing.

After processing, the images are presented to a radiologist as a series of two-dimensional images. The radiologist then interprets and decides, based on knowledge and experience, the site of the plaque build-up. Problems with this method include the nonintuitive method of viewing the images, where the set of 2D images are viewed one at a time and the 3D model is interpreted. This takes up a great deal of time and effort that could be expended at more important tasks. Moreover, each radiologist gives a different measure of the site and extent of the plaque according to their own judgement. Thus, there is a large variability in the diagnosis of coronary artery atherosclerosis.

The aim of the study was to improve the diagnostic accuracy of coronary arterial atherosclerosis by providing an intuitive approach to visualization. Multiple techniques were exploited to achieve this, including nonlinear diffusion filtering, region growing segmentation, and VR visualization. Accurate detection of the site and extent of atherosclerosis would facilitate complete and timely treatment of the disease and therefore the mortality rate.

6.3 METHODOLOGY

An electrocardiograph (ECG)–gated computed tomography angiography (CTA) medical dataset was obtained from OsiriX DICOM Viewer in DICOM format. This image dataset contained 452 slices and was used as a model to test our algorithms and methodology. The ECG–gated property reduces blurring due to motion by accounting for the motion of the beating heart and adjusting the images according to it.

The Perona-Malik model of a nonlinear diffusion filter (Perona & Malik, 1990) was used with the varying values of the constant K. This filter defines the scale space along with a class of algorithms that realize the definition using a diffusion process. The diffusion coefficient can be chosen to vary spatially in such a way that it favours smoothing within a region and prevents the smoothing on region boundaries resulting in a filtered image with sharp region boundaries.

At locations where the gradient between the foreground and the background is minimum, g, the universal diffusion coefficient should be high and vice versa (Figure 6.2). The result is blurring within the region without any interaction between separate regions.

The following function is used to calculate the diffusion coefficient, g, at a point:

$$g(\nabla I) = e^{\left(-\left(\frac{\|\nabla I\|}{K}\right)^2\right)} \tag{6.1}$$

where,

g = diffusion coefficient
∇I = gradient of the image
K = constant that may either be fixed by hand or calculated using the noise estimator described by Canny (1986)

The images are then examined and compared both quantitively using the plots of the resolution, SNR and CNR, and qualitatively by analysing the quality of the image and observing whether the fine details were clearly visible determine which value best improved the image characteristics while still preserving the edges of the elements.

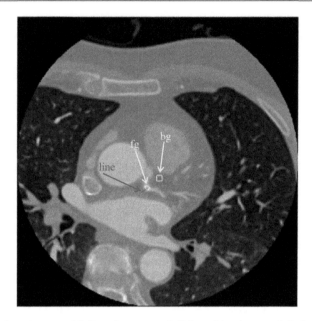

Figure 6.2 Raw image with line, foreground (fg), and background (bg).

The resolution was obtained using the full-width half max (FWHM) at the line.

$$FWHM = 2\sqrt{2\ln2}\,\sigma_{line} = 2.355\sigma_{line} \tag{6.2}$$

where

σ_{line} = standard deviation of the line

The following equations were used to obtain the SNR and CNR:

$$SNR = 20^{*}\log\left(\mu_{fg}\,/\,\sigma_{fg}\right) \tag{6.3}$$

$$CNR = \left(\mu_{fg} - \mu_{bg}\right)/\,\sigma_{bg} \tag{6.4}$$

where

μ_{fg} = mean of the foreground
μ_{bg} = mean of the background
σ_{fg} = standard deviation of the foreground
σ_{bg} = standard deviation of the background σ

To find the best value of the constant, K for the CTA dataset, the filter was applied to the slice 115 repeatedly while varying the K from 10–300 at intervals of 10. Slice number 115 was used as it clearly shows the coronary artery. The characteristics of SNR, CNR, and resolution were analyzed at each iteration using the regions shown in Figure 6.2 and Equations 6.2, 6.3, and 6.4.

The results of the resolution, SNR, and CNR were recorded and plotted against K after normalization. To find the K that would produce the image with the best quality, the product of the reciprocal of resolution, the SNR, and the CNR was plotted against K. The reciprocal of resolution was used since a lower resolution is better. The K value at the peak of the graph was

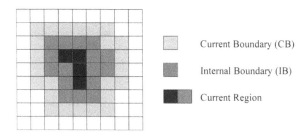

Current Boundary (CB)

Internal Boundary (IB)

Current Region

Figure 6.3 Schematic showing current boundary (CB), internal boundary (IB), and current region.

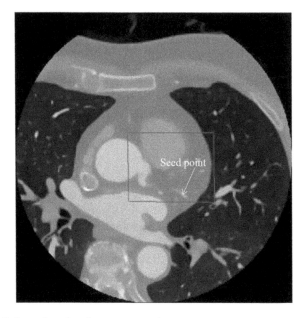

Seed point

Figure 6.4 Selected region for segmentation.

taken as the optimum value for the filtering of these CTA images. This K was then used to filter the whole CTA dataset using MATLAB.

The Hojjatoleslami and Kittler region growing method (Hojjatoleslami & Kittler, 1998) was used to segment the image dataset in MATLAB. The two novel discontinuity measures used in this method to control the region growing process are the average contrast measure (ACM) and the peripheral contrast measure (PCM). To understand the two measurements, the terms current boundary (CB) and internal boundary (IB) are introduced. CB is the set of pixels that surround the current region and IB are the set of pixels that make the boundary of the current region. This is illustrated in Figure 6.3.

The number of voxels inside the selected region was calculated and the seed point was set to be in the middle of that region. The code passes through the expanse of the region and finds the highest intensity present in the region. The highest intensity can be predicted to be of the coronary artery since a contrast agent is used. A second pass is made where all pixels of that intensity are selected while the remaining pixels are discarded. This results in a binary image with the coronary artery as white and the remaining image as black.

Due to a lack of time and computational power, only a small region (where the left coronary artery is most likely to be) of thirty-two (32) slices was segmented. Figure 6.4 shows the region selected for segmentation as well as the seed point.

The segmented dataset of forty slices was written as a DICOM dataset using the dicomwrite function in MATLAB. The DICOM dataset was loaded in 3D Slicer software where the 3D model was reconstructed. A 3D model is built using the segmentation editor and model maker tools. The model was saved as a vtk (Visualization Toolkit) file format.

The vtk file was imported to version 5.4.1(OpenVR) of Paraview which has virtual reality support. After adjusting the lighting and colours of the 3D model, it was sent to OpenVR. The model can now be seen and manipulated using the virtual reality devices. The operator is able to grab, rotate, clip through, and measure the 3D model of the coronary artery.

6.4 RESULTS

The plots in Figures 6.5 and 6.6 show the variation of resolution, SNR and CNR with a varying K. Figures 6.7 and 6.8 show the normalized variation of resolution, SNR and CNR, and (1/Resolution)*SNR*CNR with a varying K. Note that the points at 0 indicate the measure of the image properties of the original image and not of $K = 0$ since equating K to 0 would result in an undefined solution according to the equation. The variables were normalized to enable an easier comparison since each variable is equally important.

Figure 6.7 shows the reciprocal of resolution, SNR, and CNR plotted against K varying from 10 to 300. The best resolution is when $K = 100$

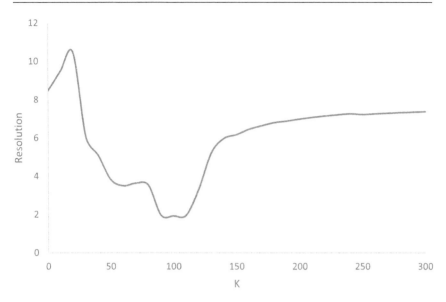

Figure 6.5 Resolution against *K*.

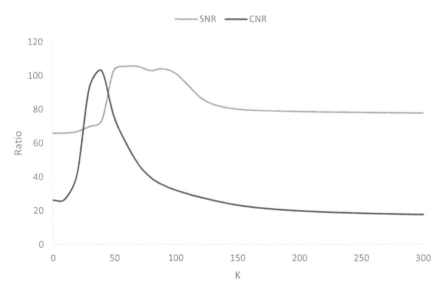

Figure 6.6 SNR and CNR against *K*.

measuring a value of 1.92, the maximum SNR is at $K = 60$ at a value of 105.45, and the maximum CNR is measured to be 103.05 at $K = 40$.

Figure 6.8 shows a normalized plot of the product of the reciprocal of resolution, the SNR and the CNR. The plot shows two peaks at $K = 50$ and $K = 90$ with the peak at 90 being slightly lower than that of 50. At 50, the

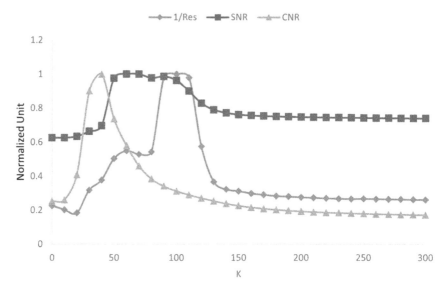

Figure 6.7 Normalized plot of 1/Resolution, SNR and CNR against *K*.

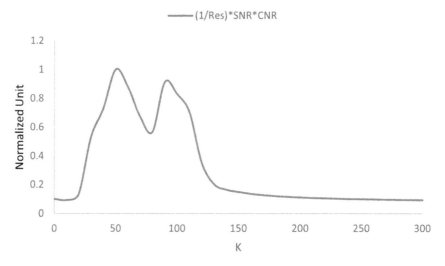

Figure 6.8 Normalized plot of (1/Resolution)*SNR*CNR against *K*.

resolution is recorded as 3.82 which is 50% more than the optimum resolution. The SNR is 97% of its maximum at 102.97 and the CNR is at 73% of its maximum at 75.85. At 90, the resolution, SNR, and CNR are measured to be 1.95 (98% of the max), 104.00 (98% of the max), and 35.10 (34% of the max) respectively.

Although the resolution and SNR are closer to the maximum at *K* = 90, the CNR is much lower. This made the fine details and part of the coronary artery disappear which is an undesirable result. This can be seen from the Figures 6.9 and 6.10. At $K = 50$, an appropriate balance is maintained between reduction in noise, preservation of edges, and conservation of the fine details. This is essential in coronary artery images since the artery diameter may be of a minute 1.9 mm and therefore a K value of 50 was chosen for further processing.

The filtered images of slices 95 to 127 were segmented using the Hojjatoleslami region growing method in MATLAB. The grey level and PCM and ACM measures can be seen in Figures 6.11 and 6.12. The results of three slices (110, 115, and 120) are shown in the Figures 6.13, 6.14, and 6.15.

It can be seen clearly that the results of both the ACM and PCM are very close. While the grey level remains almost constant, the ACM and PCM both increase till the ACM reaches its maximum at pixel number 25729 and the PCM reaches its maximum at pixel number 32516. As the grey level decreases, the ACM and PCM also decrease indicating the formation of a region. The ACM and PCM form another peak, a valley, and a peak. This is an indication of the presence of another region. Qualitative analysis shows that the coronary artery forms several regions, but they all join together as one when depicted in 3D.

The segmented slices are written as a DICOM set and exported to 3D Slicer. A 3D model is built using the segmentation editor and model maker tools. Figure 6.16 shows the resultant model of the segmented part of the coronary artery.

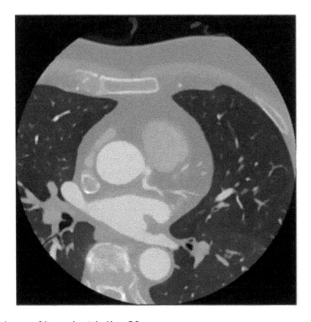

Figure 6.9 Image filtered with $K = 50$.

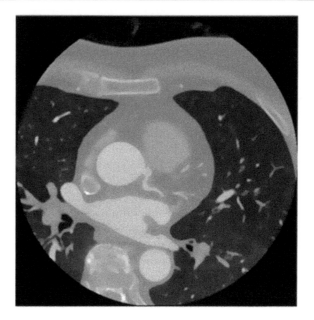

Figure 6.10 Image filtered with *K* = 9.0.

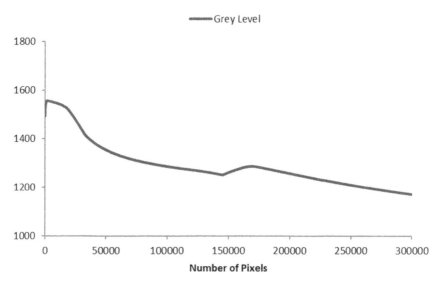

Figure 6.11 Grey level plot.

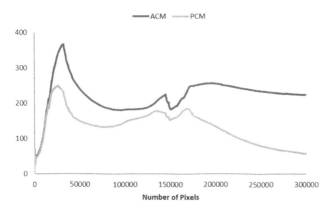

Figure 6.12 ACM and PCM plot.

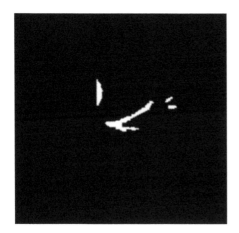

Figure 6.13 Segmentation results of slice 110.

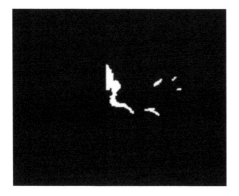

Figure 6.14 Segmentation results of slice 115.

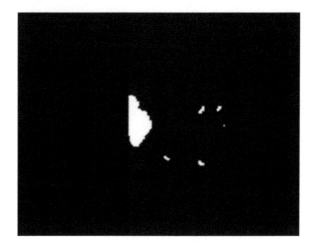

Figure 6.15 Segmentation results of slice 120.

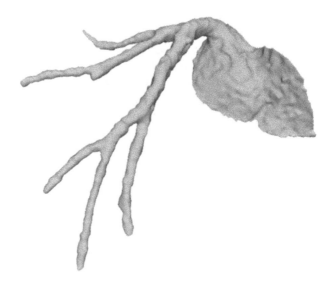

Figure 6.16 3D reconstructed model of the segmented images.

The 3D model is imported to Paraview and sent to OpenVR to be viewed in the virtual space. The operator is able to view the model by wearing the virtual reality headset and control it using the controllers. Paraview provides the ability to grab and zoom, rotate and clip in all planes, and to measure distances between two points. Figures 6.17, 6.18, 6.19, 6.20, and 6.21 show the 3D model in different orientations in Paraview.

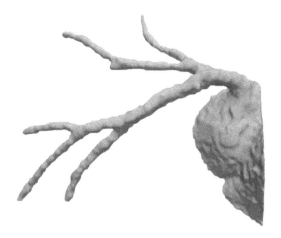

Figure 6.17 Top view.

Figure 6.18 Side A view.

Figure 6.19 Front view.

Figure 6.20 Side B view.

Figure 6.21 Bottom view.

6.5 DISCUSSION

The present study successfully developed a complex system for the creation of three-dimensional (3D) models of coronary arteries in virtual reality using computed tomography angiography (CTA) datasets. The process involved filtering the raw images using the Perona and Malik model of anisotropic nonlinear diffusion filtering, followed by segmentation using the Hojjatoleslami and Kittler region growing method. The segmentation resulted in binary images, with the coronary artery appearing as bright regions and the remaining image appearing dark. The segmented images were then reconstructed using 3D Slicer and imported into Paraview, which supported virtual reality to display the models using the HTC Vive device.

However, this process was not without challenges. The limited availability of datasets, due to patient confidentiality, restricted the optimization of input parameters. Additionally, the filtering and segmentation processes required significant computational power, and parallel processing may improve efficiency. Furthermore, the validation of the results requires the cooperation of radiologists. Collaborating with experts from different fields could lead to faster and higher-quality results.

A lot of challenges are associated with using VR techniques, especially when the resolution of images is taken in perspective. One of the main challenges is that low-resolution images may not provide enough detail to create an accurate 3D model. VR methods rely on creating 3D models of medical images to allow healthcare professionals to visualize and manipulate the data in an immersive way. If the images are low resolution, the resulting 3D model may be inaccurate and not provide enough detail for accurate diagnosis or treatment planning.

Another challenge is that low-resolution images can cause motion sickness or other discomfort for the user when viewed through a VR headset. This is because the brain expects a certain level of detail and realism when viewing images in VR, and low-resolution images may not meet those expectations. This can lead to nausea, dizziness, and other discomfort for the user. In addition, low-resolution images can also lead to longer processing times, as the computer may need to perform additional processing to create an accurate 3D model. This can lead to longer wait times for healthcare professionals who need to access the data quickly.

To address these challenges, it is important to ensure that medical images are of high enough resolution to create accurate 3D models for VR methods. It may also be necessary to develop new algorithms and processing techniques that can help to create accurate 3D models from low-resolution images. Additionally, it is important to consider the user experience and take steps to minimize discomfort when using VR methods with low-resolution images.

6.6 SUMMARY AND CONCLUSION

Virtual reality (VR) is a promising and advantageous technology that can be utilized for intuitive and precise diagnosis of medical conditions. In this study, we investigated the application of VR in the diagnosis of coronary artery atherosclerosis, which has demonstrated the potential of VR as a valuable tool for medical imaging. The proposed approach utilizes the Perona-Malik model of nonlinear diffusion filter with the equation that favors high contrast regions over low contrast areas, with a value of K set to 50. Furthermore, region growing segmentation was performed using the peripheral contrast measure to detect the regions of interest. The segmented regions were reconstructed in 3D Slicer to generate a 3D model that can be viewed and manipulated in VR using the HTC Vive and Paraview. This technique provides clinicians with the ability to meticulously examine the coronary artery, allowing them to pinpoint the location of atherosclerotic plaque and possible calcifications. This information can be used to make more informed prognosis and to pre-plan surgical procedures, potentially reducing the time spent in surgeries and increasing the accuracy of the procedure.

The processes of filtering and segmentation that were performed using MATLAB necessitated considerable computational resources. In addition, the results of the system cannot be validated without the collaboration of radiologists. Because the data went through multiple steps before generating the final VR images, this could potentially lead to the loss of data and the introduction of noise. Moreover, the quality of the VR renders is heavily reliant on the resolution of the medical imaging equipment used. Lower resolutions can result in subpar quality renders that create inconsistencies between the renders and reality. However, by utilizing high-quality medical imaging equipment and fostering interdisciplinary collaborations, this technique has the potential to improve and produce dependable VR renders from medical images.

Another main benefit of immersive technology is that it allows for a more intuitive and natural way of interacting with medical images. Rather than looking at 2D images on a screen, medical professionals can now visualize and interact with 3D models in a more immersive and realistic way. This can help with diagnosis, treatment planning, and patient education.

For example, virtual reality headsets can be used to immerse medical professionals in a 3D model of a patient's anatomy, allowing them to explore and manipulate the image in a more natural and intuitive way. This can help with surgical planning and simulation, as well as with patient education and communication.

In addition, immersive technology can also help to reduce the learning curve for new medical professionals. By providing a more immersive and interactive way of understanding medical images, immersive technology can help to speed up the learning process and improve the overall quality of medical education. As the technology continues to evolve and become more accessible, we can expect to see more widespread adoption of these technologies in medical settings.

Apart from this there are several ways to improve the field of virtual reality and ensure that it continues to advance and grow in the future. For example:

- It is important to develop more sophisticated and user-friendly VR hardware. Currently, VR technology is still relatively new, and the hardware can be quite expensive and complicated to use. To encourage wider adoption of VR, it is important to make the hardware more accessible, affordable, and user-friendly.

- Another suggestion is to enhance the quality and realism of VR content. The more realistic and immersive the VR experience, the more effective it will be. Therefore, it is essential to continue to improve the quality of VR content and to ensure that it accurately simulates the real world.

- The issue of motion sickness is quite common with VR–driven technology. Motion sickness is a common problem for some people when using VR. To address this, researchers and developers should continue to investigate ways to reduce or eliminate motion sickness in VR, such as through improvements to hardware and software.

- It is also possible to expand the range of applications for VR. While VR is already being used in a variety of fields, including gaming and education, there is still significant potential for the technology to be applied in new and innovative ways. Therefore, it is important to continue to explore new applications for VR and to encourage innovation in the field.

If the researches using VR can be cross pollinated it can bring transformation in the field of medicine. VR is a complex and interdisciplinary field that requires input from a range of experts, including computer scientists, designers, and psychologists. To improve the field of VR, it is essential to continue to foster collaboration and cross-disciplinary research. As VR becomes more accessible, more sophisticated, and more widely used, it has the potential to transform a wide range of industries and change the way we interact with technology and with each other.

ACKNOWLEDGEMENTS

This research was conducted at the Department of Biomedical Engineering in the College of Engineering at Imam Abdulrahman bin Faisal University, as a component of a senior design project under the guidance of Dr. Mahbubunnabi Tamal and Engr. Kamran Hameed Khwaja. To facilitate the scientific and technical writing of this study, the School of Interdisciplinary Engineering & Sciences (SINES) at NUST provided a guide to consolidate the research into a comprehensive scientific document.

REFERENCES

Canny, J. (1986). A Computational Approach to Edge Detection. *IEEE Transactions on Pattern Analysis and Machine Intelligence, PAMI-8* (6), 679–698. doi: 10.1109/tpami.1986.4767851

Dargar, S., Kennedy, R., Lai, W., Arikatla, V., & De, S. (2015). Towards Immersive Virtual Reality (iVR): A Route to Surgical Expertise. *Journal of Computational Surgery*, 2(1), 1–26. doi: 10.1186/s40244-015-0015-8

Dodge, J. T., Brown, B. G., Bolson, E. L., & Dodge, H. T. (1992). Lumen Diameter of Normal Human Coronary Arteries. Influence of Age, Sex, Anatomic Variation, and Left Ventricular Hypertrophy or Dilation. *Circulation*, 86(1), 232–246. doi: 10.1161/01.cir.86.1.232

Egger, J., Gall, M., Wallner, J., Boechat, P., Hann, A., Li, X., ... Schmalstieg, D. (2017). HTC Vive MeVisLab Integration via OpenVR for Medical Applications. *PLOS ONE*, 12(3), e0173972. doi: 10.1371/journal.pone.0173972

Farahani, N., Post, R., Duboy, J., Ahmed, I., Kolowitz, B., Krinchai, T., ... Pantanowitz, L. (2016). Exploring Virtual Reality Technology and the Oculus Rift for the Examination of Digital Pathology Alides. *Journal of Pathology Informatics*, 7(1), 22–22. doi: 10.4103/2153-3539.181766

Hojjatoleslami, S.A. & Kittler, J. (1998). Region growing: a new approach. *IEEE Transactions on Image Processing*, 7(7), 1079–1084. doi: 10.1109/83.701170

Kim, Y., Yoo, S. H., Chun, J., Kim, J.-H., Youn, Y. H., & Park, H. (2023). Relieving Anxiety through Virtual Reality Prior to Endoscopic Procedures. *Yonsei Medical Journal*, 64(2), 117–122.

King, F. (2015). *An immersive virtual reality environment for diagnostic imaging*. (Dissertation/Thesis), ProQuest Dissertations Publishing. Retrieved from http://ud.summon.serialssolutions.com/2.0.0/link/0/eLvHCXMwnV07T8MwED6VsiCG8hSPIlliToljn51OFa-2UwfEwlRVtSN1SUpLOvDrOTtOiQB1YIysWCfb9_nznc8fgEh6cfQDE4TErJ8q00c0JkWZSatpZ9NWoZ2h14Z5eNOTiXgZqXEo6neRgmq2a5D0yG2KuQua3xExlkR3pE4Hy_fIyUi5dGvQ1NiDfY7aeqoyYe2x3culHNzHodXeLbf_Bco-51m2IE6w28_l72yqqGrh13-83vhvo4_g8KmRhD-Gls1PoFPLO7Dg7acwuM_Zwse1CRHZZrFypSaMSKZj7qxRIceI-DJT3dmjdUg_eemjM7gdPr8-jqPaxmlYuOvpt4HiHNp5kdsLYHGSKc7dRFk6UCkaKcHnBpMZZpJLIy6hu6unq93N13BALASruEYX2h-r0t5AqzRfe ussqQ

Lee, S., Shetty, A. S., & Cavuoto, L. (2023). Modeling of Learning Processes using Continuous Time Markov Chain (CTMC) for Virtual Reality (VR)-based Surgical Training in Laparoscopic Surgery. *IEEE Transactions on Learning Technologies*, 1–13. doi: 10.1109/TLT.2023.3236899

Mazuryk, T., & Gervautz, M. (1999). *Virtual Reality – History, Applications, Technology and Future*.

Perona, P., & Malik, J. (1990). Scale-Space and Edge Detection Using Anisotropic Diffusion. *IEEE Transactions on Pattern Analysis and Machine Intelligence*, 12(7), 629–639. doi: 10.1109/34.56205

Chapter 7

Accelerating rehabilitation through AR/VR solutions

Enrique Calderon-Sastre and Gunarajulu Renganathan
Hiroshima University, Hiroshima, Japan

Poongavanam Palani
Indian Institute of Technology Madras, Chennai, India

Priyanka Ramasamy and Yuichi Kurita
Hiroshima University, Hiroshima, Japan

Saša Ćuković
Swiss Federal Institute of Technology – ETH Zurich, Institute of
Biomechanics, Zurich, Switzerland

7.1 INTRODUCTION

Rehabilitation is the set of interventions performed to regain or optimize physical, mental, or social functions previously compromised due to illness, injury, trauma, or aging (Cieza et al. 2020; Stucki et al. 2018; Stucki, Cieza, and Melvin 2007). The purpose of rehabilitation is not oriented to prevention but to restore functionality or reduce the damage of the body component caused by disease, injury, or trauma. Currently, world health is facing a multi-paradigm of concerns, such as a sustained increase in the aged population, more people with chronic diseases, and a shortfall in specialized rehabilitation personnel, which have increased the demand for rehabilitation services now and in the coming years. In addition to the demographic factors and the unmet demand for rehabilitation professionals, the COVID-19 pandemic has also increased the need for rehabilitation services due to some disabling conditions due to disease.

It is estimated that as far as 2019, 2.41 billion people (nearly one-third of the world population in that year) would benefit from rehabilitation services (Cieza et al. 2020). As part of the global efforts made to increase the visibility of rehabilitation, in 2017, the World Health Organization (WHO) carried out "Rehabilitation 2030: a call for action" (World Health Organization 2017), a summit where over 200 different stakeholders were gathered to propose a collaborative plan aiming for making more visible the lack of unmet need for rehabilitation in the world and the role that can have the

DOI: 10.1201/9781003306078-10

rehabilitation in achieving the United Nations' Sustainable Development Goals by 2030 (Gimigliano and Negrini 2017).

The rehabilitation field covers three main types of therapies: occupational, physical, and speech therapy. Occupational therapy helps to reduce the pain, disability, or injury that hinders the patient from doing activities of daily living, including but not limited to self-care, leisure, work, household, or school tasks. Speech therapy aims to overcome the genetic or pathological problems that complicate communication, including articulation and fluency, among others. Finally, physical therapy treatments include massages, regulated exercise, water, light, heat, cold, ultrasound, and electricity (Cameron and Monroe 2007). This book chapter will mainly focus on physical rehabilitation and show illustrative examples of other rehabilitation types or applications when necessary. In addition to prevention, cure, and support, rehabilitation is often seen as one of the four main healthcare strategies (Stucki, Cieza, and Melvin, 2007). Besides, having a healthy and functional society significantly impacts the economy because it can directly impact the productivity of society. From a 2019 study, musculoskeletal disorders, which are included in physical rehabilitation treated diseases, represented the highest contribution to worldwide prevalence (Cieza et al. 2020).

7.1.1 Brief explanation of the state of the art of VR/ AR systems

Virtual Reality (VR) is a set of technologies capable of creating "a computer-generated three-dimensional environment that gives an immersion effect" (Lioce et al. 2020). This environment, also known as the VR environment, is often achieved with the use of head-mounted devices (HMD) and/or haptic interfaces. On the other hand, augmented reality (AR) is a type of VR in which the computer-generated digital information is overlapped with elements of the real environment (Lioce et al. 2020) with the aim of enhancing the experience in the most natural and imperceptible way. AR is achieved with more portable devices compared with VR, but the immersion level is also different. Technology has always been to the service of humanity. In this case, cutting-edge technologies like AR, VR, and recently mixed reality (MR) have proved to help reduce the workload of selective rehabilitation services, automate the therapy sessions, make the treatments more cost-effective, or serve as a complement to impart better therapy sessions. In addition to aiding in therapy impartation, Chang et al. (2021) have shown that these systems have proved to be an excellent ally for professional therapy training to overcome the unsatisfied demand for rehabilitation professionals.

Virtual reality and augmented reality systems' prices have become more affordable, making it easier for clinics, hospitals, and recurrent patients to afford a VR/AR system to take therapy.

The general reduction of VR/AR system prices summed to an increased acceptance of general users (due to better user interfaces and more immersive scenarios), device ubiquity, and finally, the COVID-19 pandemic, which caused millions of people to stay at home for several months for work or interact with other people remotely, dramatically accelerated the adoption and usage of VR/AR systems. This demand increase also means an increase in the projects developed and the research projects oriented to healthcare. During the COVID-19 pandemic, the area (excluding videogames and entertainment sectors) in which more change occurred regarding immersive technologies was healthcare (PERKINSCOIE and XR Association 2021).

The main advantages of using immersive technologies (AR/VR) for physical rehabilitation lie in the capacity of these systems to create different adaptable environments and games that can suit the patient's needs using the feedback provided by system-included or added sensors. Because these systems are highly immersive, they can increase the attention span during the therapy session, making it better for situations like pain distraction and exposure therapy (Yu, Yan, and Sundstedt 2022). The feedback data can also be used to generate a record for the patient, optimize the therapy sessions and predict the next steps of the treatment.

The usage and developmental growth of VR/AR technologies for rehabilitation can be seen in Figure 7.1, which shows the number of publications that included one of the keywords proposed in each of the used databases for carrying out the state-of-the-art survey during the selected years of study (2015–2022) in which we can see an increasing trend in AR/VR usage for

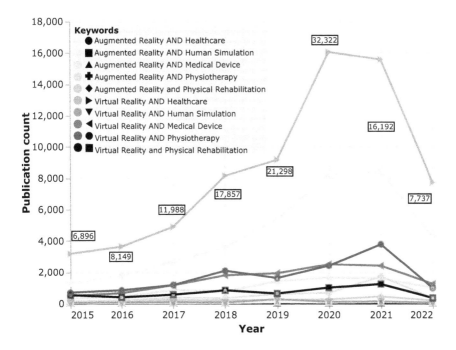

Figure 7.1 Yearly paper count based on the selected keywords.

the purposes related with the selected keywords. The black box shows the accumulated number of papers for the corresponding year.

A plot of the three central databases used for searching the papers can be seen in Figure 7.2. We can see a clear dominance of virtual reality applications over augmented reality and an increasing research trend in these fields. Given the recent and growing relevance of the research field, we consider it essential to include a review in this chapter.

This book chapter reviews the state-of-the-art AR/VR projects and products used in rehabilitation, taking a seven-year period from 2015 to the first half of 2022. The rest of this chapter is organized as follows: Section 7.2 details the methodology used to determine the criteria for searching, excluding, and selecting the papers summarized. Section 7.3 presents the currently existing AR and VR technologies suitable for physical rehabilitation and their classification. Section 7.4 lists the majority of diseases that have benefited from AR/VR technologies. Section 7.5 presents the state-of-the-art review of the selected papers with detailed insights into AR/VR product development and regulations. Section 7.4 shows the discussion and conclusions obtained from this book chapter. Section 7.6 explains the approach taken from the design and development perspective for physical rehabilitation devices as well as standards and regulations. Section 7.7 discusses the application and benefits of using these technologies, emerging risks, design requirements, and future research directions. Section 7.8 closes this book chapter with the conclusions that emerged from the development of this work.

7.2 SEARCH STRATEGY

The systematic review was conducted in accordance with the PRISMA statement for reporting systematic reviews and meta-analyses. The following question was framed during the screening process: "What are the essential design criteria/components needed for the developing of an AR/VR based Physical rehabilitation system?" We used the following electronic databases for screening the comprehensive articles: IEEE Explore, ACM, PubMed/MEDLINE, and Web of Science. The search keywords used for this review include Augmented Reality 'and' Physical Rehabilitation, Virtual Reality 'and' Physical Rehabilitation, Augmented Reality 'and' Physiotherapy, Virtual Reality 'and' Physiotherapy, Augmented Reality 'and' Human Simulation, Virtual Reality 'and' Human Simulation, Augmented Reality 'and' Medical Device, Virtual Reality 'and' Medical Device, Augmented Reality 'and' Healthcare, Virtual Reality 'and' Healthcare. The publication period should be between 01-Jan 2015 to 20-Jun 2022. The time period was chosen based on the announcement of two of the first mainstream AR and VR devices, which are Microsoft Hololens and Oculus Rift, respectively.

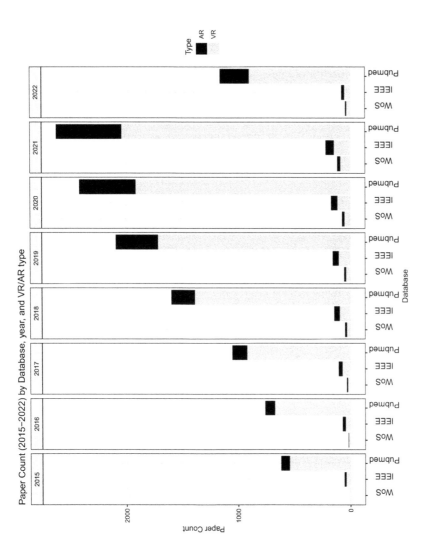

Figure 7.2 Paper count arranged by year, database, and type.

Inclusion criteria: (1) be related to physical rehabilitation therapy, simulation, and design approaches; (2) be written in English; (3) discuss VR or AR applications; (4) be focused explicitly on physical rehabilitation; and (5) include patient study groups.

Exclusion criteria: Articles related to non-medical technologies and applications were excluded.

The PRISMA Chart (Figure 7.3) shows that 66 research articles were screened and included after proper scrutiny. This review article gives multiple research outlines and development approaches. Several research gaps, novel research methodologies, and design standards were included in this study. The preceding question of interest focuses on targeted patients, age group, therapy modes, technology means, physiotherapy, or rehabilitation performance. This review extracts information pertaining to the hardware, software, patients included, disease state, developmental statistics, measurement assessments, and outcomes.

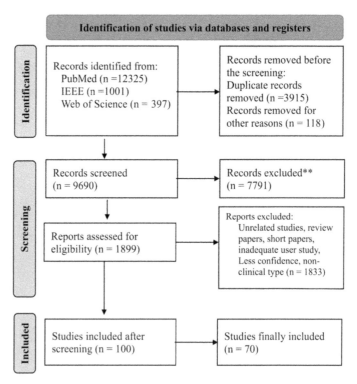

Figure 7.3 PRISMA Chart depicts the article screening process for this review.

7.3 EXISTING AR/VR TECHNOLOGIES FOR PHYSICAL REHABILITATION

The list of existing technologies can be divided based on whether the physical rehabilitation targets the upper or lower limbs. One other division among these technologies is the type of experience they provide. As for the experience, it can be immersive, where the patient feels they are part of the environment, or non-immersive, where the gaming environment is distinctively different from that of the real world.

For upper extremity therapy, handheld controllers become an integral part. These controllers are similar to a joystick found in videogame control. These controllers are ergonomically designed and lightweight. Along with program controls, some of the mentioned devices have inertial sensors to identify motion and tilt. In certain advanced technologies, such as HTC VIVE Focus or Oculus, an inbuilt hand recognition algorithm eliminates the requirement for a handheld device. It uses markerless trackers to map the whole-body segments and perform pose estimation from the tracked landmarks. The game or VR environment will be displayed on a monitor. For a semi-immersive experience, large monitors can be employed.

Balance boards such as Nintendo Wii Balance Board or Sensamove's Sensbalance MiniBoard have been utilized for lower extremity therapy. The participants must stand on these balance boards equipped with pressure and tilt sensors. The parameters measured for identifying stability are the center of pressure, mediolateral symmetry, and/or anterior-posterior symmetry.

Technology development has recently led to the widespread utilization of AR/VR in different fields. This has led to the emergence of low-cost systems that can be affordable and portable, making AR/VR a household name. This calls for standardizing and laying rules over such systems. Hence FDA (U.S. Food and Drug Administration) approval becomes an inevitable requirement to permit AR/VR applications to be part of a rehabilitation regimen. Some of the devices, such as the Relieve VRx, have received FDA approval under 513(f)(2)(De Novo).

The list of new AR/VR technologies employed in rehabilitation can be found in Table 7.1. Most of the custom rehabilitation activities are designed for use based on these platforms.

7.4 AR/VR TECHNOLOGY AS HEALTHCARE TREATMENT OPTIONS

This section presents some of the most common diseases that have benefited from the inclusion of immersive technologies into traditional rehabilitation methods. Each subsection provides insight into the disease as well as the improvements made by VR and AR compared to the traditional approach.

Table 7.1 List of new AR/VR technologies for rehabilitation activities

Product name	Manufacturer	Year	Device type	Immersive/ Non-immersive	Target area	Sensors	Clinical study
IREX VR	GestureTek Healthcare	2001	Video	Immersive	• Upper Extremity • Lower Extremity • Balance • Fine motor control	• Camera • Gesture control technology	(Levac et al. 2016)
PlayStation II Eye Toy VR	Sony	2003	Color Webcam	Non-Immersive (FOV - Approx. 100 degrees)	• Upper Extremity stroke rehabilitation • Neurorehabilitation • Dynamic balance	• 3D audio • Microphone • Camera • Motion controller • Accelerometer, gyroscope	(Yavuzer et al. 2008)
Wii Balance Board	Nintendo	2007	Balance board	Non-immersive	• Lower extremity (static and dynamic balance) • Balance • Mobility	• Pressure sensors • Bluetooth	(Madshaven et al. 2021; Weaver, Ma, and Laing 2017)
Sensbalance MiniBoard	Sensamove	2010	Balance board	Non-immersive	• Lower extremity (static and dynamic balance) • Balance • Mobility	• Inertial sensors	(Valodwala and Desai 2019)
Samsung Gear VR	Samsung Electronics	2015	Head-mounted displays	Immersive (FOV 101 degrees)	• Pain management • Cognitive behavioral therapy • Kinesiophobia	• Inertial measurement unit • Touchpad • Proximity sensor	–

Device	Company	Year	Display	FOV	Application	Sensors	References
HoloLens	Microsoft Corporation	2015	AR	(FOV about 120 degrees)	• Upper extremity • Lower extremity	• Visible light cameras • I.R. camera • Time of Flight depth sensor • Inertial sensor	(Vergel et al. 2020; Anton et al. 2018; Martin et al. 2020; Held et al. 2020)
Oculus Rift	Oculus VR, LLC, Menlo Park, CA, USA	2016	Head-mounted displays	Immersive (FOV about 115 degrees)	• Neurorehabilitation	• Optical sensors • Audio • Electromagnetic sensors	(Baldominos, Saez, and Pozo 2015; Holmes et al. 2017)
Oculus Touch	Facebook Technologies	2016	Handheld analog stick	Immersive	• Hand	• Capacitive sensors • Motion tracking LEDs	
HTC Vive Focus	HTC Corporation, New Taipei City, Taiwan	2016	Head-mounted displays	Immersive (FOV 120 degrees)	Remote diagnosisCognitive therapyPhysical therapyPain management	• Tracking cameras • G-sensor • Gyroscope • Proximity sensor Controller - • Hall sensors • Capacitive sensors • G-Sensor • Gyroscope	(Lerner et al. 2020; Sipatchin, Wahl, and Rifai 2021) (Elor et al. 2022; REAL™ system and XRHealth)
Oculus Go	Facebook Technologies	2018	Head-mounted displays and controller	Mixed (FOV about 101 degrees)	• Vision therapy • Cognitive therapy • Physical therapy	• Inertial sensor • Camera • Proximity sensor	(Hassandra et al. 2021)

(Continued)

Table 7.1 (Continued)

Product name	Manufacturer	Year	Device type	Immersive/ Non-immersive	Target area	Sensors	Clinical study
Lenovo Mirage Solo	Lenovo	2018	HMD	(FOV about 110 degrees)	• Upper extremity • Lower extremity	• P-Sensor • Gyroscope • Accelerometer • Magnetometer	–
Oculus Quest	Facebook Technologies	2019	Head-mounted displays	Immersive (FOV about 100 degrees)	• Upper Extremity	• Optical sensors • Audio • Electromagnetic sensors	(Madshaven et al. 2021; Carnevale et al. 2022)
H.P. Reverb G2	H.P.	2020	HMD + Controller	Mixed Reality (FOV about 114 degrees)	• Upper extremity • Lower extremity	• Eye Tracking • Pupillometry sensor • Pulse monitor • Heart Rate Sensor • Face Camera	–
Relieve VRx (formerly EaseVRx)	AppliedVR	2021	Head-mounted device	Immersive	• Pain treatment (lower back) • Cognitive behavioral therapy	• Microphone • Breathing amplifier	(Garcia et al. 2021)

7.4.1 Upper limb

The upper limb comprises of the hand, wrist, forearm, elbow, and upper arm. Damage to any of the previously mentioned components can be caused for many reasons and diseases including, but not limited to stroke, sports, work-related injuries, arthritis, or congenital disorders. Upper limb rehabilitation demands long-term therapy sessions to achieve good results because of the complexity of the upper limb and the systems involved in proper functioning (Das and Kurita 2020). Project Star Catcher (Elor, Teodorescu, and Kurniawan 2018) is a virtual reality game made using HTC Vive to impart therapy to patients with hemiparesis using a modified version of constraint-induced therapy (CIP), which includes shorter but intensive training periods compared with traditional CIP. The system can change the physical-psychological binding to influence the use of the weaker arm (using an in-game reward system that gives a better reward if the weak arm is used more) and provides immediate feedback to the users about their performance. The system was tested on nine stroke survivors and six users with upper-limb impairments.

Upper limb rehabilitation includes recovery of movement-functional damage and therapy for becoming familiar with prosthetics for activities of daily living (ADL). Upbeat (Melero et al. 2019) is an augmented reality platform designed to help the prosthetic rehabilitation process in upper limb amputees using a dance game with a virtual instructor who imparts the therapy as dance choreography. The system uses Microsoft Kinect to track the user's position and a Myo armband for collecting electromyography (EMG) signals. The gamified experience, achieved through the dance experience, can improve the motivation of the user to take rehabilitation sessions. Another Kinect-based solution is the exergame proposed by Muñoz et al. (2019), which was tested on ten patients.

7.4.2 Lower limb

The lower limb includes the hip, thigh, knee, leg, ankle, and foot. In the same way as the upper limb, the lower limb can be affected by many different reasons, and depending on the cause, additional rehabilitation therapy can be applied. Gao et al. (2021) show an evaluation of the virtual reality effect on lower limb function in children with cerebral palsy considering many existing research projects, and they proposed an efficacy model based on their findings. Experimental results showed an improvement in treatment efficacy of 30%. For ankle rehabilitation, Covaciu et al. (2021) presented a solution for people affected by stroke. The VR system combined with an electromyogram can be used to create effective exercises based on the gathered data. In addition to improvement on different performance metrics, therapy motivation preservation is also an important parameter to consider a therapy method as effective and thus obtain better outcomes. Bergmann et al. (2018) presented a comparison between no VR and robot-assisted gait training (RAGT) therapy for subacute stroke patients. It was found across the participants a lower therapy drop-out rate in the group that used the VR and RAGT therapy methods.

AR has also seen a rise in lower limb rehabilitation because it can overcome some user experiences in VR for a reduced number of patients, such as lower limb identification (Das et al. 2021) while in the VR environment. As AR is less immersive than VR, people with these problems can safely use AR rehabilitation systems. Chang et al. (2022) analyzed the AR rehabilitation platforms available. They identified the projects depending on the application: lower limb rehabilitation of elderly adults, lower limb rehabilitation of stroke patients, and lower limb rehabilitation of Parkinson's patients. Bennour et al. (2018) showed an AR system based on video projectors and an optoelectronic motion capture device for modifying some footprint parameters on the patient and, at the same time, "determine the error in footprint modifications and the effects of footprint modifications on lower-limb flexion/extension angles". Modification of footprint parameters could be useful for specific pathologies rehabilitation protocols. Chen et al. (2020) proposed a system capable of imparting AR-assisted Tai Chi training, showing improvement Berg Balance Scale (BBS) for a patient-tailored set of exercises compared with the no AR version of complete traditional Tai Chi.

7.4.3 Parkinson's Disease

Parkinson's disease (PD) is a neurogenerative disease characterized by motor symptoms such as bradykinesia, tremor, and postural balance disorder and also non-motor symptoms such as cognitive decline (Rizos et al. 2014). In addition to drug-based treatment, while treating PD, it is essential to promote physical activity as much as possible. Hence AR and VR play a crucial role in providing safe environments for physical activity performance and evaluation of the exercise using the system-incorporated sensors. Physical rehabilitation exercises can have a significant impact on improving gait, strength, and coordination. Cikajlo and Potisk (2019) conducted a parallel study to evaluate the performance of patients in a pick-and-place task with the use of 3D virtual reality using a 3D Oculus Rift CV1 for one group and only one laptop for the other group while tracking user movements with the Leap motion controller. The 3D group showed better performance in five exercise metrics. 3D virtual reality group usage presented more enjoyment.

Another study involving immersive technologies for PD treatment is the one by Lei et al. (2019), in which they focused on analysing the effect of VR systems used in PD for gait and balance improvement. The results indicate that VR systems outperformed the traditional systems in balance function, mobility, and step and stride length. In addition to the performance metrics, the patients that used VR systems showed more significant effects after therapy on their confidence level and quality of life improvement.

7.4.4 Stroke

Stroke is a widespread brain injury that affects the human body differently depending on the brain region where the blood obstruction occurs (either by ischemic or hemorrhagic stroke). Still, the most common effects include paralysis, speech problems, vision problems, and memory loss. Due to the many disabling sequelae of stroke, VR monitoring systems have also been implemented (Postolache et al. 2021). In the United States, stroke is the fifth leading cause of death (Virani et al. 2021) and worldwide, in the category of neurological disorders, stroke demands the highest number for rehabilitation, with approximately 86 million people (Cieza et al. 2020). Most of the physical rehabilitation for stroke is oriented to promote neuroplasticity by doing repetitive and challenging tasks. Karácsony et al. (2019) presented a VR game and an electroencephalogram (EEG) motor imagery brain-computer interface (MI-BCI). In this type of rehabilitation, immersive systems are helpful because they use the game (Xu et al. 2021) or create an environment to improve or retain the motivation of the user while performing repetitive tasks for long periods and simultaneously record treatment data from the sensors included in the system.

Rogers et al. (2019) evaluated a system for goal-directed and exploratory upper-limb using Elements VR (a VR system designed to enhance the neuroplastic recovery process using tangible interfaces) applied to stroke rehabilitation and tested it on 21 adults with sub-acute stroke. The results show that the therapy provided with this system can facilitate motor and cognitive recovery.

7.4.5 Sclerosis

Multiple sclerosis (MS) is an auto-immune, neurodegenerative, and inflammatory disorder that affects the patient's central nervous system. This disturbs the neuromuscular control of the human which affects the communication flow between the brain and the rest of the motor organs. Some of the consequences of MS are problems in mobility, hand function, vision, fatigue, cognition, bowel function, sensory, spasticity, pain, depression, and tremor (Kister et al. 2013), which severely affect the capability of the patient to perform ADL. MS is the most common non-traumatic disabling disease that affects young adults (Dobson and Giovannoni 2019).

Physical rehabilitation for this disorder mainly includes exercises to improve strength, endurance, flexibility, and mobility (Burks, Bigley, and Hill 2009). Most VR solutions aimed to impart MS rehabilitation focus on gait and balance function. A recent review showed the comparison of VR systems with traditional approaches in the cognitive and motor processes. The patients that used VR-based systems showed a significant improvement both in gait and balance, as well as memory skills, attention, and visual-spatial abilities (Maggio et al. 2019). Park et al. (2020) presented a VR system tested on 40 adults to impart cognitive-motor rehabilitation with enhancement in motivation and cognitive function.

7.4.6 Pain management

Numerous studies have suggested that VR therapies can help with acute pain, and there is evidence that they can also help with chronic pain. The general approach uses VR to distract and relax the user, typically with soothing sights and sounds or engaging content that draws the user's attention away from pain, influencing both sensory and psychological components of pain perception. In both hospitalized and outpatient settings, studies have found the technique effective for pain associated with localized pain from injury and illness, surgical procedures, labour, wound-dressing changes, and chronic neck and lower back pain. In some studies, the outcomes of VR pain-management therapy are comparable to traditional physical rehabilitation approaches and medication options, which can also have adverse side effects (Nambi et al. 2021).

7.5 STATE OF ART REVIEW (TOP 5 ARTICLES)

This article discusses several possible technologies for physical rehabilitation using VR and AR platforms with novel navigation and performance systems. Using digital technologies to simulate a non-invasive paradigm based on acoustic, vibrotactile, and haptic control-based innovations is essential in developing more efficient rehabilitation systems. The five most viewed articles based on the systematic presentation of AR and VR-based rehabilitation of patients and some simulation-based training for the staff were discussed in this section. The discussion was based on either specific criteria of the group or samples dedicated to the participants' list, particular disease or research requirement involved, technology specification of VR and AR, sessions, and outcome results obtained from the executed research. The five most relevant articles were tabulated below in Table 7.2.

7.6 DESIGN AND DEVELOPMENT APPROACHES FOR PHYSICAL REHABILITATION

7.6.1 Traditional research and development of AR/VR devices

For a completely immersive experience, it is necessary to have a combination of haptic, audio, and visual perceptions of the environment. The most advanced form of VR experience is the immersive type with the provision of an HMD where the patient feels they are a part of the virtual experience.

Table 7.2 Top five state of the art articles with clinical measures

Study	Group/sample	Research requirement /Type of disease	Type of AR/VR	Sessions	Outcome measures
(Wang et al. 2017)	VRG (n = 12) ARG (n = 12)	Remote medical training	Google glass (VR) and Microsoft HoloLens (AR)	Conducted as a pilot study based on the availability of mentors for each group	Microsoft HoloLens is utilized to enhance the view of a rural emergency room and serves as a potential application for medical training remotely
(Hodge et al. 2018)	VRG (n = 7)	Alzheimer's type dementia	VR environment set up through Unity platform	Randomized sessions depending on the diagnosis criteria of the dementia	Development of intensively designed prototype and extensively personalized based on comfort
(Zhao et al. 2018)	VRG (n = 9)	Visually impaired people (VIPs)/three types of feedback-based controls for canes	VR system supports I. Vibrotactile feedback, physical resistance, and spatial 3D audio feedback	Formative study (Tutorial 15-min session, indoor and outdoor navigation) and evaluation study (1-hour session)	Performance effect of canes using VR in different environments and evaluate the efficacy of the feedback controls
(Staropoli et al. 2018)	Simulator group (n = 11) Comparison group (n = 11)	Post-graduate student of year 3 (PGY-3) serves as a surgeons/ simulator training with residents	Eye surgical simulator (VR Magic Holding AG, Mannheim, Germany)	30–50 live cataract surgeries based on the completion of two introduction sessions of micro and cataract surgeries	Reduces the risk of surgical accidents with prior simulation training for new PGY-3 students
(Rogers et al. 2019)	VRG (n = 21)	Sub-acute stroke patients of 42–94 years	Several VR-based rehabilitative games for stroke survivors	Weekly, three 30–40mins sessions of virtual rehabilitation	Simultaneous evaluation on both cognitive and motor skills improvement after stroke

On the other hand, the less advanced type is the non-immersive type, where the modules are limited to a monitor and a simple controller, which can be a mouse, keyboard, or joystick. AR technologies differ from that of VR owing to the fact that AR helps visualize engineered elements in the real world while VR will ultimately be virtual. Thus, the components of AR/VR technologies play a vital role in rendering the requirements. A general schematic of the system is shown in Figure 7.4.

It can be seen from Figure 7.4 that the entire process of developing an AR/VR system for rehabilitation is engineered to cater to the needs of the patients with the help of a physician. Physicians and physiotherapists have explored task design for providing targeted rehabilitation. The AR/VR system enhances patients' experience when performing these tasks. Also, the physician's effort in tracking the patient's progress will be reduced. It can be seen as an equally shared effort between physician and patient, whose workload is alleviated by the AR/VR system.

7.6.1.1 Patient side

Capturing the motion of the human and identifying the human activities is integral in designing an AR/VR system that forms the input. It requires a multi-sensor system, each working in coherence with the other. Many researchers have applied sensor fusion techniques to obtain accurate measurements. Following are some of the sensors, part of the movement recording system.

(i) **Motion capture system:** To record the various motions of humans, Wang et al. (2017) used the Leap motion sensor on a PC to identify the gestures using the dedicated software development kit. Also, Baldominos et al. (2015) used Intel RealSense (released in 2014) to monitor the abduction and adduction of the rotator cuff. Motion capturing/tracking sensors are required to be highly precise, so sensing technologies like electromagnetic sensors and reflective markers have long been employed. Commercial systems such as Qualisys and Microsoft Kinect have also been employed in motion tracking for AR/VR applications.

(ii) **Time of flight camera (ToF):** This is found to be embedded in smart glasses and HMD devices for AR/VR applications. It is a charge-coupled device (CCD) that uses a modulated infrared (IR) light source for sensing the images.

(iii) **Inertial sensors:** The inertial sensors contain an accelerometer, gyroscope, and magnetometer. The angles of the different planes, such as the roll, pitch, and yaw angle, can be calculated using a simple complementary filter or a Kalman filter. Machine learning algorithms have also been recently implemented to perform sensor fusion and identify the angles. Inertial sensors provide position-sensing abilities and can be embedded in wearable devices such as the HMD, handheld controllers, and haptic gloves.

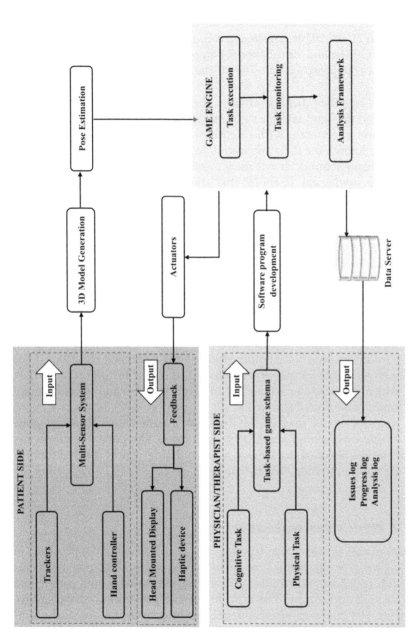

Figure 7.4 General schematic for AR/VR system with feedback to patient and doctor.

These tracked sensor outputs are implemented in the 3D model generation to estimate the user's pose. The output from the AR/VR system is received by augmentative devices such as the head-mounted display, haptic feedback device, and/or audio feedback device (Okumura and Kurita 2021). Erhardsson et al. (2020) implemented commercially available devices such as the HTC Vive and Beat Saber for upper extremity rehabilitation. This study shows the prospects of using off-the-shelf devices in rehabilitation.

(i) *Head-mounted display (HMD)*: The device has a display that wraps around the head and fits snugly over the eyes, providing a highly immersive experience. With recent advancements, HMDs have become fairly known for their application in VR games. As seen in Table 7.1, the manufacturers have made it available to the population with varying technological amenities that allow its application in healthcare. Many of these devices have received FDA approval which further aids their contribution to rehabilitation.

(ii) *Haptic feedback device*: The tactile/haptic feedback can be rendered using desktop or wearable devices. For tasks that concentrate on whole-body movement, wearable devices are preferred as opposed to the desktop devices, such as devices from force dimensions and 3D systems. Wearable devices can be a suite with embedded sensors or targeted devices. Gutiérrez et al. (2021) use a haptic thimble that acts as vibration and/or pressure haptic feedback over the fingertips for reaching and grasping activities as part of the study involving spinal cord injury patients. Another study on the combined effect of HMDs with wearable haptics was conducted by Ilaria Bortone et al. (2020), which involved an assessment of cerebral palsy and developmental dyspraxia-affected children.

(iii) *Audio feedback device*: This feedback usually comes from the game engine designed for the AR/VR application. Directional microphones can be embedded in HMDs, or the audio devices in the desktop PC/laptop can provide this feedback.

7.6.1.2 Physician/physiotherapist

The traditional approach involves the active involvement of the physician in deciding the type of treatment required for the patient. This requires a customizable task flow and intuitive progress log that benefits both patient and physician/physiotherapist. The task design can target motor or cognitive functions, and dual cognitive tasks can also be considered. The dual cognitive task involves the assessment of both motor and cognitive task assessment as seen in Exergames (Harrington, Koon, and Rogers 2020; Nahum and Bavelier 2020; Tadayon, Wataru, and Yuichi Kurita 2020).

The data server logs the information about the progress made by the patient. Recent technology allows machine learning (ML) and deep learning (DL) algorithms to analyse progress and aid decision-making. These logs can be accessed via smartphones or can be received via email. For clinical setups, the physiotherapists generate the reports, and the physician analyses the data to decide on the future exercise prescription.

7.6.1.3 Software

In AR/VR, the environmental elements and the 3D models can be designed using platforms such as Unity, Blender, Google VR, Unreal Engine 4, CryEngine, 3ds Max, Maya, and Oculus Medium. Most of these platforms can be programmed in the C++ programming language. The virtual environment thus created encourages the patients to actively carry out their rehabilitation activities without being bored or losing focus over their training period.

Most physical rehabilitation technologies revolve around task-specific game designs, making the repetition more engaging than conventional therapy techniques. One must concentrate on the elements of game theory to utilize the broad spectrum of advantages. Care must be taken when composing the strategy, designing the environment, and setting the game's theme and rewards.

7.6.1.4 Limitations of AR/VR usability

1. *Cyber sickness*: The patients incur motion sickness when using HMDs and/or are standing on a balancing board. It increases the unwillingness to try out the rehabilitation exercises, which can be investigated via questionnaires like Simulation Sickness Questionnaire (Sevinc and Berkman 2020). Also, Zielasko and Riecke (2021) have conducted a study that shows that sitting posture produces more motion sickness, since it does not generate vestibular and proprioceptive feedback, than the activities that involve walking and active interaction with the virtual environment.
2. *High processing speed/High-end hardware*: The quantum of data being processed necessitates the presence of a high-end processor. This processing power is required to make the AR/VR environment more relevant to the real world.
3. *Latency*: The time lag between the user-generated movement and the AR/VR environment response should be as minimal as possible. It requires increasing the transparency of the two processes.
4. *Game theory*: There is a requirement to understand the game strategy and conflict plan for different age groups. The ecological environment developed for one age group may not be suitable for another. The user should be provided with an engaging game theory and an appropriate environment for active participation.

7.6.2 FDA regulations for AR/VR product development

In consideration of the complexities in the development of the AR/VR medical device, the US Food and Drug Administration has taken the initiative to give some special consideration to the development of AR/VR devices (AAMI, 2012).

1. Well-informed consent is essential for collecting clinical data
2. Additional safeguarding practices should be implemented for studies involving children.
3. For a novel device, risks and benefits assessment will be examined by FDA. through the De Novo request form. It provides a marketing pathway to classify novel devices with general and special controls, which is also a risk-based classification process.
4. Substantial equivalence is essential as part of 510 (K) premarket notification to include AR/VR capabilities in the existing devices.
5. FDA's multiple-function device policies are needed when the device is integrated with consumer hardware and software.
6. Risk-benefit information is essential for the determination of device effectiveness. FDA may also approve devices with higher uncertainty rates upon properly examining the risk and uncertainty ratio balanced by other factors.

7.7 DISCUSSION

7.7.1 Application and benefits

The design approaches and application enhancement are always concerned with the medical conditions and therapies to which the prototype development of AR or VR might be employed. However, various domains influence the interfacing parameters, whether VR/AR, which is already available in the markets to boost the treatment of patients. Let us discuss a few significant domains.

7.7.1.1 Mental health and concerned disorders

In the past, exposure therapy management was handled only by psychological therapists in order to ensure a protected and comfortable environment to train and rehabilitate. This environment was represented by the surrounding objects or actions. The environment includes enhancing the parameters like stress, fatigue, anxiety, and so on, and making the patients train overtime to manage their mental states depending on the situations concerned. Virtual reality–based cognitive treatment helps therapists to deal with the measure of the mental strength of the patients and how well the exposure therapy supports overcoming traumatic incidents (American Psychological Association, 2017). Several research studies have found that the contribution of VR in exposure therapy is increasing and explores its effectiveness in treating many neurological disorders such as autism, hyperactivity deficit, schizophrenia spectrum, and so on.

Assessing cognitive function is vital while observing physical tasks such as motor functions, balance, and gait, which is a crucial requirement in improving immersion and motivation and helps increase the human's ADL.

7.7.1.2 Surgical limitations and pediatric diagnosis

AR supports the preliminary understanding of the surgery process and allows the surgeons to analyse the patient's anatomy through 3D visualizations while discussing the different surgical techniques (Ćuković et al. 2013). Adapting to this kind of pre-operative planning would vastly support the alternative approach of switching to more precise technology. Moreover, with these less-invasive procedures, it is possible to reduce complications, improve outcome measures, and shorten the operative time.

Exciting VR/AR applications help treat adolescents and senior adults and focus on the pediatric population to diagnose children with major mental disorders of cerebral palsy, autism spectrum disorders, and so on. In addition, it is observed that ophthalmology-based treatments have been done with promising VR/AR-based therapy findings.

7.7.2 Emerging risks

Integrating VR/AR-based applications has many associated risks and is vulnerable to the attractive 3D environments used to increase the patient's interest. In this article, we are reviewing some of the risks concerned with reducing effectiveness. VR/AR–based rehabilitation and therapeutic conditions can easily make therapists habitual users. This habitual change may have severe consequences, creating new problems, neglecting other important activities, and missing routine daily tasks (Food and Drug Administration, 2016).

Seizures, collisions, and falls are more frequently observed for VR/AR users, and it is mandatory to increase the safety requirements during therapeutic sessions. Owing to the associated risks, the discomforts and injuries are more familiar with the limited development of the prototypes. The distress conditions occur only during the repetitive sessions for motion syndromes and long-term rehabilitation of the upper and lower limbs.

7.7.3 Design standard requirements

This book chapter also reviews regulatory standards, policies, guidelines, and reports which are useful for the development of AR/VR as a medical device. The standard design and development process also includes generic home-based usage for home therapy applications.

1. **QMS/FDA QSR:** The most preliminary and essential requirement is the development of quality management systems (QMS), which includes a formal framework of policy documents, procedures, and processes. These requirements are indicated by the notifying body to ensure that the device developed follows safety protocols and procedures as intended. QMS development and implementation are expected from the organizational standpoint in which the design and development plans are achieved through the process developed in the QMS forms and procedures or local regulations (Example: US FDA QSR). US QSR is generally aligned with ISO 13485 standard in the United States. The key stages of the QMS/QSR included storage, distribution, rework, installation, support, services, and disposal metrics.

2. **Risk Management ISO 14971 / 21 CFR 820.30:** Each organization developing a medical device should perform risk management activities to ensure the designed device is risk free. Manufacturers should have well-detailed documentation of risk assessment plans, identification methods, analyzing techniques, and estimating the foreseeable hazards and associated risks. This traceability matrix helps in controlling/eliminating the risk assessed. ISO 14971 has six stages for performing the risk management process, including risk analysis, risk evaluation, risk control, overall residual risk acceptability, risk management report, and production and postproduction information. It also covers hazard analysis, fault-free analysis, failure modes, and effects analysis (FMEA) (Salisbury 2021).

3. **Software development life cycle IEC 62304:** IEC 62304 is an EU standard that FDA recognizes as an approved consensus standard to comply with regulatory mandate requirements. The central idea of IEC 62304 is to establish and maintain the traceability between the user needs/system requirements, software testing, and risk control processes involved in software development. It is often illustrated via V-Model and Agile control practices (Salisbury 2021).

7.7.4 Future research directions

Immersive systems have helped a significant amount to endure some of the challenges brought by the COVID-19 pandemic, such as home isolation, mental-health problems (Ellis et al. 2020), remote education (Wang et al. 2017), and social-distance monitoring (Arpaia et al. 2021; Mamone et al. 2020; Priyan et al. 2021) by allowing the creation of virtual environments where realistic simulations can be held and reducing the communication gap in work-related meetings.

Regarding the healthcare field, immersive systems will continue to help in vocational training such as surgery and rehabilitation as the development kits (Vidal-Balea et al. 2021) and are more intuitive to develop applications, and the cost of AR/VR equipment is lowering. Integration of more sensors and systems to get more data will continue (Brunete et al. 2021). AR development is cheaper because of the variety of devices that can run AR applications (ranging from smartphones and tablets to computers). AR/VR mental health rehabilitation systems are likely to continue growing because of their capability to recreate tailored scenarios for exposure therapy with a lot of detail (Hodge et al. 2018) as well as monitoring and detection systems (Bayahya, Alhalabi, and AlAmri 2021). As the AR/VR capable systems evolve, more physical rehabilitation therapy improvements are possible due to a higher integration between software and system-integrated sensors.

7.8 CONCLUSION

AR/VR devices have a high potential for home-based rehabilitation treatments. Nevertheless, the intended treatment should be successfully administered in clinical practice. Hence, the manufacturers need to develop a device under the regulatory scope. Also, the regulatory requirements can be adapted in the early phase design if these processes and procedures posted by FDA were included. This book chapter will be a recommendation for engineers who are interested in developing AR/VR medical devices. These inputs will make the device safe and effective and improve the patient's condition and clinician satisfaction.

ACKNOWLEDGEMENTS

We authors would like to thank Hiroshima University and the Indian Institute of Technology Madras for their support and encouragement throughout the work.

REFERENCES

AAMI, AT. "Guidance on the Use of Agile Practices in the Development of Medical Device Software." *Association for the Advancement of Medical Instrumentation* 21 (2012): 22–78.

American Psychological Association. 2017. *Ethical Principles of Psychologists and Code of Conduct.* Washington DC: American Psychological Association. http://www.apa.org/ethics/code/index.aspx

Anton, David, Idoia Berges, Jesús Bermúdez, Alfredo Goñi, and Arantza Illarramendi. 2018. "A Telerehabilitation System for the Selection, Evaluation and Remote

Management of Therapies." *Sensors* (Basel, Switzerland) 18 (5). https://doi. org/10.3390/S18051459

Arpaia, Pasquale, Egidio De Benedetto, Concetta Anna Dodaro, Luigi Duraccio, and Giuseppe Servillo. 2021. "Metrology-Based Design of a Wearable Augmented Reality System for Monitoring Patient's Vitals in Real Time." *IEEE Sensors Journal* 21 (9): 11176–11183. https://doi.org/10.1109/JSEN.2021.3059636

Baldominos, Alejandro, Yago Saez, and Cristina García del Pozo. 2015. "An Approach to Physical Rehabilitation Using State-of-the-Art Virtual Reality and Motion Tracking Technologies." *Procedia Computer Science* 64: 10–16. https:// doi.org/10.1016/j.procs.2015.08.457

Bayahya, Areej Y., Wadee Alhalabi, and Sultan H. AlAmri. 2021. "Smart Health System to Detect Dementia Disorders Using Virtual Reality." *Healthcare* 9 (7): 810. https://doi.org/10.3390/healthcare9070810

Bennour, Sami, Baptiste Ulrich, Thomas Legrand, Brigitte M. Jolles, and Julien Favre. 2018. "A Gait Retraining System Using Augmented-Reality to Modify Footprint Parameters: Effects on Lower-Limb Sagittal-Plane Kinematics." *Journal of Biomechanics* 66: 26–35. https://doi.org/10.1016/j.jbiomech.2017.10.030

Bergmann, Jeannine, Carmen Krewer, Petra Bauer, Alexander Koenig, Robert Riener, and Friedemann Müller. 2018. "Virtual Reality to Augment Robot-Assisted Gait Training in Non-Ambulatory Patients with a Subacute Stroke: A Pilot Randomized Controlled Trial." *European Journal of Physical and Rehabilitation Medicine* 54 (3). https://doi.org/10.23736/s1973-9087.17.04735-9

Bortone, Ilaria, Michele Barsotti, Daniele Leonardis, Alessandra Crecchi, Alessandra Tozzini, Luca Bonfiglio, and Antonio Frisoli. 2020. "Immersive virtual environments and wearable haptic devices in rehabilitation of children with neuromotor impairments: a single-blind randomized controlled crossover pilot study." *Journal of Neuroengineering and Rehabilitation* 17 (1): 1–14. https://doi.org/10.1186/ s12984-020-00771-6

Brunete, Alberto, Ernesto Gambao, Miguel Hernando, and Raquel Cedazo. 2021. "Smart Assistive Architecture for the Integration of IoT Devices, Robotic Systems, and Multimodal Interfaces in Healthcare Environments." *Sensors* 21 (6): 2212. https://doi.org/10.3390/s21062212

Burks, Jack S., George Kim Bigley, and Harry Haydon Hill. 2009. "Rehabilitation Challenges in Multiple Sclerosis." *Annals of Indian Academy of Neurology* 12 (4): 296. https://doi.org/10.4103/0972-2327.58273

Cameron, Michelle H., and Linda G. Monroe. 2007. *Physical Rehabilitation*. Elsevier. https://doi.org/10.1016/B978-0-7216-0361-2.X5001-7

Carnevale, Arianna, Ilaria Mannocchi, Mohamed Saifeddine Hadj Sassi, Marco Carli, Giovanna De De Luca, Umile Giuseppe Longo, Vincenzo Denaro, and Emiliano Schena. 2022. "Virtual Reality for Shoulder Rehabilitation: Accuracy Evaluation of Oculus Quest 2." *Sensors* 22 (15): 5511. https://doi.org/10.3390/ S22155511

Chang, Hongbin, Yang, Song, and Xuanzhen Cen. 2022. "Effectiveness of Augmented Reality for Lower Limb Rehabilitation: A Systematic Review." Edited by Wen-Ming Chen. *Applied Bionics and Biomechanics* 2022 (July): 1–10. https://doi. org/10.1155/2022/4047845

Chang, Todd P., Trevor Hollinger, Thomas Dolby, and Joshua M. Sherman. 2021. "Development and Considerations for Virtual Reality Simulations for Resuscitation Training and Stress Inoculation." *Simulation in Healthcare: The*

Journal of the Society for Simulation in Healthcare 16 (6): e219–e226. https://doi.org/10.1097/SIH.0000000000000521

Chen, Po-Jung, I-Wen Penn, Shun-Hwa Wei, Long-Ren Chuang, and Wen-Hsu Sung. 2020. "Augmented Reality-Assisted Training with Selected Tai-Chi Movements Improves Balance Control and Increases Lower Limb Muscle Strength in Older Adults: A Prospective Randomized Trial." *Journal of Exercise Science Fitness* 18 (3): 142–147. https://doi.org/10.1016/j.jesf.2020.05.003

Cieza, Alarcos, Kate Causey, Kaloyan Kamenov, Sarah Wulf Hanson, Somnath Chatterji, and Theo Vos. 2020. "Global Estimates of the Need for Rehabilitation Based on the Global Burden of Disease Study 2019: A Systematic Analysis for the Global Burden of Disease Study 2019." *The Lancet* 396 (10267): 2006–2017. https://doi.org/10.1016/S0140-6736(20)32340-0

Cikajlo, Imre, and Karmen Peterlin Potisk. 2019. "Advantages of Using 3D Virtual Reality Based Training in Persons with Parkinson's Disease: A Parallel Study." *Journal of NeuroEngineering and Rehabilitation* 16 (1): 119. https://doi.org/10.1186/s12984-019-0601-1

Covaciu, Florin, Adrian Pisla, and Anca Elena Iordan. 2021. "Development of a Virtual Reality Simulator for an Intelligent Robotic System Used in Ankle Rehabilitation." *Sensors* 21 (4): 1–17. https://doi.org/10.3390/s21041537

Cukovic, Sasa, Frieder Pankratz, Antonio Uva, Goran Devedzic, Vanja Lukovi, Michele Fiorentino, and Tanja Zecevic Lukovic. 2013. "Conceptual Augmented Reality Framework for Spinal Disorders Representation and Diagnosis." In *Proceedings of the 2nd Regional Conference-Mechatronics in Practice and Education-MechEdu*, pp. 05–06.

Das, Swagata, and Yuichi Kurita. 2020. "ForceArm: A Wearable Pneumatic Gel Muscle (PGM)-Based Assistive Suit for the Upper Limb." *IEEE Transactions on Medical Robotics and Bionics* 2 (2): 269–281.

Das, Swagata, Wataru Sakoda, Priyanka Ramasamy, Ramin Tadayon, Antonio Vega Ramirez, and Yuichi Kurita. 2021. "Feature Selection and Validation of a Machine Learning-Based Lower Limb Risk Assessment Tool: A Feasibility Study." *Sensors* 21 (19): 6459.

Dobson, R., and G. Giovannoni. 2019. "Multiple Sclerosis – A Review." *European Journal of Neurology* 26 (1): 27–40. https://doi.org/10.1111/ene.13819

Ellis, Louise A., Matthew D. Lee, Kiran Ijaz, James Smith, Jeffrey Braithwaite, and Kathleen Yin. 2020. "COVID-19 as 'Game Changer' for the Physical Activity and Mental Well-Being of Augmented Reality Game Players During the Pandemic: Mixed Methods Survey Study." *Journal of Medical Internet Research* 22(12): E25117 https://www.jmir.org/2020/12/E25117. https://doi.org/10.2196/25117

Elor, Aviv, Michael Powell, Evanjelin Mahmoodi, Mircea Teodorescu, and Sri Kurniawan. 2022. "Gaming beyond the Novelty Effect of Immersive Virtual Reality for Physical Rehabilitation." *IEEE Transactions on Games* 14 (1): 107–115. https://doi.org/10.1109/TG.2021.3069445

Elor, Aviv, Mircea Teodorescu, and Sri Kurniawan. 2018. "Project Star Catcher." *ACM Transactions on Accessible Computing* 11 (4): 1–25. https://doi.org/10.1145/3265755

Erhardsson, Mattias, Margit Alt Murphy, and Katharina S. Sunnerhagen. 2020. "Commercial Head-Mounted Display Virtual Reality for Upper Extremity Rehabilitation in Chronic Stroke: A Single-Case Design Study." *Journal of*

NeuroEngineering and Rehabilitation 17 (1): 154. https://doi.org/10.1186/s12984-020-00788-x

Food and Drug Administration. "Postmarket management of cybersecurity in medical devices." Silver Spring: Food and Drug Administration (2016).

Gao, Chao, Yongli Wu, Junting Liu, Runhan Zhang, and Manting Zhao. 2021. "Systematic Evaluation of the Effect of Rehabilitation of Lower Limb Function in Children with Cerebral Palsy Based on Virtual Reality Technology." Edited by Zhihan Lv. *Journal of Healthcare Engineering* 2021 (March): 1–11. https://doi.org/10.1155/2021/6625604

Garcia, Laura M., Brandon J. Birckhead, Parthasarathy Krishnamurthy, Josh Sackman, Ian G. Mackey, Robert G. Louis, Vafi Salmasi, Todd Maddox, and Beth D. Darnall. 2021. "An 8-Week Self-Administered At-Home Behavioral Skills-Based Virtual Reality Program for Chronic Low Back Pain: Double-Blind, Randomized, Placebo-Controlled Trial Conducted During COVID-19." *Journal of Medical Internet Research* 23 (2): e26292. https://doi.org/10.2196/26292

Gimigliano, Francesca, and Stefano Negrini. 2017. "The World Health Organization 'Rehabilitation 2030: A Call for Action'." *European Journal of Physical and Rehabilitation Medicine* 53 (2): 155–168. https://doi.org/10.23736/S1973-9087.17.04746-3

Gutiérrez, Álvaro, Nicola Farella, Ángel Gil-Agudo, and Ana de los Reyes Guzmán. 2021. "Virtual reality environment with haptic feedback thimble for post spinal cord injury upper-limb rehabilitation." *Applied Sciences* 11 (6): 2476. https://doi.org/10.3390/app11062476

Harrington, Christina N., Lyndsie Marie Koon, and Wendy A. Rogers. 2020. "Design of Health Information and Communication Technologies for Older Adults." In *Design for Health*, 341–363. Elsevier. https://doi.org/10.1016/B978-0-12-816427-3.00017-8

Hassandra, Mary, Evangelos Galanis, Antonis Hatzigeorgiadis, Marios Goudas, Christos Mouzakidis, Eleni Maria Karathanasi, Niki Petridou, et al. 2021. "A Virtual Reality App for Physical and Cognitive Training of Older People With Mild Cognitive Impairment: Mixed Methods Feasibility Study." *JMIR Serious Games* 9 (1): e24170. https://doi.org/10.2196/24170

Held, Jeremia Philipp Oskar, Kevin Yu, Connor Pyles, Janne Marieke Veerbeek, Felix Bork, Sandro-Michael Heining, Nassir Navab, and Andreas Rüdiger Luft. 2020. "Augmented Reality-Based Rehabilitation of Gait Impairments: Case Report." *JMIR MHealth and UHealth* 8 (5): e17804. https://doi.org/10.2196/17804

Hodge, James, Madeline Balaam, Sandra Hastings, and Kellie Morrissey. 2018. "Exploring the Design of Tailored Virtual Reality Experiences for People with Dementia." In *Conference on Human Factors in Computing Systems – Proceedings* 2018-April (April). https://doi.org/10.1145/3173574.3174088

Holmes, Dominic E., Darryl K. Charles, Philip J. Morrow, Sally McClean, and Suzanne M. McDonough. 2017. "Leap Motion Controller and Oculus Rift Virtual Reality Headset for Upper Arm Stroke Rehabilitation." In *Virtual Reality: Recent Advances in Virtual Rehabilitation System Design*, 83–102. Nova Science Publishers, Inc.

Karácsony, Tamás, John Paulin Hansen, Helle Klingenberg Iversen, and Sadasivan Puthusserypady. 2019. "Brain Computer Interface for Neuro-Rehabilitation With Deep Learning Classification and Virtual Reality Feedback." In *Proceedings of the 10th Augmented Human International Conference 2019*, 1–8. New York, NY, USA: ACM. https://doi.org/10.1145/3311823.3311864

Kister, Ilya, Tamar E. Bacon, Eric Chamot, Amber R. Salter, Gary R. Cutter, Jennifer T. Kalina, and Joseph Herbert. 2013. "Natural History of Multiple Sclerosis Symptoms." *International Journal of MS Care* 15 (3): 146–158. https://doi.org/10.7224/1537-2073.2012-053

Lei, Cheng, Kejimu Sunzi, Fengling Dai, Xiaoqin Liu, Yanfen Wang, Baolu Zhang, Lin He, and Mei, Ju. 2019. "Effects of Virtual Reality Rehabilitation Training on Gait and Balance in Patients with Parkinson's Disease: A Systematic Review." Edited by Imre Cikajlo. *PLOS ONE* 14 (11): e0224819. https://doi.org/10.1371/journal.pone.0224819

Lerner, Dieter, Stefan Mohr, Jonas Schild, Martin Göring, and Thomas Luiz. 2020. "An Immersive Multi-User Virtual Reality for Emergency Simulation Training: Usability Study." *JMIR Serious Games* 8 (3). https://doi.org/10.2196/18822

Levac, Danielle E., Stephanie M. N. Glegg, Heidi Sveistrup, Heather Colquhoun, Patricia Miller, Hillel Finestone, Vincent DePaul, Jocelyn E. Harris, and Diana Velikonja. 2016. "Promoting Therapists' Use of Motor Learning Strategies within Virtual Reality-Based Stroke Rehabilitation." Edited by Jeffrey M. Haddad. *PLOS ONE* 11 (12): e0168311. https://doi.org/10.1371/journal.pone.0168311

Lioce, L. (Ed.), J. Lopreiato (Founding Ed.), D Downing (Assoc. Ed.), T.P. Chang (Assoc. Ed.), J.M. Robertson (Assoc. Ed.), M. Anderson (Assoc. Ed.), D.A. Diaz (Assoc. Ed.), A.E. Spain (Assoc. Ed.), and Terminology and Concepts Working Group. 2020. "Healthcare Simulation Dictionary." *Healthcare Simulation Dictionary –Second Edition*. https://doi.org/10.23970/simulationv2

Madshaven, Julie Madelen, Tonje Fjeldstad Markseth, David Bye Jomås, Ghislain Maurice Norbert Isabwe, Morten Ottestad, Frank Reichert, and Filippo Sanfilippo. 2021. "Investigating the User Experience of Virtual Reality Rehabilitation Solution for Biomechatronics Laboratory and Home Environment." *Frontiers in Virtual Reality* 2 (May). https://doi.org/10.3389/frvir.2021.645042

Maggio, Maria Grazia, Margherita Russo, Marilena Foti Cuzzola, Massimo Destro, Gianluca La Rosa, Francesco Molonia, Placido Bramanti, Giuseppe Lombardo, Rosaria De Luca, and Rocco Salvatore Calabrò. 2019. "Virtual Reality in Multiple Sclerosis Rehabilitation: A Review on Cognitive and Motor Outcomes." *Journal of Clinical Neuroscience* 65 (July): 106–111. https://doi.org/10.1016/j.jocn.2019.03.017

Mamone, Virginia, Miriam Di Fonzo, Nicola Esposito, Mauro Ferrari, and Vincenzo Ferrari. 2020. "Monitoring Wound Healing with Contactless Measurements and Augmented Reality." *IEEE Journal of Translational Engineering in Health and Medicine* 8. https://doi.org/10.1109/JTEHM.2020.2983156

Martin, Guy, Louis Koizia, Angad Kooner, John Cafferkey, Clare Ross, Sanjay Purkayastha, Arun Sivananthan, Anisha Tanna, Philip Pratt, and James Kinross. 2020. "Use of the HoloLens2 Mixed Reality Headset for Protecting Health Care Workers During the COVID-19 Pandemic: Prospective, Observational Evaluation." *Journal of Medical Internet Research* 22 (8): e21486. https://doi.org/10.2196/21486

Melero, Marina, Annie Hou, Emily Cheng, Amogh Tayade, Sing Chun Lee, Mathias Unberath, and Nassir Navab. 2019. "Upbeat: Augmented Reality-Guided Dancing for Prosthetic Rehabilitation of Upper Limb Amputees." *Journal of Healthcare Engineering* 2019 (March): 1–9. https://doi.org/10.1155/2019/2163705

Muñoz, Gabriel Fuertes, Ramón A. Mollineda, Jesús Gallardo Casero, and Filiberto Pla. 2019. "A RGBD-Based Interactive System for Gaming-Driven Rehabilitation of Upper Limbs." *Sensors* (Basel, Switzerland) 19 (16). https://doi.org/10.3390/S19163478

Nahum, Mor, and Daphne Bavelier. 2020. "Video Games as Rich Environments to Foster Brain Plasticity." 117–136. https://doi.org/10.1016/B978-0-444-63934-9.00010-X

Nambi, Gopal, Walid Kamal Abdelbasset, Saud F. Alsubaie, Ayman K. Saleh, Anju Verma, Mohamed A. Abdelaziz, and Abdulaziz A. Alkathiry. 2021. "Short-Term Psychological and Hormonal Effects of Virtual Reality Training on Chronic Low Back Pain in Soccer Players." *Journal of Sport Rehabilitation* 30 (6): 884–893. https://doi.org/10.1123/JSR.2020-0075

Okumura, Takumi, and Yuichi Kurita. 2021. "Cross-Modal Effect of Presenting Visual and Force Feedback That Create the Illusion of Stair-Climbing." *Applied Sciences* 11 (7): 2987.

Park, Ji Su, Young Jin Jung, and Gihyoun Lee. 2020. "Virtual Reality-Based Cognitive–Motor Rehabilitation in Older Adults with Mild Cognitive Impairment: A Randomized Controlled Study on Motivation and Cognitive Function." *Healthcare* 8 (3): 335. https://doi.org/10.3390/HEALTHCARE8030335

PERKINSCOIE, and XR Association. 2021. "XR Industry Insider 2021 XR Survey." Vol. 5.

Postolache, Octavian, D. Jude Hemanth, Ricardo Alexandre, Deepak Gupta, Oana Geman, and Ashish Khanna. 2021. "Remote Monitoring of Physical Rehabilitation of Stroke Patients Using IoT and Virtual Reality." *IEEE Journal on Selected Areas in Communications* 39 (2): 562–573. https://doi.org/10.1109/JSAC.2020.3020600

Priyan, Lasiya, Md Gapar Md Johar, Mohammed Hazim Alkawaz, and Rabab Alayham Abbas Helmi. 2021. "Augmented Reality-Based COVID-19 SOP Compliance: Social Distancing Monitoring and Reporting System Based on IOT." In *2021 IEEE 12th Control and System Graduate Research Colloquium, ICSGRC 2021 – Proceedings*, 183–188. Institute of Electrical and Electronics Engineers Inc. https://doi.org/10.1109/ICSGRC53186.2021.9515234

Rizos, A., P. Martinez-Martin, P. Odin, A. Antonini, B. Kessel, T. Klemencic Kozul, A. Todorova, et al. 2014. "Characterizing Motor and Non-Motor Aspects of Early-Morning off Periods in Parkinson's Disease: An International Multicenter Study." *Parkinsonism & Related Disorders* 20 (11): 1231–1235. https://doi.org/10.1016/j.parkreldis.2014.09.013

Rogers, Jeffrey M., Jonathan Duckworth, Sandy Middleton, Bert Steenbergen, and Peter H. Wilson. 2019. "Elements Virtual Rehabilitation Improves Motor, Cognitive, and Functional Outcomes in Adult Stroke: Evidence from a Randomized Controlled Pilot Study." *Journal of NeuroEngineering and Rehabilitation* 16 (1): 56. https://doi.org/10.1186/s12984-019-0531-y

Salisbury, Joseph Peter. 2021. "Using Medical Device Standards for Design and Risk Management of Immersive Virtual Reality for At-Home Therapy and Remote Patient Monitoring." *JMIR Biomedical Engineering* 6 (2): e26942. https://doi.org/10.2196/26942

Vergel, Serrano Ramiro, Pedro Morillo Tena, Sergio Casas Yrurzum, and Carolina Cruz-Neira. 2020. "A Comparative Evaluation of a Virtual Reality Table and a HoloLens-Based Augmented Reality System for Anatomy Training." *IEEE Transactions on Human-Machine Systems* 50 (4): 337–348. https://doi.org/10.1109/THMS.2020.2984746

Sevinc, Volkan, and Mehmet Ilker Berkman. 2020. "Psychometric Evaluation of Simulator Sickness Questionnaire and Its Variants as a Measure of Cybersickness in Consumer Virtual Environments." *Applied Ergonomics* 82 (January): 102958. https://doi.org/10.1016/j.apergo.2019.102958

Sipatchin, Alexandra, Siegfried Wahl, and Katharina Rifai. 2021. "Eye-Tracking for Clinical Ophthalmology with Virtual Reality (VR): A Case Study of the HTC Vive Pro Eye's Usability." *Healthcare* (Basel, Switzerland) 9 (2). https://doi.org/10.3390/HEALTHCARE9020180

Staropoli, Patrick C., Ninel Z. Gregori, Anna K. Junk, Anat Galor, Raquel Goldhardt, Brian E. Goldhagen, Wei Shi, and William Feuer. 2018. "Surgical Simulation Training Reduces Intraoperative Cataract Surgery Complications Among Residents." *Simulation in Healthcare: Journal of the Society for Simulation in Healthcare* 13 (1): 11–15. https://doi.org/10.1097/SIH.0000000000000255

Stucki, Gerold, Jerome Bickenbach, Christoph Gutenbrunner, and John Melvin. 2018. "Rehabilitation: The Health Strategy of the 21st Century." *Journal of Rehabilitation Medicine* 50 (4): 309–316. https://doi.org/10.2340/16501977-2200

Stucki, Gerold, Alarcos Cieza, and John Melvin. 2007. "The International Classification of Functioning, Disability and Health: A Unifying Model for the Conceptual Description of the Rehabilitation Strategy." *Journal of Rehabilitation Medicine* 39 (4): 279–285. https://doi.org/10.2340/16501977-0041

Tadayon, Ramin, Wataru Sakoda, and Yuichi Kurita. 2020. "Stealth-Adaptive Exergame Design Framework for Elderly and Rehabilitative Users." In *International Conference on Human-Computer Interaction*. Springer, Cham, pp. 419–434.

Valodwala, Khushboo C., and Anjan R. Desai. 2019. "Effectiveness of Dynamic Balance Training with and without Visual Feedback on Balance in Ambulatory Stroke Patients." *Journal of Clinical and Diagnostic Research*. https://doi.org/10.7860/JCDR/2019/40001.12834

Vidal-Balea, Aida, Óscar Blanco-Novoa, Paula Fraga-Lamas, and Tiago M. Fernández-Caramés. 2021. "Developing the Next Generation of Augmented Reality Games for Pediatric Healthcare: An Open-Source Collaborative Framework Based on Arcore for Implementing Teaching, Training and Monitoring Applications." *Sensors* 21 (5): 1–24. https://doi.org/10.3390/s21051865

Virani, Salim S., Alvaro Alonso, Hugo J. Aparicio, Emelia J. Benjamin, Marcio S. Bittencourt, Clifton W. Callaway, April P. Carson, et al. 2021. "Heart Disease and Stroke Statistics—2021 Update." *Circulation* 143 (8): E254–743. https://doi.org/10.1161/CIR.0000000000000950

Wang, Shiyao, Michael Parsons, Jordan Stone-McLean, Peter Rogers, Sarah Boyd, Kristopher Hoover, Oscar Meruvia-Pastor, Minglun Gong, and Andrew Smith. 2017. "Augmented Reality as a Telemedicine Platform for Remote Procedural Training." *Sensors* (Basel, Switzerland) 17 (10). https://doi.org/10.3390/S17102294

Weaver, Tyler B., Christine Ma, and Andrew C. Laing. 2017. "Use of the Nintendo Wii Balance Board for Studying Standing Static Balance Control: Technical Considerations, Force-Plate Congruency, and the Effect of Battery Life." *Journal of Applied Biomechanics* 33 (1): 48–55. https://doi.org/10.1123/jab.2015-0295

World Health Organization. 2017. "Rehabilitation 2030: The Need to Scale up Rehabilitation." *Rehabilitation*.

Xu, Yangfan, Meiqinzi Tong, Wai Kit Ming, Yangyang Lin, Wangxiang Mai, Weixin Huang, and Zhuoming Chen. 2021. "A Depth Camera-Based, Task-Specific Virtual Reality Rehabilitation Game for Patients with Stroke: Pilot Usability Study." *JMIR Serious Games* 9 (1): 1–12. https://doi.org/10.2196/20916

Yavuzer, G., A. Senel, M. B. Atay, and H. J. Stam. 2008. "'Playstation Eyetoy Games' Improve Upper Extremity-Related Motor Functioning in Subacute Stroke: A Randomized Controlled Clinical Trial." *European Journal of Physical and Rehabilitation Medicine* 44 (3): 237–244. http://www.ncbi.nlm.nih.gov/pubmed/18469735

Yu, F. U., H. U. Yan, and Veronica Sundstedt. 2022. "A Systematic Literature Review of Virtual, Augmented, and Mixed Reality Game Applications in Healthcare." *ACM Transactions on Computing for Healthcare* 3 (2). https://doi.org/10.1145/3472303

Zhao, Yuhang, Cynthia L. Bennett, Hrvoje Benko, Edward Cutrell, Christian Holz, Meredith Ringel Morris, and Mike Sinclair. 2018. "Enabling People with Visual Impairments to Navigate Virtual Reality with a Haptic and Auditory Cane Simulation." https://doi.org/10.1145/3173574.3173690

Zielasko, Daniel, and Bernhard E. Riecke. 2021. "To Sit or Not to Sit in VR: Analyzing Influences and (Dis)Advantages of Posture and Embodied Interaction." *Computers* 10 (6): 73. https://doi.org/10.3390/computers10060073

Chapter 8

Overcoming phobias

Harnessing the power of immersive virtual reality therapy

Agnieszka Popławska

SWPS University of Social Sciences and Humanities, Faculty of
Psychology in Sopot, Sopot, Poland

Jacek Lebiedź

Gdańsk University of Technology, Faculty of Electronics,
Telecommunications and Informatics, Gdańsk, Poland

Przemysław Bąbel

Jagiellonian University, Institute of Psychology, Kraków, Poland

8.1 INTRODUCTION

The goal of the chapter is to review the different therapeutic techniques
used in the treatment of various forms of phobias, with particular emphasis
on virtual reality treatment. We define different types of phobias, including
social ones. We also describe treatment techniques – adopted from behavioral therapy – which have been developed to aid the treatment of phobias.
Particular emphasis has been placed on flooding, implosive therapy and systematic desensitization. We review the results of virtual reality treatment,
which show that one of the most effective and most emotionally engaging
techniques is that known as cave automatic virtual environment (CAVE) –
literally a room that one enters and is automatically completely immersed
in a virtual reality. In this context, a description of the possibilities on offer
at the Immersive 3D Visualization Lab built on the premises of Gdańsk
University of Technology, is a substantial and significant part of the chapter. The laboratory, which, unlike any other such laboratory in the world,
features a spherical walk simulator, offers people the possibility to move
around the CAVE while they are completely immersed in 3D virtual reality. We also present a few applications that make use of virtual reality and
have been developed to serve as therapeutic tools in the treatment of phobias. Thus, our chapter combines a narrative review of the literature with a
detailed description and discussion of the technical and practical issues in
applying CAVE in the treatment of phobias.

DOI: 10.1201/9781003306078-11

8.1.1   Background and driving forces

We can observe virtual reality permeating actual reality in our daily lives. Today, virtual reality is used to enhance the attractiveness of computer games, events, museum exhibitions, and so on. It is also used for educational purposes and to train people – for example, to teach people how to manage complex machinery, to train doctor's social skills to break bad news or to depict complex chemical compounds (Barett et al., 2015; Ochs et al., 2019). Attempts have been made to train police officers with the use of virtual reality. The sensation of realness provided by virtual reality has been shown to be so convincing that in situations of real-life threats that followed, training done via virtual reality proved to be nearly as effective as that done using traditional methods (Bertram et al., 2015; Freitas et al., 2021). Virtual reality has also found its place in marketing where it is often used to increase the sales of products and services by visually enhancing marketing communication. The term itself was first coined in the middle of the 20th century and was popularized with the advent of the so-called virtual reality helmet, which immersed users in a virtual reality and allowed them to view it from first-person perspective. These initial devices were not enough to create the illusion of reality but over the years they were greatly improved and today virtual reality devices allow users to experience virtual reality with a sense of unprecedented striking realism.

Therapists have also embraced virtual reality. Studies conducted with the use of a virtual bar show that smokers who participate in sessions where they are exposed to known triggers (cue exposure treatment – CET) significantly cut down on the number of cigarettes they smoke daily (Lee et al., 2004). Similarly, full-blown gambling addicts, subjected to therapy in 'virtual casinos' report a significant decrease in their urge to gamble in comparison to their counterparts from the control group (Park et al., 2015). Another field that makes use of virtual reality is the treatment of phobias (Wrzesien et al., 2015; Gromer et al., 2018). Thanks to the possibility of immersing a participant in a highly convincing digitally created virtual world, we can now effectively treat persistent phobias as well as anxiety and obsessive-compulsive disorders (OCD). This type of therapy may be referred to as exposure to virtual reality (Bouchard et al., 2006; Abate et al., 2011; Freitas et al., 2021; Wallach et al., 2009).

8.2   VARIOUS TYPES OF PHOBIAS

Phobias are a sub-type of anxiety disorders. People who suffer from a phobia do not just experience fear in particular situations, they also avoid fear-inducing situations and live in constant fear of finding themselves in fear-inducing situations (Moldovan and David, 2014). People who suffer from phobias are aware that their reactions and feelings are inadequate and unfounded, yet they cannot overcome their irrational fears as they find them so overpowering and overwhelming. Symptoms of phobias are persistent and recurrent. Phobias may occur in singular (isolated) forms – such as when someone is afraid of the color red, or animals, or has a fear of heights. The list of such phobias is very long as they are brought on by various objects and situations (e.g. riding a lift or crossing a bridge). Another form of phobias are social phobias, which manifest themselves during interactions with other people or in situations of social exposure – when people have a strong fear of being judged by others and of being embarrassed. They often afflict adolescents and manifest as a fear of being judged by others as if they were adults and not teenagers. The most complex of phobias is agoraphobia – literally the fear of open spaces. It is usually the outcome of anxiety neurosis and is often co-morbid in people who suffer from various mental illnesses. It is worth emphasizing that people who suffer from phobias experience tremendous anxiety and live in constant fear of finding themselves in a situation that scares them. Fear-related thoughts are intrusive and uncontrollable, much like they are in obsessive-compulsive disorder (Bilikiewicz, 2003).

8.3   AVAILABLE TREATMENTS FOR PHOBIAS

The most effective ways to treat phobias are methods used in behavioral therapy, which are also used by cognitive-behavioral therapists. These methods are as follows: flooding, implosive therapy, systematic desensitization, and modeling. The first three treatment methods are based on establishing a hierarchy of fear-inducing scenarios (flooding does not always require the establishment of a hierarchy), where the ones that evoke the least fear are situated at the bottom and the ones that evoke the greatest fear are situated at the top.

Flooding consists of confronting clients with phobia-inducing scenarios of two varieties. The client is either exposed to an extremely strong fear-inducing stimulus (thus, the process resembles throwing somebody in at the deep end) or is gradually presented with fear-inducing stimuli beginning from the one they are least afraid of and ending with the one they are most afraid of. This sort of treatment is only possible when there is mutual trust between the client and the therapist.

Implosive therapy is very similar as it encourages clients to vividly imagine a fear-inducing scenario and experience all the emotions it evokes in them. Therapists begin the process by exposing their clients to stimuli that are at the bottom of their fear-hierarchy (and then work on them until the client's fear subsides), gradually working their way up (Morganstern, 1973). The difference between flooding and implosive therapy is that in the first one clients are actually exposed to phobic stimuli whereas in the latter they only imagine them. The goal of both these techniques is for the clients to experience none of the negative outcomes they associate with the phobic stimuli (Bąbel and Ziółkowska, 2014).

In contrast, modeling comprises of clients observing people who do not suffer from their phobia in a scenario they, the clients, find fear-inducing. By witnessing that no harm has been done to others in a scenario they themselves dread, clients can learn to fear the scenario less.

Systematic desensitization is a method that allows for substantial improvement in the process of overcoming a phobia in a matter of months and works by gradually exposing clients to the object of their fear. The treatment takes place in three stages. Initially, clients are taught relaxation techniques and are instructed how to relax their muscles. Next, with the help of a therapist they establish a hierarchy of fear-inducing scenarios, where the most frightening scenarios are at the top of the hierarchy. The last stage is the actual desensitization stage – the attempt to expose clients to phobic stimuli from their fear-hierarchy when they are calm and relaxed. The procedure is repeated as many times as is needed until the most fear-inducing scenario in the fear-hierarchy no longer evokes any fear in clients. That's when clients are confronted with the object of their greatest fear, the top of the tops in their fear-hierarchy. This takes place solely in their imagination and brings marked improvement in 80–90% of phobia cases. The long-term effects of this type of treatment are visible in follow-up screenings done a year or two after treatment (Bąbel and Ziółkowska, 2014).

8.4   VIRTUAL REALITY IN THE TREATMENT OF PHOBIAS

Virtual reality offers therapists the possibility to immerse clients in an artificial reality and expose them to freely chosen phobic stimuli. This type of therapy is known as virtual exposure therapy (Abate et al., 2011; Bouchard et al., 2012; Wallach et al., 2009). Research shows that exposure to fear-inducing stimuli is of key importance if treatment of phobias is to be effective and the results are to be permanent (Rothbaum et al., 2000).

In implosive therapy for example, we can use virtual reality exposure to desensitize clients by gradually exposing them to phobic stimuli in different scenarios. This can be of particular use if clients do not have a vivid imagination and clearly struggle with imagining scenarios where they are exposed to fear-inducing stimuli. This sort of therapy significantly increases treatment effectiveness of quite a few phobias including fear of heights, fear of flying, arachnophobia, and even post-traumatic stress disorder (PTSD) (Albakri et al., 2022; Gromer et al., 2018; Kisker et al., 2021; Krzystanek et al., 2021; Moldovan and David, 2014; Rothbaum et al., 1999).

Freitas et al. (2021) compared efficacy of virtual reality therapy exposure versus in vivo therapy exposure among participants suffering from phobias by using a meta-analysis. The results showed that a virtual reality exposure treatment can have a positive effect in the treatment of most phobias. However, a few specific phobias needed the standard procedures, which were more effective. In the experiment conducted by Wiens et al. (2022) there were two groups of spider-phobic individuals who received either in vivo or virtual reality exposure treatment. There were no differences in efficacy between these two conditions – after the treatment, the negative emotional ratings of spiders were reduced. In a meta-analysis conducted by Fodor et al. (2018), VR interventions were found to be more effective than control conditions (e.g., waitlist, placebo, relaxation) in reducing anxiety and depression symptoms among people with specific phobias. A recent review of the literaure provided by Krzystanek et al. (2021) showed that effectiveness of virtual reality exposure treatment is equal to in vivo exposure therapy. In addition, an average to large effect size for virtual reality exposure treatment was found compared to the psychological placebo conditions. The conclusion from the literature review is that virtual therapy can be effective in the treatment of anxiety and several specific types of phobias and confirm its equivalence with standard procedures.

Research conducted by Wallergard et al. (2011) shows that the CAVE can also be used to treat social phobia. Participants were asked to make a speech and solve an arithmetic problem in front of a panel of judges. Pulse measurements taken inside the CAVE were no different from those taken in real-life situations of social exposure – in both conditions the researchers noted an increase in pulse when clients spoke in front of a panel of judges.

Many other experiments were conducted in which researchers immersed participants in virtual reality using various methods. Results of these experiments show that participants experience stronger emotions when they are exposed to emotional stimuli within the CAVE than during a 3D presentation (Ochs et al., 2019; Valentijn et al., 2010). In a study that dealt with fear of heights, researchers compared participants' levels of anxiety in a scenario where they were exposed to gradually increasing heights either via a head mounted display (HMD) or inside the CAVE. Results show that participants' felt greater anxiety in the CAVE than when they wore the HMD (Juan and Perez, 2009). Researchers also point to the fact that participants prefer virtual reality driven phobia exposure therapy to real-life phobia exposure therapy. Sessions in the CAVE are cheaper, are less time consuming and allow therapists to tailor fear-inducing stimuli to clients' individual needs (Powers and Emmelkamp, 2008).

Applications used to treat clients should be built with the following rules in mind. First of all, participants should have a safe place within the CAVE where they can take shelter when they feel overwhelmed by anxiety. Second of all, clients should feel in control of the situation. Third, clients should have the possibility to move freely around the room and if need be, they should have a designated 'safe haven' they can go to at any given time during the session. Furthermore, phobic stimuli ought to be displayed in neutral scenarios and not purposefully attack or scare participants. Last but not least, the level of participants' fear ought to be gradually increased by a skilled and experienced therapist who is in charge of overseeing the whole session (Hagemann et al., 1999; Meyerbröker and Morina, 2021).

Although VR is highly effective in treatment of phobias, some ethical concerns regarding the use of VR in treatment have been raised (Kellmeyer, 2018; Martloth et al., 2020; Parsons, 2021). Thus, the use of VR in any treatment should be guided by ethical priorities (Kellmeyer et al., 2019) and an ethical framework for the clinical use of VR should be developed (Martloth et al., 2020).

8.5   VIRTUAL REALITY SYSTEMS

Virtual reality can be defined in many different ways depending on what standpoint we adopt. From a technical point of view, it is understood as a user interface that creates the illusion of reality that 'feels like the real thing' to the participant even though it is digitally generated by a computer. Hence, we often speak of immersing subjects in a virtual reality – this is achieved by stimulating subjects' various senses through the use of specially constructed devices (e.g., the HMD affects vision). It is also important that subjects feel they can interact with the virtual reality they are in, which is possible thanks to appropriate input such as a steering wheel in a driving simulator. All this enhances participants' imagination. Hence, virtual reality is often called i^3 or $3{\times}i$ (both the terms refer to the first letters of the following three words: *immersion*, *interaction*, and *imagination*) (Burdea and Coiffet, 2003).

Since the very beginning, virtual reality has always appealed to the senses. One of the first such appliances, the Sensorama, designed by Morton Heilig in 1962, was a motorcycle driving simulator. In order to achieve maximum immersion, the appliance made use of a color stereoscopic motion picture as well as stereo sound and smells (used to signal to users that they have just passed a bar), wind (a fan situated near users' heads) and a vibrating seat (Burdea and Coiffet, 2003). Nowadays, technical capabilities are of course much greater but most virtual reality devices still mostly appeal to our sense of sight. This explains the huge popularity of virtual reality helmets that 'focus' solely on visual stimuli (e.g., Oculus Rift and HTC Vive), although the first such device to be patented in 1960 was one called *stereoscopic-television apparatus for individual use* which offered not only screens and headphones but also a smell diffuser (Burdea and Coiffet, 2003).

The virtual reality helmet is considered to be the basic tool of virtual reality. It consists of integrated input and output devices. Immersion is governed by the use of two screens (or one screen split in two halves) that display separate images for each eye so that the virtual reality they create is perceived as spacious (stereoscopy); very often headphones are also used. Interaction is possible thanks to an apparatus that traces head movements – this not only allows the virtual reality device to adjust the visual image displayed to the position of the users' heads (so that looking around is more natural for the user) but also gives the users much more control over the speed and the precision of movements (Jażdżewski and Trzosowski, 2015; Czerniawski et al., 2015). However, people who suffer from motion sickness should rather steer clear of such devices. Studies show that the more dynamic scenarios within virtual reality appliances can bring on unpleasant sensations in users – such as nausea – in a relatively short time, even in people who do not usually suffer from such afflictions (Jażdżewski and Trzosowski, 2015).

Virtual reality CAVEs are much safer in this respect. Such CAVEs have screens instead of walls – images are projected on all of them so that the user is fully immersed in a virtual world. Users feel more comfortable in the CAVE than they do wearing a helmet because virtual reality helmets are rather uncomfortable both to mount and wear and use of a CAVE does not require them to wear one. What is more, in a CAVE users can see their own body and the tools in their hands which also makes interaction easier (when wearing a virtual reality helmet, people cannot see the hand-held joystick-like device in their hands; they can only see the avatars of their own hands and the hand-held controllers). Users can also see other subjects of their simulation and thereby can share their experiences with them. Thus, the CAVE allows for deeper immersion in virtual reality. Much like when wearing a helmet, the CAVE is perceived as spacious thanks to cinema-like light glasses that discern which images displayed on the screens are targeted at which eye. Thanks to special tracking markers attached to users' glasses, these images are dynamically adjusted to the position of the observer, which in turn creates the illusion that objects within virtual reality are parallactically moving with every turn of our head.

8.6 APPLICATIONS OF THE IMMERSIVE 3D VISUALIZATION LAB

The Immersive 3D Visualization Lab is located on the campus of the Gdańsk University of Technology at the Faculty of Electronics, Telecommunications and Informatics. Its CAVE is the only one of its kind in Poland, featuring no less than six screen-walls that together create a cube (Figure 8.1a) (Lebiedź and Mazikowski, 2014b; Mazikowski and Lebiedź, 2014; Lebiedź and Redlarski, 2016; Lebiedź and Mazikowski, 2021; Lebiedź and Wiszniewski, 2021). The level of virtual reality immersion offered by this laboratory is so high that it can be successfully used in treating phobias by exposing phobia-sufferers to phobic stimuli in virtual reality (Lebiedź, 2015). What is more, thanks to the introduction of a transparent spherical walk simulator (which resembles a hamster wheel, Figure 8.1b), clients can now freely move around in the virtual reality and have control over how near or far they are from phobic stimuli (Lebiedź and Mazikowski, 2014a).

Such a novel solution as the CAVE allows for the design of virtual reality applications which are of much support in the treatment of phobias. Thanks

(a)

(b)

Figure 8.1 The CAVE in the Immersive 3D Visualization Lab (a), the CAVE complete with the spherical walk simulator (b).

to the spherical walk simulator, clients can freely move around virtual reality saturated with phobic stimuli. In the case of sets (the size of a small room), they can use the limited space of the floor screen to walk around instead of using the walk simulator.

Regardless of whether the spherical walk simulator is used or not, all clients must be accompanied by a therapist at all times during a session in the CAVE; the therapists should also have the possibility to control the virtual reality (Żołnowski, 2014; Byczkowski, 2017). Thus, there are always two users of the application – the patient and the therapist. The therapist is also supported by a graphic designer who prepares the set and supplies all the necessary 3D models (Żołnowski and Lebiedź, 2014). Once clients enter the virtual reality they can move around it as they please. Therapists stand outside the CAVE (near the control cockpit) and monitor clients' behavior by controlling phobic stimuli (their features, size, position, and visibility).

In terms of the features of the Immersive 3D Visualization Lab, and that of the virtual reality helmets (Oculus Rift, HTC Vive, etc.), the Faculty of Electronics, Telecommunications and Informatics of Gdańsk University of Technology prepared a few applications that show their potential in the supporting treatment of peristerophobia (fear of pigeons, Figure 8.2)

(a)

Figure 8.2 An application that supports the treatment of peristerophobia (Żołnowski, 2014) – the therapist's view (a) and the client's view of the set with pigeons (b).

(b)

Figure 8.2 (Continued)

(Żołnowski, 2014; Żołnowski and Lebiedź, 2014), arachnophobia (Figure 8.3a and b) (Dobrzeniecki and Pluskota, 2015; Smoliński, 2021), glassophobia (Figure 8.3c) (Badziak et al., 2014), and acrophobia (Malinowska et al., 2015) (Figure 8.4). The first application was developed with the use of programming tools specifically dedicated to virtual reality – Vizard by WorldViz, whereas the other ones were developed using Unity by Unity Technologies, which is primarily used to develop video games.

The detailed scenario for supporting arachnophobia treatment with the use of virtual reality is described in the next section. Generally, scenarios of all prepared applications are based on gradual confrontation of a client with phobic stimuli, starting from that which is less frightening and ending with the one that causes the greatest fear. For example, in the application for

(a)

(b)

(c)

Figure 8.3 An application that supports arachnophobia treatment (Dobrzeniecki and Pluskota, 2015) – a patient's view of a spider walking on a table (a); another application that supports arachnophobia treatment (Smoliński, 2021) – photo of spiders near the patient's feet on the CAVE floor (b); an application that supports glossophobia treatment (Badziak et al., 2014) – a patient's view of a classroom with students who have just arrived and are about to take a seat (c).

(a)

(b)

Figure 8.4 An application that supports acrophobia treatment (Malinowska et al., 2015) – a patient's view of heights (a); visualization in the CAVE in the Immersive 3D Visualization Lab (b).

supporting acrophobia treatment (Malinowska et al., 2015), different levels of increasing perceived height are used. A client can visit a higher level (Figure 8.4) only if the lower level was passed without fear (Figure 8.5). If anxiety persists, the client can always return to a virtual safe room.

(a)

(b)

Figure 8.5 Different levels of increasing height perceived by a client using the application supporting acrophobia treatment (Malinowska et al., 2015) run in the Immersive 3D Visualization Lab.

(c)

Figure 8.5 (Continued)

8.7 PRACTICAL ASPECTS OF PHOBIA TREATMENT WITH THE USE OF VIRTUAL REALITY

Theoretically, the CAVE could be used to conduct all three kinds of behavioral therapy – that is flooding, implosive therapy, and systematic desensitization. In the case of flooding, immersion in virtual reality can replace real-life exposure to phobic stimuli, whereas in the case of implosive therapy and systematic desensitization it will enhance clients' imagination. This is particularly important in cases of clients who are reluctant when it comes to visualizing their fears and those whose imagination is not vivid enough.

From a practical point of view, using the CAVE would be very difficult in systematic desensitization therapy. This technique is predicated on the assumption that all phobic scenarios ought to be envisioned in a state of deep relaxation, achieved by relaxing muscles, something that would be difficult to achieve in the CAVE. What is more, the key element of systematic desensitization is an immediate return to relaxation techniques when the client experiences fear and anxiety upon envisioning a phobic stimulus, and only resuming visualization of phobic stimuli when they have completely calmed down (Wolpe, 1958; Wolpe and Wolpe, 1999). In other words, systematic desensitization consists of repeatedly visualizing phobic stimuli and alternating that with a deep relaxation session. Such a procedure can be implemented with the use of a virtual reality helmet. Clients sit comfortably in a chair or rest on a chaise longue and the therapist can turn the application off when it is time for the deep relaxation sessions. This would be much more difficult to do in the CAVE and would be also futile as the ability to freely move around it is its main feature and it is of no use in this case.

Flooding takes one of the following forms: (1) exposing the client to the phobic stimulus they fear most (Type 1) or (2) gradually confronting him or her with phobic stimuli, starting from the one that evokes the smallest fear and ending with that which is most frightening to him or her (Type 2). The first form is referred to as flooding, whereas the latter is called graded flooding (Moulds and Nixon, 2006). Both forms can be used in the CAVE.

By implementing the first form of flooding in the CAVE, we give the participants an opportunity to interact with phobic stimuli which in real-life are not readily available. For example, it would be hard to implement the first type of flooding *in vivo* in the case of aerodromophobia (fear of flying) – for financial reasons (the sheer cost of the flight), organizational reasons (getting to the airport, adjusting therapy hours to that of the departure hours of planes), and particularly for safety reasons (no possibility to escape flooding after the plane has taken off when we feel our fear has gotten the best of us). In contrast to *in vivo* flooding, the CAVE offers a cheap, easy to set up, and most of all, safe way to conduct flooding in case of treating aerodromophobia, given that there would be an appropriate application on hand.

Although existing applications allow for Type 1 flooding of clients suffering from peristerophobia (Żołnowski, 2014; Żołnowski and Lebiedź, 2014), arachnophobia (Dobrzeniecki and Pluskota, 2015; Smoliński, 2021), glossophobia (Badziak et al., 2014), and acrophobia (Malinowska et al., 2015), in the CAVE this type of flooding can just as well be done *in vivo*. Nevertheless, even in this case, the CAVE has advantages over other techniques. First of all, it is easier to control virtual reality than close encounters of the third degree with real-life phobic stimuli, especially those related to animals, as is the case in peristerophobia and arachnophobia; because of this, therapy conducted with the use of virtual reality is safer. Second of all, it is easier to schedule a session in a CAVE than *in vivo*. Third of all, many applications are readily available so the cost of treatment in a CAVE vs. that of real-life treatment can be substantially smaller. To sum up, the CAVE allows for Type 1 flooding in the case of phobias in which fear-inducing stimuli are virtually inaccessible and also facilitates the treatment of phobias in which phobic stimuli are more readily accessible.

Type 1 flooding is based on briefly exposing a person to their most feared phobic stimuli without any possibility to escape the situation or avoid the stimuli (Moulds and Nixon, 2006; Polin, 1959). In the CAVE this technique demands that we set the application in such a way that upon entering the CAVE, the client encounters the phobic stimulus that has the highest rank in their hierarchy. For example, if the client suffers from peristerophobia, then a typical session involving Type 1 flooding in the virtual reality might match the following description. The client, who is first briefed about the nature of this treatment and then clearly told what to expect, enters the CAVE and immediately realizes he or she is on the street where there are many pigeons, which from time-to-time pluck to fly – both individually and in groups. The weakness of this method is that it cannot stop the client from leaving the

CAVE, whereas the success of this classic method of phobia treatment is predicated on the fact that clients cannot indeed escape. However, the fact that participants can physically leave the CAVE at any given moment may act as a negative reinforcement and thereby increase their level of anxiety (Bąbel and Ziółkowska, 2014). Thus, graded flooding in a CAVE can lead to better and more long-lasting therapeutic results.

It is worth emphasizing that from the perspective of treatment conducted in the CAVE, there is no significant difference between graded flooding and implosive therapy. Both techniques differ only when they are used outside of virtual reality – the first one is done *in vivo*, whereas the other one is done in clients' imaginations. Because implosive therapy, in principle, makes use of the imagination, then from the theoretical standpoint we ought to assume that graded flooding in virtual reality facilitates implosive therapy. Thus, this is how we will from now on refer to this use of virtual reality in our chapter. Nevertheless, from a practical point of view, graded flooding and implosive therapy are one and the same method when done with the use of virtual reality.

Implosive therapy is preceded by establishing a hierarchy of fear-inducing stimuli. The hierarchy has to be precise, that is, the difference in the intensity of fear from one level to the other should be similar. However, the treatment itself begins when the therapist instructs the client to imagine a stimulus from the lowest level of the hierarchy. Work on that first image continues until the client reports that their fear has subsided and they are ready to work on the next stimulus in the hierarchy, and this therapeutic cycle is repeated again and again until all the stimuli in the fear hierarchy have been exhausted (Stampfl and Levis, 1967; Troester, 2006).

A typical hierarchy of fear-inducing stimuli for a person who suffers from arachnophobia would probably look a lot like this:

(1) A drawing of a spider seen from across the room.
(2) A drawing of a spider seen from the middle of the room (Figure 8.6a).
(3) A drawing of a spider seen close-up.
(4) A spider mascot on a table seen from the middle of the room (Figure 8.6b).
(5) A spider mascot on a table, seen close-up.
(6) Reaching your hand out towards a spider mascot.
(7) A small, live spider in a terrarium seen from across the room.
(8) A small, live spider in a terrarium seen from the middle of the room (Figure 8.6c).
(9) A small, live spider in a terrarium seen close-up.
(10) Reaching your hand out towards a terrarium with a small, live spider.
(11) A big, live spider on a table seen from across the room.
(12) A big, live spider on a table seen from the middle of the room (Figure 8.3a).
(13) A big, live spider on a table seen close-up.

(14) Reaching your hand out towards a table where there is a big, live spider.

(15) Reaching your hand out towards a big, live spider on a table.

(a)

(b)

Figure 8.6 An application that facilitates arachnophobia treatment (Dobrzeniecki and Pluskota, 2015) – client's view of a table with a drawing of a spider, as seen from the middle of the room (a); a client's view of a spider mascot (toy) as seen from the middle of the room (b); a client's view of a small terrarium with a small spider inside, as seen from the middle of the room (c).

(c)

Figure 8.6 (Continued)

Each session of implosive therapy in a CAVE consists of three consecutive stages repeated in a cycle: (1) stepping into the scenario, (2) withdrawing from the scenario when fear gets the best of us and we no longer feel in control of the situation, (3) calming down and regaining composure before resuming the process of exposing oneself to phobic stimuli. The client moves from the bottom to the top of their fear hierarchy. Therapists are present at all times and monitor clients' behavior – when they see that the client does not show signs of fear, they use the application interface to access a higher-level scenario from the client's fear hierarchy. Each session goes on for no longer than 60 minutes (usually it lasts between 30 to 60 minutes) and always ends just when the client no longer shows fear in response to phobic stimuli from a particular level of their fear hierarchy – when a particular fear has been overcome. During the following session, the client is exposed to phobic stimuli from the level of their fear hierarchy which they mastered during their last session. Therapy in the CAVE ends when the client does not show fear even when they are faced with a fear-inducing stimuli from the very top of their fear hierarchy. At the same time, therapy may be continued *in vivo*. Upon ending therapy in the CAVE, it is worth encouraging the client to revisit all the levels of their fear hierarchy through exposure to real-life phobic stimuli. This is not only the best means to evaluate the effectiveness of the implosive therapy facilitated by immersion in virtual reality, but also allows for the generalization of its outcomes to real-life threats.

8.8 CONCLUSIONS

Classic approaches to the treatment of phobias require the client to be exposed to real-life fear-inducing stimuli or to imagine such stimuli. Virtual reality, which is a synthesis of both these approaches, brings out all of their advantageous features. On the one hand, the visualized stimulus feels like the real thing and does not require the client to use their imagination; on the other hand, the client is aware that this is not in fact a real-life stimulus and this may facilitate the therapeutic process. What is more, all stimuli used in virtual reality scenarios are very precisely controlled by therapists, which is not the case in scenarios involving real-life objects or those that require clients to visualize them. Thus, the use of virtual reality looks to be very promising in improving the effectiveness of phobia treatment. This conclusion is predicated on the promising results obtained during the process of implementing the described applications. However, to confirm this hypothesis, we need to design new therapeutic scenarios and complementary applications and test them in experimental studies on phobia treatment.

ACKNOWLEDGEMENTS

We want to thank our students quoted in the chapter for preparing and testing the applications described in the chapter.

REFERENCES

Abate, A. F., Nappi, M., and Ricciardi, S. (2011). AR based environment for exposure therapy to mottephobia. *Virtual and Mixed Reality*, Part 1, HCII 2011, LNCS 6773, 3–11.

Albakri, G., Bouaziz, R., Alharthi, W., Kammoun, S., Al-Sarem, M., Saeed, F., and Hadwan, M. (2022). Phobia exposure therapy using virtual and augmented reality: A systematic review. *Applied Sciences* 12(3), 1672.

Badziak, K., Przybyłowska, N., Tatara, A., and Wiatrowska, A. (2014). Phobia treatment "Shyspy". *Student project of the subject Virtual Reality*. Gdańsk, Poland: FETI GUT.

Barrett, T., Stull, A. T., Hsu, T. M., and Hegarty, M. (2015). Constrained interactivity for relating multiple representations in science: When virtual is better than real. *Computers & Education* 81, 69–81.

Bąbel, P., and Ziółkowska, A. M. (2014). Terapia behawioralna zaburzeń lękowych (Behavioral therapy for anxiety disorders, in Polish). *Postępy Psychiatrii i Neurologii (Advances in Psychiatry and Neurology)* 23, 3–9.

Bertram, J., Moskaliuk, J., and Cress, U. (2015). Virtual training: Making reality work? *Computers in Human Behavior* 43, 284–292.

Bilikiewicz, A. (2003). *Psychiatria (Psychiatry*, in Polish). Warszawa, Poland: PZWL.

Bouchard, S., Côté, S., St-Jacques, J., Robillard, G., and Renaud, P. (2006). Effectiveness of virtual reality exposure in the treatment of arachnophobia using 3D games. *Technology and Health Care* 14(1), 19–27.

Bouchard, S., Robillard, G., Loranger, C., and Larouche, S. (2012). Description of a treatment manual for in virtuo exposure with specific phobia. *Virtual Reality in Psychological, Medical and Pedagogical Applications*, ed. C. Eichenberg (Rijeka: InTech), 82–108.

Burdea, G. C., and Coiffet, P. (2003). *Virtual Reality Technology* (Second Edition). Hoboken, NJ: Wiley-Interscience.

Byczkowski, K. (2017). Wykorzystanie zanurzenia w rzeczywistość wirtualną do badania zachowania człowieka (The use of immersion in virtual reality to study human behavior, in Polish). *Master's thesis*. Gdańsk, Poland: FETI GUT (supervisor J. Lebiedź, consultant A. Popławska).

Czerniawski, M., Florczak, M. P., and Florczak, M. J. (2015). Demonstrator możliwości kasku wirtualnego Oculus Rift w zastosowaniach dla wielu użytkowników (Multiuser demonstrator of opportunities of Oculus Rift virtual helmet, in Polish). *Engineering Diploma Project*. Gdańsk, Poland: FETI GUT (supervisor J. Lebiedź).

Dobrzeniecki, R., and Pluskota, R. (2015). Help in treating phobias. *Student project of the subject Virtual Reality*. Gdańsk, Poland: FETI GUT (the development of an application prepared for the AppCamp 2014 competition organized by Kainos).

Freitas, J., Velosa, V., Abreu, L., Jardim, R. L., Santos, J., Peres, B., and Campos, P. F. (2021). Virtual reality exposure treatment in phobias: A systematic review. *The Psychiatric quarterly* 92(4), 1685–1710.

Fodor, L. A., Coteț, C. D., Cuijpers, P., Szamoskozi, Ş., David, D., and Cristea, I. A. (2018). The effectiveness of virtual reality based interventions for symptoms of anxiety and depression: A meta-analysis. *Scientific Reports* 8, 10323.

Gromer, D., Madeira, O., Gast, P., Nehfischer, M., Jost, M., Mueller, M., Muehlberger, A., and Pauli, P. (2018). Height simulation in a virtual reality CAVE system: Validity of fear responses and effects of an immersion manipulation. *Frontiers in Human Neuroscience* 12, 372.

Hagemann, B., Tessmann, H., Yeaster, M., and Huang, M. (1999). Arachnophobia therapy through virtual reality. http://www.umich.edu/~psychvr/spider/

Jażdżewski, P. D., and Trzosowski, R. W. (2015). Gra dla wielu osób z wykorzystaniem kasków wirtualnych Oculus Rift (Multiplayer video game using virtual helmets Oculus Rift, in Polish). *Engineering Diploma Project*. Gdańsk, Poland: FETI GUT (supervisor J. Lebiedź).

Juan, M. C., and Perez, D. (2009). Comparison of the levels of presence and anxiety in an acrophobic environment viewed via HMD or CAVE. *Presence* 18(3), 232–248.

Kellmeyer, P. (2018). Neurophilosophical and ethical aspects of virtual reality therapy in neurology and psychiatry. *Cambridge Quarterly of Healthcare Ethics* 27(4), 610–627. doi: 10.1017/S0963180118000129

Kellmeyer, P., Biller-Andorno, N., and Meynen, G. (2019). Ethical tensions of virtual reality treatment in vulnerable patients. *Nature Medicine* 25, 1185–1188. doi: 10.1038/s41591-019-0543-y

Kisker, J., Gruber, T., and Schöne, B. (2021). Behavioral realism and lifelike psychophysiological responses in virtual reality by the example of a height exposure. *Psychological Research: An International Journal of Perception, Attention, Memory, and Action* 85(1), 68–81.

Krzystanek, M., Surma, S., Stokrocka, M., Romańczyk, M., Przybyło, J., Krzystanek, N., and Borkowski, M. (2021). Tips for effective implementation of virtual reality exposure therapy in phobias—A systematic review. *Frontiers in Psychiatry* 12, 737351.

Lebiedź, J. (2015). Człowiek zanurzony w rzeczywistości wirtualnej na przykładzie Laboratorium Zanurzonej Wizualizacji Przestrzennej (A human immersed in virtual reality on the example of Immersive 3D Visualization Lab, in Polish). *Człowiek zalogowany 4, Człowiek społeczny w przestrzeni Internetu (Man online 4, The social man in Internet space*, ed. M. Wysocka-Pleczyk, B. Gulla), Kraków, Poland: Biblioteka Jagiellońska, 108–115.

Lebiedź, J., and Mazikowski, A. (2014a). A. Launch of the Immersive 3D Visualization Laboratory. *Szybkobieżne Pojazdy Gąsienicowe (Fast Tracked Vehicles)* 34(1), 49–56.

Lebiedź, J., and Mazikowski, A. (2014b). Innovative Solutions for Immersive 3D Visualization Laboratory. *22nd International Conference on Computer Graphics, Visualization and Computer Vision WSCG 2014 – Communication papers proceedings* (ed. V. Skala), Plzeň, Czech Republic, 315–319.

Lebiedź, J., and Mazikowski, A. (2021). Multiuser stereoscopic projection techniques for CAVE-type virtual reality systems. *IEEE Transactions on Human-Machine Systems* 51(5), 535–543.

Lebiedź, J., and Redlarski, J. (2016). Applications of Immersive 3D Visualization Lab. *24th International Conference on Computer Graphics, Visualization and Computer Vision WSCG 2016 – Poster Papers Proceedings* (ed. V. Skala), Plzeň, Czech Republic, 69–74.

Lebiedź, J., and Wiszniewski, B. (2021). CAVE applications: From craft manufacturing to product line engineering. *VRST 2021: ACM Symposium on Virtual Reality Software and Technology.*

Lee, J., Lim, Y., Graham, S. J., Kim, G., Wiederhold, B. K., Wiederhold, M. D., Kim, I. Y., and Kim, S. I. (2004). Nicotine craving and cue exposure therapy by using virtual environments. *CyberPsychology & Behavior* 7(6), 705–713.

Malinowska, J., Sadowski, R., and Sadowski, R. G. (2015). System wspomagający terapię implozywną leczenia fobii z użyciem jaskini rzeczywistości wirtualnej (System to support implosive phobias treating with use of virtual reality cave, in Polish). *Engineering Diploma Project.* Gdańsk, Poland: FETI GUT (supervisor J. Lebiedź, consultant A. Popławska).

Mazikowski, A., and Lebiedź, J. (2014). Image projection in Immersive 3D Visualization Laboratory. *18th Intl. Conf. in Knowledge Based and Intelligent Information and Engineering Systems KES 2014*, Gdynia, Poland, *Procedia Computer Science* 35, 842–850.

Marloth, M., Chandler, J., and Vogeley, K. (2020). Psychiatric interventions in virtual reality: Why we need an ethical framework. *Cambridge Quarterly of Healthcare Ethics* 29(4), 574–584. doi:10.1017/S0963180120000328

Meyerbröker, K., and Morina, N. (2021). The use of virtual reality in assessment and treatment of anxiety and related disorders. *Clinical Psychology & Psychotherapy* 28(3), 466–476.

Moldovan, R., and David, D. (2014). One session treatment of cognitive and behavioral therapy and virtual reality for social and specific phobias. Preliminary results from a randomized clinical trial. *Journal of Cognitive and Behavioral Psychotherapies* 14(1), 67–83.

Morganstern, K. P. (1973). Implosive therapy and flooding procedures: A critical review. *Psychological Bulletin* 79(5), 318–334.

Moulds, M. L., and Nixon, R. D. V. (2006). In vivo flooding for anxiety disorders: proposing its utility in the treatment posttraumatic stress disorder. *Journal of Anxiety Disorders* 20, 498–509.

Ochs, M., Mestre, D., de Montcheuil, G., Pergandi, J.-M., Saubesty, J., Lombardo, E., Francon, D., and Blache, P. (2019). Training doctors' social skills to break bad news: evaluation of the impact of virtual environment displays on the sense of presence. *Journal on Multimodal User Interfaces* 13, 41–51.

Parsons, T. D. (2021). Ethical challenges of using virtual environments in the assessment and treatment of psychopathological disorders. *Journal of Clinical Medicine* 10(3), 378. doi: 10.3390/jcm10030378

Park, C.-B., Park, S. M., Gwak, A. R., Sohn, B. K., Lee, J.-Y., Jung, H. Y., Choi, S.-W., Kim, D. J., and Choi, J.-S. (2015). The effect of repeated exposure to virtual gambling cues on the urge to gamble. *Addictive Behaviors* 41, 61–64.

Polin, A. T. (1959). The effects of flooding and physical suppression as extinction techniques on an anxiety motivated avoidance locomotor response. *Journal of Psychology* 47, 235–245.

Powers, M. B., and Emmelkamp, P. M. G. (2008). Virtual reality exposure therapy for anxiety disorders: A meta-analysis. *Journal of Anxiety Disorders* 22, 561–569.

Rothbaum, B. O., Hodges, L., Alarcon, R., Ready, D., Shahar, F., Graap, K., Pair, J., Hebert, P., Gotz, D., Wills, B., and Baltzell, D. (1999). Virtual reality exposure therapy for PTSD Vietnam veterans: A case study. *Journal of Traumatic Stress* 12(2), 263–271.

Rothbaum, B. O., Hodges, L., Smith, S., Lee, J. H., and Price, L. (2000). A controlled study of virtual reality exposure for the fear of flying. *Journal of Consulting Clinical Psychology* 68, 1020–1026.

Smoliński, T. (2021). Wykorzystanie zanurzenia w rzeczywistość wirtualną w terapii implozywnej leczenia fobii (The use of immersion in virtual reality to the implosive phobias treating, in Polish). *Master's thesis*. Gdańsk, Poland: FETI GUT (supervisor J. Lebiedź, consultant A. Popławska).

Stampfl, T. G., and Levis, D. J. (1967). Essentials of implosive therapy: a learning-theory-based psychodynamic behavioral therapy. *Journal of Abnormal Psychology* 72, 496–503.

Troester, J. D. (2006). Experiences with implosive therapy. *Clinical Social Work Journal* 34, 349–360.

Valentijn, T. V., Tan, E. S., and Molenaar, D. (2010). The emotional and cognitive effect of immersion in film viewing. *Cognition and emotion* 24(8), 1439–1445.

Wallach, H. S., Safir, M. P., and Bar-Zvi, M. (2009). Virtual reality cognitive behavior therapy for public speaking anxiety: A randomized clinical trial. *Behavior Modification* 33(3), 314–338.

Wallergård, M., Jönsson, P., Österberg, K., Johansson, G., and Karlson, B. (2011). A virtual reality version of the Trier Social Stress Test: A pilot study. *Presence* 20(4), 325–336.

Wiens, S., Eklund, R., Szychowska, M., Miloff, A., Cosme, D., Pierzchajlo, S., and Carlbring, P. (2022). Electrophysiological correlates of in vivo and virtual reality exposure therapy in spider phobia. *Psychophysiology* 59(12), e14117. doi: 10.1111/psyp.14117

Wolpe, J. (1958). *Psychotherapy by reciprocal inhibition*. Palo Alto, CA: Stanford University Press.

Wolpe, J., and Wolpe, D. (1999). *Wolni od lęku. Lęki i ich terapia (Free from fear. Fears and their therapy*, in Polish). Kraków, Poland: WiR Partner.

Wrzesien, M., Burkhardt, J.-M., Botella, C., Alcañiz, M. (2015). Towards a virtual reality- and augmented reality-mediated therapeutic process model: A theoretical revision of clinical issues and HCI issues. *Theoretical Issues in Ergonomics Science* 16(2), 124–153.

Żołnowski, M. (2014). Wspomaganie leczenia fobii zanurzeniem w rzeczywistość wirtualną (Help in treating phobias by immersion in virtual reality, in Polish). *Master's thesis*. Gdańsk, Poland: FETI GUT (supervisor J. Lebiedź, informal consultant A. Popławska).

Żołnowski, M., and Lebiedź, J. (2014). Wspomaganie leczenia fobii za pomocą zanurzenia w rzeczywistość wirtualną. Prototyp systemu (Help in treating phobias by use of immersion in virtual reality. System prototype, in Polish). *ICT Young Conference*. Gdańsk, Poland: FETI GUT.

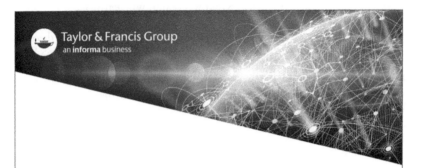

Milton Keynes UK
Ingram Content Group UK Ltd.
UKHW031132141024
449569UK00006B/242